DEVIL OF THE DOMESTIC SPHERE

DRUGS and ALCOHOL
Contested Histories

DEVIL

of the

DOMESTIC

SPHERE

Temperance, Gender, and

Middle-class Ideology,

1800–1860

Scott C. Martin

NORTHERN ILLINOIS UNIVERSITY PRESS

DeKalb

© 2008 by Northern Illinois University Press

Published by the Northern Illinois University Press, DeKalb, Illinois 60115

Manufactured in the United States using recycled, acid-free paper

All Rights Reserved

Design by Shaun Allshouse

Library of Congress Cataloging-in-Publication Data

Martin, Scott C., 1959–

Devil of the domestic sphere : temperance, gender, and middle-class ideology,

1800–1860 / Scott C. Martin.

p.   cm.

Includes bibliographical references and index.

ISBN 978-0-87580-385-2 (clothbound : alk. paper)

1. Temperance—United States—History—19th century. 2. Sex role—

United States—History—19th century. 3. Women—Suffrage—United States—

19th century. 4. Feminism—United States—History—19th century.

5. United States—Social conditions—19th century. 6. United States—

Moral conditions—19th century. I. Title.

HV5229.M36 2008

178′.1097309034—dc22

2007037991

For my family

my parents, Edward and Magdalene McGuire;

my children, Nathaniel, Ross, Alec, and Daniella;

and most of all for Lara.

Contents

Illustrations

Acknowledgments

In the course of writing a book over a number of years, one incurs many debts. My research and writing have been aided by a Wood Fellowship from the College of Physicians of Philadelphia, and a Frederick B. Artz Summer Research Fellowship from the Oberlin College Archives. I have also benefited from support provided by Bowling Green State University: a yearlong Faculty Improvement Leave, a semester's fellowship at BGSU's Institute for the Study of Culture and Society, and travel and research funds from the Graduate Program in Policy History. All of these facilitated my work, and I am grateful for them. In addition, portions of Chapter 3 appeared in a different form in "'A Star that Gathers Lustre from the Gloom of Night': Wives, Marriage and Gender in Early Nineteenth-Century American Temperance Reform," *Journal of Family History* 29, no. 3 (July 2004): 274–92.

I could not have completed this book without the assistance and support of family and friends. My family supported my efforts, not complaining when research trips or writing deadlines made me unavailable for other pursuits. My friends and colleagues shared conversation, expertise, and experience while providing encouragement. Though I appreciate all the aid I have received, I would like to thank in particular Richard Godbeer, Carol Lasser, Jon Miller, Rob Buffington, and Lara Lengel. They have contributed much to whatever is of value in the book, and for that I thank them.

DEVIL OF THE DOMESTIC SPHERE

INTRODUCTION

Temperance Literature and Misogyny

Between 1800 and 1860, more American women supported temperance reform than any other benevolent cause. Though various individuals or groups of women agitated for an array of issues and positions—prison reform, sexual equality, religious reformation, educational improvement, and moral uplift, to name but a few—the battle against intoxicating beverages was the only movement to generate nearly universal female enthusiasm. Beginning early in the century, the wives, daughters, sisters, and mothers of male foes of drunkenness rallied to the temperance cause, lending their support individually, or in concert with local efforts. By the late 1820s, previously disjointed and uncoordinated efforts against intemperance coalesced into a national movement, thereby providing greater scope for women's interest and participation. At first, women contented themselves with aiding male temperance activities, either as fellow, if auxiliary, organizers, workers, and fund-raisers, or as passive observers whose presence provided moral support and an air of respectability and decorum. By the 1830s, however, women bridled at male restrictions on their advocacy of a cause that they regarded as peculiarly important to them. With the tremendous increase in male drinking during the early nineteenth century, many American women found themselves the innocent victims of spousal and parental abuse or neglect. Disqualified by their sex from demanding relief in the legal or political arenas, women turned to the temperance movement to press their claims.[1]

Here, too, they discovered that gender conventions limited and constrained them, as male-dominated temperance societies usually relegated them to secondary status within the movement. Many women, convinced of the importance of the battle against intemperance, labored on in the shadow of male reformers, hoping that their support of temperance men would ultimately be the most effective means of ameliorating the plight of the drunkard's wife and family. But as the 1830s progressed, some women registered their dissatisfaction with the dominance of male reformers by establishing temperance societies and publications run by and for their sex, often to the exclusion of men. Whichever camp they gravitated toward, women in all parts of the United States raised the temperance standard in large numbers by the 1840s. The Daughters of Temperance, a society that sprang from female enthusiasm for alcohol reform during that decade, boasted 20,000 members at the height of its influence, making it the largest women's organization of any kind before the Civil War.[2]

Despite the extent and importance of antebellum women's participation in alcohol reform, little is known about the character, dynamics, or ideological dimensions of female temperance activism. Over the past three decades, scholars in a variety of disciplines have contributed a handful of articles focusing on some aspect of women and the antebellum temperance movement, but no monographs have been published. In large measure, the American historical profession has ignored this area of women's history in favor of other topics. This becomes particularly clear when considering the amount of scholarly attention devoted to women's participation in the other major antebellum reform movement, antislavery. A search of any library catalogue or electronic database will produce few entries for women and antebellum temperance but yield scores, if not hundreds, of books and articles on women and antislavery.[3] What has caused this disparity in scholarly and historical attention?

The answer, I believe, lies at the intersection of the conventional wisdom about the American experience with alcohol reform and the politics of women's history. Despite a growing body of historical evidence to the contrary, academicians and the lay public alike generally regard the nineteenth- and early twentieth-century effort to restrict or outlaw the production and use of alcohol as an abject failure. In this view, the temperance movement and alcohol reform sprang from the self-righteous meddling of intolerant busybodies and produced only disdain for federal law and the growth of organized crime. This viewpoint, however myopic, might not inhibit scholarly interest in antebellum women's struggle against the liquor trade were it not for widespread opinion among women's historians that antislavery, and not temperance, provided the seedbed for women's rights activism and modern feminism.[4] To be sure, one could hardly underestimate the importance of women's advocacy of abolition, and the organizational and political experience they gained by participating in the antislavery movement, in the history of women's rights. But, as Carol Mattingly has pointed out, scholars have too often taken the assertions of women's rights advocates like Elizabeth Cady Stanton and Susan B. Anthony as the unvarnished truth, failing to subject their claims about temperance reform to critical analysis. In their massive *History of Woman Suffrage,* Stanton, Anthony, and Matilda Josyln Gage portrayed temperance reform by the late 1840s as a cause hopelessly compromised by conservative men who refused to countenance discussion of women's rights. Writing decades later, they contended that after being marginalized by men once states enacted prohibitory laws in the early 1850s, most

> liberal men and women now withdrew from all temperance organizations, leaving the movement in the hands of time-serving priests and politicians, who, being in the majority, effectually blocked the progress of the reform for the time . . . in 1853, intelligent women saw that the most direct way to effect any reform was to have a voice in the laws and lawmakers.

Elaborating on this theme, Anthony's biographer, Ida Husted Harper, declared in 1898 that her subject and kindred spirits like Stanton abandoned temperance societies because they "would not accept the principle of woman's rights." In Harper's account, once-activist female temperance societies like the one Stanton and Anthony helped establish in New York State fell "into the hands of a body of conservative women" who declined to challenge male dominance of the movement. According to these influential activists, then, temperance women played little part in the unfolding struggle for suffrage and women's rights.[5]

A growing body of scholarship has demonstrated the inaccuracy, or at least inadequacy, of this position. The *History of Woman Suffrage,* a major source for women's history during the mid- to late-nineteenth century, can hardly be taken at face value. Stanton, Anthony, and Gage represented the history of their campaign for women's rights in ways that suited their political and ideological needs in the 1880s, when the volumes were written. Their dismissal of temperance women may have reflected thirty years of hindsight, as well as competition for female support for their cause occasioned by the resurgence of an organized women's temperance movement in the 1870s and 1880s. Though the most radical women's rights advocates did leave the temperance movement in the early 1850s, other women stayed, believing that intemperance constituted a significant enough evil to justify continuing to work in secondary and constrained roles. This may provide at least a partial explanation of why feminist scholars, who have done the bulk of the work on women's history, continue to emphasize antislavery reform as the predominant source of women's rights activism.[6] As noted above, conventional wisdom holds that the drive for black liberation and civil rights produced a laudable success, while the crusade to eliminate liquor from American society ended in a misguided failure. Hence it is understandable that feminist historians seeking to link contemporary struggles for women's rights to earlier reforms prefer to find their intellectual and moral forebears among the ranks of abolitionists, rather than prohibitionists.

Devaluing temperance as a significant source of women's activism, however, ignores important connections between alcohol reform and gender ideology during the early nineteenth century. Antebellum temperance reformers prompted debate about the proper roles that men and women should play in the era's expanding capitalist society and explored questions about gender raised by the dramatic increase in drinking and intemperance that characterized the first few decades of the nineteenth century. These discussions circulated to every corner of the United States, for the temperance movement quickly embraced the new and cheaper printing technologies and more efficient methods of distribution that produced the incredible proliferation of print media during the antebellum years. Temperance advocates produced more literature, and made it more easily available to the public, than any other reform cause during the nineteenth century. With wide dissemination of its ideas and arguments about women and gender, temperance literature shaped the vocabulary available for later discussions of temperance, women's rights, and market capitalism. Significantly, late nineteenth- and early twentieth-century public discourse on prohibition and women's suffrage, both pro and con, employed arguments and rhetorical strategies that can be traced back to discussions about gender in antebellum temperance literature. As Ian Tyrrell, Janet Giele, Carol Mattingly, and others have shown, women's antebellum temperance work provided a base for the postwar revival of female temperance activism. The daughters of antebellum temperance women participated in the Ohio Women's Crusade of the 1870s and helped establish the Woman's Christian Temperance Union, one of the nineteenth century's largest and most influential women's organizations. Late nineteenth-century women's temperance activism, in turn, contributed directly to the passage of the Eighteenth Amendment and politicized women in ways that generated public support and enthusiasm for the enactment of the Nineteenth Amendment. In a broader sense, the concepts, images, and assumptions that emerged from antebellum temperance literature changed the American cultural landscape in ways that persist to the present. In particular, the preoccupation of American popular culture with women as victims of male violence and excess owes much to ideological work done in antebellum temperance literature.[7]

This book aims at reinvigorating historical interest in women and temperance before the Civil War. It foregrounds the temperance movement, and the voluminous literature it generated, as a primary site for the production and dissemination of new and reconfigured ideas about women and gender during the first six decades of the nineteenth century. Four themes run throughout the book. First, the evolution of the temperance

movement and the emergence of the American middle class were inti-
mately connected. By the early nineteenth century, the erosion of older,
pre-Revolutionary conceptions of social order and economic rank paved
the way for a newer system of understanding and describing socioeconomic status, one that would ultimately become the modern American
class structure. Central to this process was the formation of a middle class
created by the recognition of common interests and concerns among successful lawyers, physicians, and other professionals, as well as prosperous
farmers, merchants, skilled artisans, and other groups of financially secure, if not wealthy, Americans. In seeking to define and justify itself in relation to those above and below in the American socioeconomic order,
this nascent middle class emphasized the moral advantages of middling
status, finding depravity in both the lavish excesses of the rich and the abject squalor of the poor. At this early point in the process of class formation, before the American bourgeoisie could take its moral authority and
social influence for granted, intemperance raised questions about gender,
social status, and political economy that threatened middle-class coalescence and identity. Attempts to resolve these questions exerted a lasting
influence on the trajectories of temperance reform and gender ideology
that ramified beyond the middle class.[8]

Second, temperance literature, which provides most of the sources for
this study, is conceived broadly to include sermons, tracts, newspaper articles, medical writing, and reform periodicals, as well as fiction, drama, and
poetry. One could hardly underestimate the extent of temperance publishing. In an 1851 retrospective on fifty years of temperance reform, antiliquor advocate John Marsh provided publication figures for popular
tracts and pamphlets published by the American Tract Society. The society
issued nearly five million copies of temperance publications by 1851. The
profusion of temperance literature was part of the explosive growth of
American print culture but also reflected the particular ideological needs
of the nascent middle class. Most discussions about temperance, whether
conducted in the expansive print media of the era or in public assemblies
or private gatherings, took place in the context of middle-class formation
in the United States. The images and ideas about women, and male and
female roles, presented in the various genres of temperance literature, I argue, helped produce an ideology of gender particularly suited to the re-
quirements of the emerging American middle class.[9]

Third, temperance was central to the articulation of middle-class gender ideology, and especially ideas about women, in ways that other reforms and social issues were not. Middle-class identity and authority depended heavily on positing the existence of a female private sphere in
which women exerted a salutary moral influence on men hardened by
their struggles and exertions in the male public sphere. Intemperance,
which increased precipitously during the early nineteenth century, threatened

more than any other evil to erase the distinction between public and private at the precise historical moment when the emerging middle class needed to take it for granted. When the market invaded the domestic sphere, in the form of drunken husbands and fathers returning to their firesides, home could not provide a suitable sheltered environment for the exercise of female moral influence. If the cultivation of virtue in a gendered domestic sphere proved impossible, then claims to middle-class moral preeminence and social authority evaporated as well. Hence middle-class advocacy of temperance reform, which coincided with the process of class coalescence during the antebellum years, necessarily bespoke not just conviction about the evils of drink but also the articulation and defense of a class-specific ideology of gender.[10]

Finally, a strand of misogyny runs throughout temperance ideology, shaping women's prospects and experiences in the middle class and beyond. Denunciations of women as causes of intemperance and snares for men, or the celebration of their victimization, often coexisted with, and even underpinned, more positive assessments of women's role in the emerging middle class. This was particularly true of domesticity, which claimed an exalted position for women even as it sought to limit and circumscribe their supposedly superior moral influence. The misogynist tendencies in the temperance movement reflect the persistence of older attitudes toward women that became partially submerged, only to resurface periodically as new ideologies of gender emerged in the early nineteenth century. Indeed, as we shall see in a later discussion of the gender politics of the Maine Law, misogyny exerted a significant and lasting effect on the tactics and goals of temperance reform.[11]

Not surprisingly, then, much of the ideological work done by temperance advocates in tracts, sermons, pamphlets, books, orations, newspaper and magazine articles, and other products of the antebellum era's burgeoning print culture revolved around delimiting and delineating male and female attributes as they related to the problems caused by drunkenness. Physicians, clergymen, civic leaders, politicians, scholars, and ordinary citizens, male and female, weighed in on the necessity of protecting women from male drunkenness and the propriety of women's participation in alcohol reform. This diverse group of Americans concerned with temperance also considered thornier questions: why did more men than women drink, and what should American society make of women who, like men, neglected their familial and social duties to become drunkards? If women exerted real moral power over men, why did they fail to eradicate male drunkenness? How could women protect the domestic sphere from intemperance without entering the public sphere to militate for reform and thereby compromising their feminine virtue? In a larger sense, what implications did women's interest and participation in temperance reform have for middle-class efforts to solidify claims to social and cultural authority?

I have approached middle-class attempts to answer these questions with the sensibilities and concerns of a cultural rather than a women's historian. This orientation reflects both my training and interests, as well as the nature of the material. Despite the large number of antebellum women who gravitated toward temperance as a distinctively female issue, relatively few records of female temperance societies, or accounts of individual reform activity, have survived. Women's historians have published some fine studies of female temperance activities in particular locales or regions, but, owing to a paucity of source materials, these usually comprise a small part of a larger investigation of reform activity or women's activism.[12] Much of what can be learned about women's relationship to the temperance movement, I rapidly discovered, derives from sources not devoted solely, or even primarily, to discussions of women or gender. It is here that an ideological analysis of the intersection of temperance and gender proves most useful. The voluminous temperance literature produced largely by middle-class authors often addressed obliquely, or inadvertently, issues such as the proper roles of women, male and female qualities, and the gendered aspects of bourgeois political economy. By examining temperance reform as a primary site for the elaboration and development of middle-class ideology, one learns a great deal about women's participation in the battle against liquor and the reciprocal relationship between class and gender in the emerging American socioeconomic order. Certainly, this approach is not without problems: it privileges middle-class discourse over other voices and risks marginalizing or ignoring altogether the experiences of immigrants and women of color. But given the dearth of primary or secondary sources on Irish, German, African American, and working-class women's temperance activities, studying women and temperance in the context of middle-class ideology offers a starting point for the detailed local studies that will be necessary to illuminate the broader range of women's experience with temperance reform.

A similar point could be made about the difficulties surrounding an international comparative perspective on women and temperance during the antebellum years. It would be illuminating to compare American women's relationship to the temperance movement with those of Canadian or English women. Primary research into the Canadian and British campaigns against liquor are beyond the scope of this study, however, and the secondary literature does not permit meaningful comparisons. In all three nations, women perceived temperance as a woman's issue, rooted in notions of domesticity and protection of the home. But aside from the insight that fewer middle- and upper-class English women appear to have been engaged in the early temperance movement than in the United States, there is insufficient scholarship to provide the basis for rigorous comparisons, especially using the class and gender analysis employed here. A comparative perspective on middle-class women's involvement in temperance reform in Canada and Britain might occasion a reappraisal of the American experience, but it will have to await more detailed study by scholars in British and Canadian history.[13]

Another caveat concerns the uneven progress of temperance reform throughout the United States. Certainly, temperance activism and the middle-class ideology that underpinned it emerged to the greatest extent in areas where market capitalism took hold earliest and strongest. Not surprisingly, then, many of the sources for this work come from the Northeast, the center for many of the developments on which temperance depended: publishing innovations, reform enterprises, capitalist transformation, and middle-class coalescence. One might expect that temperance reform and its attendant gender ideology would not loom as large in other areas of the country, such as the South and West, where the market and middle class assumed smaller, or at least different, proportions. The South, for example, with different class and gender dynamics and a much smaller middle class than the North, might seem less fertile ground for temperance reform. To an extent, this was the case, and the Northeast remained the epicenter of the Benevolent Empire throughout the antebellum era.

Despite regional variations, temperance principles and the middle-class ideology that underpinned them proved remarkably resonant in all parts of the United States. In the West, reform-minded aspirants to the bourgeoisie read the same publications and debated the same issues as their Northeastern peers. Southern temperance, though less extensive than its Northern counterpart, remained a vibrant movement throughout the prewar years and partook of much the same language, tactical changes, and ideological apparatus. The ideological appeal of temperance, like that of middle-class status, ramified well beyond its initial socioeconomic and regional origins. Unlike other reforms, such as abolitionism, temperance transcended sectional differences to garner support from all parts of the nation. Though this study draws its evidence mostly from the Northeast, there is good reason to believe that its conclusions apply well beyond that region.

The broad appeal and relative uniformity of temperance ideology become clear when comparing reform movements in different parts of the country, as John Quist did in his study of Washtenaw County, Michigan, and Tuscaloosa County, Alabama, during the antebellum era. In both counties, Quist noted, a "largely similar climate of reform existed. . . . [T]emperance shifted from the vilification of only hard liquor to total abstinence, followed the similar pattern from moral suasion to legal suasion, and then repeated this latter course." Quist did note that women appeared to play less prominent or visible roles in Southern temperance, implying that "gender roles were more circumscribed in the southern locale," perhaps reflecting a somewhat different class dynamic than in the North. Still, the "parallel development of the temperance movement in both states" underlined for Quist how temperance "was a national effort. . . .

[E]nthusiasts in both states closely monitored temperance activities elsewhere."[14] Thus while it would be a mistake to assume that patterns originating in the Northeast maintained an identical form everywhere, it would be equally incorrect to assume that those patterns exerted no influence in other parts of the country.

The first chapter begins by surveying the extent of female drunkenness in antebellum American society. It inquires why female intemperance elicited such universal disgust and why middle-class temperance reformers sought to avoid discussing it whenever possible. In part, this reticence stemmed from the fear that too much discussion of female drunkards would undermine the ideology of domesticity, which was central to emerging middle-class identity. Female drinking raised the specter of both sexual promiscuity and domestic neglect, since reformers associated drinking with carnal desire and selfish disregard of familial duty. In a larger sense, however, female drunkenness posed a profound threat to the stable gender roles on which middle-class domesticity was based by exposing their artificiality: intemperate women could be just as lustful or undutiful as men, pronouncements about inherent female morality notwithstanding. To avoid the implications of female drunkenness for established notions of gender, middle-class reformers defined "alcohol" as an unmitigated evil, a commodity unlike any other that was capable of invading the domestic sphere and corrupting even angelic women. Thus middle-class reformers shifted the focus from women—and from a more thorough consideration of the morality of untrammeled market capitalism, which the liquor trade represented—to a condemnation of what they considered an illicit item of trade.

The second chapter examines the temperance movement's two primary ways of conceptualizing women: as victims of male intemperance who elicited support for the temperance cause, or as moral exemplars encouraging men to abstain or reform. In both these guises, according to reformers, women furthered the battle against intemperance. This chapter examines these dualities of conceiving women's relationship to temperance reform in the context of middle-class ideological development. It surveys the extent and character of these roles, arguing that they overlapped and supported each other in the service of defining gender roles appropriate to middle-class ideology. Central to the discussion of these roles was the concept of "female influence," a species of moral suasion in which woman swayed man through either her pathetic suffering or her moral example. In either case, women exemplified the fidelity, piety, and submissiveness central to middle-class domesticity. Unfortunately for women, both roles placed a positive value on female suffering, depicting a woman's ability to endure suffering at the hands of a man as one of her chief virtues.

Chapter 3 considers another primary site related to temperance reform for the construction of middle-class gender ideology: medical science.

During the early nineteenth century, American physicians' attempts to improve the standing and respectability of their profession coincided with the emergence of the middle class. Medical doctors recognized that affiliating themselves with the middle class by espousing sobriety would further their professional claims. As aspirants to middle-class respectability, they eagerly provided temperance advocates with scientific proof of the deleterious effects of alcohol on the human body and mind. As they did so, they inevitably confronted questions about gender. Why were there more male than female drunkards? Did woman's physiology, reproductive functions, and "delicate" constitution produce different reactions to alcohol? This chapter focuses on the interplay between medical opinion and middle-class gender ideology. It examines the work of Charles D. Meigs, an antebellum Philadelphia physician and pioneer of American gynecology. An active temperance advocate, Meigs used popular images of women suffering from male intemperance—notably, Lydia Sigourney's story, "The Intemperate," and a widely circulated lithograph of the same name—to illustrate the "natural," physiologically determined qualities of female character: fidelity, obedience, and perseverance. Meigs bestowed a scientific imprimatur on visions of gender then being articulated in the middle class. In the process, however, he intensified and extended middle-class conceptions of women by grounding the laudable and supposedly "natural" female capacity to endure suffering in physiological structures.

Medical science, however, could not solve all the problems posed for middle-class ideology by women's role in the temperance movement. As noted, middle-class temperance reformers attributed enormous importance to "female influence": women's ability to use their superior moral and religious attributes to prevent intemperance and reform male drunkards. Chapter 4 explores how reformers conceived of female influence and reconciled its failure to eradicate drunkenness with middle-class gender ideology. Many commentators scrambled to explain why women had not striven hard enough; why some women, inadvertently or otherwise, had actually hindered reform by promoting drinking; and why female influence proved ineffective against intemperance. To explain the failure of female influence, middle-class ideologues deployed older images of corrupt woman as a snare for men, whose influence, for good or ill, lay more in their sexual attractiveness than in their moral authority. This chapter highlights both the survival of misogynist tendencies within domestic ideology and the ambivalence with which many middle-class reformers regarded women's participation in the crusade against drink.

Chapter 5 examines another middle-class ideological crisis that revolved around temperance, this one occasioned by the contradiction between the desire for free markets and the impulse to eradicate drunkenness. By the 1830s, many middle-class temperance advocates feared that the movement had reached a crisis. Not only had female influence, a moral force endorsed by the middle class, failed to eradicate intemperance, but the liquor trade appeared to be increasingly resistant to any restraint. Given the belief that alcohol could corrupt anyone, many temperance supporters fretted that their hard-won gains could be lost to an aggressive and flourishing liquor trade. Moreover, they had to tread carefully, lest condemnations of rumselling reflect badly on the system of market capitalism in which the middle class had invested, both ideologically and financially. To resolve this dilemma, middle-class ideologues extended the condemnation of liquor as uniquely evil to include the trade that produced and sold it. The liquor trade, they claimed, did not foster economic growth and a healthy market but perverted and hindered them. Temperance advocates made their case using a specious political economy buttressed by a gendered discourse that emphasized the damage inflicted upon women and the domestic sphere by the nefarious, avaricious rumseller. The definition of liquor and the liquor trade as singularly and irredeemably evil, and therefore unrepresentative of market capitalism, motivated middle-class temperance supporters to advocate prohibition, as opposed to moral suasion, by the late 1840s. The chapter details this ideological transition, using an extended discussion of gender and political economy in T. S. Arthur's *Ten Nights in a Bar-Room* to illustrate these themes.

The sixth chapter examines the implications for female activism of the shift toward prohibition discussed in the previous chapter. Female temperance advocates pursued a number of activities that ranged from informal persuasion of friends and neighbors to public advocacy against drunkenness in print and speech. Middle-class temperance supporters recognized that public activism tested the limits of domesticity, and they debated the propriety of expanded roles for women. This debate culminated in support for the Maine Law, prohibitory legislation that represented a move away from moral suasion and toward legal coercion as the temperance movement's major tactic. Both sexes supported the 1851 Maine Law and similar prohibitory legislation in other states. In the wake of its passage, however, the gender politics of the Maine Law became clear. Male temperance partisans who were ambivalent or hostile toward female activism encouraged women to retreat from public roles now that men had enacted legal protections for them against the liquor trade. Misogynist tendencies once again surfaced in temperance literature, with many writers doubting the propriety and wisdom of the kinds of public roles women had assumed in the temperance movement over the last three decades. A backlash against women's public temperance activities in the early 1850s drove feminists from the movement and resulted in the recession of female temperance activism until the early 1870s and the advent of the Women's Crusade.

The conclusion will suggest ways in which the intersection of temperance reform and gender ideology have moved beyond the middle class to shape American politics and culture. In politics, middle-class temperance and gender ideology contributed to larger discussions of women's political participation, liquor regulation, and women's role in the family and nation. Antebellum precedents influenced the development of postwar women's organizations like the Woman's Christian Temperance Union and directed the terms of debates over prohibition and the 18th Amendment into specific channels. Middle-class ideology forged in the temperance movement also provided a gendered vocabulary for discussing and debating women's role in American politics and reform well into the twentieth century. In cultural terms, middle-class ideology imparted persistent notions about female morality, sexuality, and gender roles to American society. Ideas about women's superior morality and putative guardianship of home and family, pioneered in temperance literature, continue to inform popular culture and public policy. At the level of popular culture, images of male violence against women in early temperance literature reappeared, in altered form, in many aspects of American popular entertainment. In the end, the misogyny that often characterized the middle-class temperance movement's gender politics has persisted in many ways, bespeaking great ambivalence about women's participation in American society.

Female Intemperance

Domesticity, Sex, and Middle-class Morality

Since at least the late eighteenth century, two tendencies have dominated American attitudes about temperance and women's drinking. First, moralists, physicians, reformers, and other commentators contended that female intemperance occurred rarely, owing to women's innate virtue and modesty. During the first half of the nineteenth century in particular, temperance literature portrayed women most frequently as the "unmitigated victim" of male intemperance and disposed of "females' drinking as the Romans disposed of patricide: [by] deem[ing] it too improbable to require regulation" or concern. Second, popular opinion universally regarded women's intemperance, when and if it did occur, as a far more egregious offense than its male counterpart. However deplorable male drunkenness might be, a besotted women constituted, for most Americans, a "more revolting object" than was ever conceived by "imagination's gloomiest reverie." "Heaven forbid," one clergyman implored, the discovery of even a few female drunkards, for an intoxicated wife, daughter, or mother struck him as a "spectacle . . . too dreadful to contemplate." Temperance advocates, one might conclude at first blush, considered female drunkenness so uncommon and heinous that it did not merit serious anxiety or sustained discussion.[1]

In large measure, historians and other scholars of early nineteenth-century American temperance have accepted as fact the contention that few women drank and acknowledged the double standard pertaining to male and female intemperance without much comment or analysis. Ian Tyrrell, for instance, the closest student of the antebellum temperance movement, concluded that "heavy drinking was predominantly a male pattern of behavior" in the mid-nineteenth century, making a drunken woman "a rarity." Harry Gene Levine concurred, observing that reformers' infrequent discussion of female drunkenness reflected both a low incidence of women's alcohol consumption and the social stigma attached to female inebriety. The intensity of popular repugnance toward female drunkenness, Levine argued, made the very "topic of women's intemperance . . . itself almost taboo" by the 1840s. When scholars have noted what Mark Lender termed the "special stigma" attached to female drunkenness, they have generally attributed it to the "sentimentalization and rigidification of concepts of 'ladylike' behavior and appropriate female roles" that emerged powerfully in the early nineteenth century.[2]

These interpretations are not without merit. Social disapprobation of female drinking had a long history in Europe and America by the nineteenth century and has continued, in a somewhat muted form, to the present day. Beginning in the sixteenth and seventeenth centuries, social and economic change in Europe permanently diminished female alcohol consumption to levels far below those of men. Similarly, the long-standing, disproportionate animadversion of female drunkenness in relation to its male equivalent is undeniably historical and reflects enduring attitudes toward women and "proper" female deportment.[3] Still, accepting the conventional wisdom, whatever its basis in social and historical reality, and leaving it at that, obscures as much as it illuminates. Assuming that few women in the early nineteenth-century United States drank and that any discussion of their imbibing bordered on the taboo misrepresents both the extent of female intemperance and the frequency of its discussion in temperance literature. More significantly, it forestalls questions about how, and under what specific historical circumstances, the conventional wisdom came to be. Though suspicion and discomfort with women's drinking had existed for some time, its depth and intensity increased dramatically during the early decades of the nineteenth century. Why, at that specific point in time, did Americans condemn women's drinking as never before? How was the hardening of attitudes toward female intemperance related to broader developments in early nineteenth-century American gender ideology? What constellation of ideological constructs made it merely common sense to regard a drunken woman as an object, almost without peer, of loathing and disgust?

This chapter begins by surveying the extent of female intemperance and the prevalence of its discussion in temperance literature. It then considers why and how women's drinking became so troubling and problematic a topic for the temperance movement by juxtaposing the growing discomfort concerning women's drinking with other early nineteenth-century American ideological developments: the emergence of new or reconfigured discourses of domesticity, class, sexuality, and gender. The chapter concludes by examining how, in temperance literature, reformers attempted to resolve the ideological difficulties and contradictions occasioned by women's intemperance.

The Extent and Recognition of Female Intemperance

A variety of commentators constructed an image of woman as inherently moral and temperate. Still, as they theorized away the possibility of widespread female intemperance, temperance advocates could not ignore or deny the reality of women's excessive drinking. Examination of antebellum temperance literature reveals that female drunkenness, as well as its recognition and discussion by reformers, occurred far more frequently than has been acknowledged by contemporary observers or modern scholars. The available statistical data, albeit imperfect, point to a significant number of female drunkards. Though W. J. Rorabaugh doubted that much can be learned about the "reputed 100,000 female drunkards or the more numerous women who consumed from one-eighth to one-quarter of the nation's spirituous liquor," his estimates attest to a significant female drinking population during the early nineteenth century. Reformers' own efforts at quantifying the drink problem in temperance publications revealed the pervasiveness of female drinking and intemperance. The Massachusetts Society for the Suppression of Intemperance (MSSI), for instance, estimated in 1818 that women comprised a quarter of all deaths from intemperance. Three decades later, a county poorhouse director from Pennsylvania judged that one-third of his female charges suffered from the direct effects of intemperance. Likewise, New York reformer and temperance advocate Robert M. Hartley reported that females accounted for nearly 40 percent of incarcerations for public drunkenness in New York City during 1849.[4]

Regular accounts of crimes involving drunkenness printed in popular temperance newspapers supplemented this statistical data, giving it a human face. In 1828, for instance, a temperance newspaper reprinted an article on Mary White, a Baltimore woman "taken up in the street much intoxicated and put in the Belvedere Watch House," where she hanged herself. The paper regretted that the "wretched mother" had left seven children parentless but found some solace in the fact that they were "all well behaved, and placed in good employment." During the late 1820s and early 1830s, a New York paper, *The Genius of Temperance,* in all its various incarnations, published a semi-regular "Police Office" column that described the toll of drunkenness. Susan Floyd, *Genius* readers learned in 1833, had gotten drunk after being released from the Penitentiary the day before and was recommitted the following morning. Four years later, the

paper's patrons read of Mary McMullen, whom police charged with stealing a cloak while under the influence of "pepper and gin." Similar tales of
female iniquity appeared during the 1840s in the "Chronicles of Drunkenness" section of the Sons of Temperance publication, the *New York Organ
and Temperance Safeguard*. Readers learned of thefts, deaths, injuries, and domestic discord involving drunken and disorderly women. In what must have
been a particularly egregious case, the *Organ* noted in 1847 that "a missionary
of the M. E. church, complained at the Jefferson Market Police Court, of his
wife being a habitual drunkard, and requested that she be sent to Blackwell's
Island [a notorious New York prison] as a vagrant." The "Chronicles" reported
the number of male and female arrests for public drunkenness as well, frequently remarking disapprovingly that "more than one third" were women.[5]

The recognition of female intemperance manifested itself in substantial
coverage, as well as graphic depiction, in temperance literature. Though
they did prefer to depict women as victims or moral exemplars, antiliquor
advocates pulled no punches when denouncing the pervasiveness of female drinking and intemperance. Writing in 1813, New York minister
Alexander Gunn complained that a "staggering female is no uncommon
sight," and even many women who "pretend to great refinement and delicacy" drank to excess. One wit observed that Roman law condemned female drunkards to death, wryly adding that if similar laws existed in the
United States, "would not our registers soon contain many blank pages
and alarm and consternation spread through the ranks of female beauty?"
Others struck a shriller tone. "Do not some of the Fair sex also drink deep
of the Bacchanalian spring?" demanded one doctor. "In what age do we
live? How must Morality shudder? Can such a deplorable state of things
be denied?" This attention to drunken women continued throughout the
antebellum period. A temperance paper enjoined its readers in 1844 to remember that there are drunken women, as well as besotted men, who
have "descended to the lowest depths of infamy and woe." The *Journal of
the American Temperance Union* reprinted a report in 1858 that many
Chicago men were "begging for a chance to remove to the country," to
protect their wives "from the temptation of strong drink." The *Journal* was
confident, it added ruefully, that the "amount of intemperance among
women, and not merely of the lower and laboring classes, far exceeds the
common suspicion."[6]

Like their journalistic counterparts, writers of temperance fiction displayed little reticence about women drunkards or the havoc they wrought.
Though not as common as victimized heroines, drunken female characters
did appear in novels, short stories, and purportedly "authentic" narratives
as secondary figures and, sometimes, as protagonists. A wide range of authors employed intemperate female characters, from the anonymous producers of tracts and newspaper items to prominent literary figures like T. S.
Arthur, Lydia Sigourney, Osgood Bradbury, and Walt Whitman.[7] The treat-

ment and use of female intemperance in fiction varied as well. Some authors, in what David S. Reynolds has termed the "conventional" mode of temperance writing, merely mentioned or hinted at women's drunkenness, as in the anonymous 1822 morality tale *Edmund and Margaret; Or, Sobriety and Faithfulness Rewarded*. Others, employing a more lurid style, emphasized intricate descriptions of the symptoms, progress, and consequences of female inebriety. Some narratives had intemperate wives bear an immense burden of guilt over the impact of their immorality on their families. One woman's chronic inebriation forced her husband to leave their home. This "inexpressibly wretched" woman learned that he eventually died in England, driven from his native land by her unchecked drinking. Another unfortunate woman who had encouraged her husband to drink with her repented too late her "wicked practices and false principles" that led to his death during a fit of delirium tremens. His horrid death dealt her such a "shock that a violent fever soon hurried her to the tomb." In similar fashion, Lydia Sigourney's Louisa Wilson drinks herself to death, unable to tolerate the guilt from having dropped her infant daughter in the fire while drunk, resulting in the amputation of the child's arm. Other fictional female drunkards met even ghastlier fates. Mrs. Latimer, the besotted wife in *The History of the Bottle,* lives long enough to see her youngest child die of neglect and malnutrition, only to be beaten and eventually murdered by her husband, with "the accursed instrument of all their misery, *the Bottle*."[8]

Nor did temperance writers shy away from the most grisly and disturbing images of female intemperance. A popular tract, for instance, featured an intemperate wife whose imagination became "disordered, and conjured up horrible visions." After a time she "sank in death, snoring out the few last days of her existence in a state of stupor, covered with rags and filth." An upstate New York newspaper recounted the pitiable story of a family outcast, an Albany woman with a "maimed hand." Despite having "neither beauty or education, or refinement to allure," she lost her virtue to villains for whose criminality "language has no words strong enough to mark." In the course of this "work [of] demoniac lust," the woman learned to drink, and "to love it, insanely," before being jailed for "disturbance in some midnight orgies." Sometimes, women themselves related these harrowing tales. The female-edited *Pearl,* for example, reprinted the story of a twenty-four-year-old woman in the throes of delirium tremens. The authorities had strapped the unfortunate woman to a cart with leather thongs to prevent her from injuring herself, but she struggled so that "blood gathered in her hands and feet till they became dark and swollen." Female urban missionaries of the Episcopal Church limned a number of dark pictures from their work in New York's infamous Five Points. On one foray into the slum, they encountered a naked woman, dreadfully ill and lying under a "wretched cotton quilt (which formed no contrast in color with the floor)." Upon questioning her, they discovered that she had been for some months pursuing a "course of most fearful intemperance" that had led her to take up residence with a "black man." Her intemperance accounted for part of her present illness, but the "shocking scenes in the room" greatly exacerbated her distress. Another white woman who had been beaten by the black man died the previous Sunday but had lain in the room with the sick woman until Wednesday, "the putrid body spreading contagion in every direction through the house, and especially in this narrow room." Too weak to get help, the female inebriate sickened further as she lay in this "situation beyond description."[9]

The abundance of anecdotal and statistical evidence forced an unpleasant conclusion on the opponents of alcohol: from the raucous Kentucky frontier to the staid districts of Charleston and Boston, where nearly half of those charged with common drunkenness were female, women consumed liquor and became drunkards. Local and state authorities acted on this knowledge, embodying their recognition that female drunkards would have to be dealt with in legislation and institutions. Pennsylvania, for instance, passed a law permitting relatives of anyone who became incapable of "managing his or her estate" to petition to have the person declared non compos mentis. A similar Massachusetts law provided recourse for the families of those who, "through idleness or excessive drinking of spirituous liquors, so misspend, waste, or lessen his or her estate" as to bring want or indigence. Institution builders as well as legislators attended to the problem of female intemperance. New York State's Inebriate Asylum stipulated that wages earned from inmates' labor would be sent to their families, or, if no family existed, paid "to him or her at their discharge from said Institution."[10] Clearly, Americans recognized the existence and dimensions of female intemperance.

Temperance and Domesticity

If they did not ignore female drinking and drunkenness, opponents of alcohol did manifest a certain discomfited reserve about the topic, preferring to treat it gingerly when they discussed it. In part, this restraint reflected the temperance movement's perceptions of which public relations emphases would best further its cause. As there were fewer female drunkards in any case, emphasizing male excesses and their baleful impact on defenseless wives, mothers, and children evoked more sympathy and support than did accentuating women's alcoholic transgressions.[11] Still, a fuller, more satisfactory explanation of the discomfort with female intemperance must transcend mere tactical concerns to encompass the ideological context in which they originated.

For the temperance movement's largely middle-class support base, which both produced and consumed most temperance literature, the ascendance of domestic ideology provided that context. Temperance advocates manifested concern about the impact of female drinking on domestic order from the beginning of the movement. By the 1820s at least, middle-class reformers and ideologues depicted domesticity as the model for social and familial order and assigned women the divinely ordained role of moral arbiter within it. Too much talk of dipsomaniacal women could easily undermine confidence in the system's viability and naturalness at a time when the middle class was still striving to consolidate its ideological position in American society. For an anxious middle class, it was far better to deny the possibility of widespread female drunkenness than to entertain the notion that the middle-class domestic order might not work after all. Thus middle-class reformers denominated drunkenness as a male weakness and reserved special indignation and censure for the relatively few anomalous cases of overindulgence by women, these exceptions proving the rule.[12]

Little wonder, then, that temperance literature execrated women's drinking because of its impact on the domestic circle. A drunken woman, temperance publications warned, not only made a "wreck of God's most exquisite workmanship" but, worse, forgot "her sex and her duties in this unnatural indulgence." Intemperate women thus neglected their responsibilities in all their relations to men. An intemperate wife and mother spread "shame and disgrace" over her family rather than being its "pride and ornament." One commentator considered a drunken sister or daughter even worse, praying that heaven forbid a "spectacle [that] is too dreadful to be looked upon; the evil is too great for fond affection to endure." Drunken helpmates presented an equally appalling picture. Once-lovely wives took "a kind of infernal pleasure in planting their husband's pillow with thorns," becoming a "serpent in the bosom" to bedevil their spouses.[13]

No one doubted the devastation caused by male intemperance, but reformers reminded their audiences that a woman's inebriation also "interrupted, if not forever destroyed" the "peace, order, and happiness of the whole domestic circle." Advocates of abstinence portrayed neglected children, heartbroken husbands, and the subversion of "the whole order of the family," as the fruits of female intemperance. Often they found useful object lessons in a detailed survey of the damage:

> To see a woman in this condition, setting aside all the delicacy, modesty, and sobriety of her sex; so far from managing 'her affairs with the discretion' of a goodhouse wife, that she is unable to manage them at all? . . . To behold . . . her children around her without direction, without instruction, and in vain calling upon her for the supplies of daily food, or warm and decent clothing, which it is her province to prepare for them. Her husband, nonplussed, disconcerted, grieved, and justly offended; her sex disgraced, and all, who are any way connected with her, ashamed.[14]

Though temperance literature condemned female toping as a plague on the domestic circle generally, it reserved special opprobrium for the strife and disorder caused by drunken mothers. Considering the importance Americans attributed to raising virtuous, republican children, it is not surprising that reformers directed much of their invective against women who neglected their maternal duties.[15] A mother's intemperance endangered her children's welfare and even threatened to turn her offspring into drunkards. "Oh tell it not in Gath!" a temperance convention circular implored, "of an intemperate mother over whose memory the sable pall of oblivion must be cast, and if a tear, not a word may be dropt." Orators and writers did drop words, however, conjuring up chilling images of mothers taking clothing, furniture, and other household necessities and selling them for liquor. A woman's temperance society enjoined skeptics to go to the Boston police court to witness drunken mothers being committed to the house of correction for two or three months: "What becomes of the children? Where are they in the meantime?" One can hardly overstate the vehemence with which many temperance advocates condemned maternal intemperance. Clergyman Albert Barnes, for instance, regretted that a "single such mother pollutes the air and beholds the heavens." Far better, he believed, that a drunken mother be consigned to the "unbroken sleep of death," that she might be "blotted" from human memory. "Let no marble tell the cause of her dying," he inveighed, "and speak not to the stranger at her grave of the manner of her living."[16]

It is revealing, though perhaps not surprising, that this ferocious abhorrence of maternal drinking developed alongside the ascendance of the cult of domesticity. Though drunken mothers had always been objects of scorn and ostracism, early nineteenth-century criticism of maternal imbibing was subsumed by larger concerns about the effects of paternal drinking on children. By drinking themselves, parents set a bad example for the rising generation. Many families, an Ohio moral society lamented in 1815, made a "common use of spirituous liquor. Children taste almost daily, and thereby acquire a fondness for it." Parents, they warned, did not, or would not, realize that they were "preparing their children for intemperance" by the "common use of spirits in their houses." The stakes were high, for children of "dissolute parents seldom become useful and respectable members of society."[17]

Medical commentators supported this view, urging that parental intemperance threatened children in biological as well as social terms. Here too, both sexes seemed culpable. British physician Thomas Trotter noted that the "organs of generation must equally suffer in both sexes, from frequent intoxication," resulting in debilitated offspring and a "puny race." William Carpenter, another British doctor, deployed statistical data to demonstrate a correlation between mental illness and intemperance. Hereditary disposition to insanity, in Carpenter's view, represented the major cause of mental disorder, and "such predisposition [is] frequently the result of intemperate habits on the part of the parents." Oinomania, the "irresistible propensity to swallow stimulants in enormous doses," he added, is frequently hereditary, "being derived from a parent predisposed to insanity or addicted to intemperance."[18]

In this vein, early nineteenth-century reformers criticized mothers and fathers for turning their children into inebriates. One collection of temperance poetry, for example, lambasted both parents in turn. Upon being upbraided by his father for being a drunkard, an indignant son retorted:

> How oft you've said, "Come here my son,
> And drink a little sweeten'd Rum;
> Come, drink my son, 'tis good for you;"
> And sure I thought you told me true.

In another piece of tortured verse, a young inebriate took aim at his mother:

> When restless that I could not sleep,
> Who gave me Rum well stored with sweet?
> When sick, or felt a little pain,
> Who gave me Rum or Gin again?
>   My Mother!
>
> Who first did turn my feet astray,
> And lead me in this dangerous way?
> Who bent the twigg, and let it grow
> The way that leads to pain and wo?
>   My Mother![19]

As the century unfolded, however, and new understandings of gender emerged, intemperate mothers began to receive a greater share of the blame than fathers for damaging their offspring. In an 1835 prize essay, for example, Dr. Harvey Lindsly placed the influence of parental habits and constitution on their offspring beyond doubt. If the parents' health or "intellectual power" becomes impaired by a "long course of inebriety," their "unhappy progeny" will suffer similar problems. Lindsly went on:

> Probably this effect is more striking, and its results more appalling, where the mother is a devotee of this disgusting practice, than if the father only be in the habit of it. The influence of the mother's habits over the physical as well as the moral and intellectual character of the children seems to be of a more decided nature than that of the father. How doubly awful then does the guilt of this vice appear when viewed in this two-fold aspect![20]

Unlike drunken fathers, who could exert a biological influence on their offspring only before birth, dissipated mothers, temperance literature pointed out, could harm their children post-natally as well. Nursing mothers who drank alcohol, either to strengthen themselves or to produce milk that would quiet fussy children, received particular opprobrium. What physician, Dr. Mussey demanded, "has not known a nursing mother [to] give a fretful child a good night's sleep, by taking herself, a dose of brandy at bed time?" In this manner, alcohol entered the "delicate food prepared by nature for the nourishment and growth of helpless infancy," thereby laying the "foundation for intemperance in after life." The frequency and ferocity of temperance advocates' condemnations of this practice can scarcely be exaggerated. The "pure fountain from which the God of nature designed [the infant] should derive his nourishment, must be poisoned for his pretended benefit," railed one orator. Babies imbibe spirits with "their mother's milk," fulminated another, "and they are corrupted when the first habits of life are forming." Imbibing the "poison at the mother's breast," George Bethune lamented, "it is a moral miracle if the drunkard's children be not drunkards too." For the mere convenience of quieting a restless child, the nursing mother sowed in "her infant's susceptible system, by an inevitable law, the early seeds of disease and of vitiated appetite!" The babe sleeps "like a drunkard; and for the same reason. The drunkard's appetite has been formed at the breast, or in the cradle."[21]

As the cult of domesticity took root, mothers garnered a larger share of the blame than fathers for the effects of drinking on their offspring because of women's putative role as primary nurturers of the young. Especially in the middle class, fathers, who increasingly left the home to work, did not play as great a role in routine child care as did mothers. This emerging division of labor meant that in addition to injuring their offspring genetically through prenatal intemperance and physically by drinking while nursing, inebriated mothers could also harm children through dereliction of their child rearing duties. Intemperance caused mothers to "abandon the children of their own body," noted one reformer, or to neglect them shockingly. Reportedly true stories of maternal abuse abounded, all depicting the children's plight in the worst possible terms. When in a "state of intoxication," one mother "with her infant in her arms had fallen into the fire, and both were BURNED TO DEATH!" Another intoxicated mother came home with her baby in one arm and a bag of flour in the other. In her alcoholic stupor, she threw the "child into the meal chest" and placed the flour in the cradle, then collapsed into bed. During the night, cries occasionally roused the intoxicated woman, "and once or twice she actually got up and *rocked the bag of flour*." In the morning, the woman found her child "*dead in the flour chest*."[22]

Temperance fiction abounded with tales of maternal abuse. In *Confessions of a Female Inebriate*, Mary, the ill-fated mother, accidentally overdosed her four-year-old daughter with laudanum. Her "every faculty . . . blunted by absolute intoxication," Mary could not remember how large a dose she administered and questioned her role in the child's death five days later. In what David S. Reynolds has aptly dubbed the nadir of this genre of "dark temperance sensationalism," Helen More, the protagonist of Maria Lamas's *The Glass*, discovers the son she had locked in a closet two days earlier in order to continue her drinking. To stave off hunger, the boy had "gnawed to the bone" his left arm, severing an artery and causing him to bleed to death.[23]

Even if the children did not die immediately from maternal abuse or neglect, the consequences still scandalized observers. One outraged moralist recounted "authenticated instances of mothers taking bread which charity had given" to feed their children, and then trading it for liquor. Worse, drunken mothers literally stripped "from their children the clothes which charity had given them to keep them from the cold" and sold them for "intoxicating liquors." Or, as another put it, mothers "have sacrificed food, clothing, the health, and in the result, the lives of their children for strong drink." Worse still, a mother's bad example and thirst for liquor might lead to the corruption of her children's morals. One depraved woman wallowed in a mire of intemperance and vice, raising thirteen daughters "in the way she herself pursued . . . terrible to tell, the females she employed for purposes of prostitution were the offspring of her own body." Surveying the toll of female intemperance in cities, reformer Robert M. Hartley noted that among women who engaged in "inebriating indulgences . . . utter dissoluteness, and the ruin of children, are the dreadful results." Hartley registered outrage, but no surprise, when he found that girls of "tender years, and frequently neatly dressed, modest looking, and in many instances even pretty" appeared at offices and countinghouses, ostensibly to sell nuts and fruit. This artifice gained them admission to these places of business, where, "for a miserable bribe of a few shillings, [they] submit to the most degrading familiarities." The money they earned by this immoral traffic was "eagerly grasped by the *often inebriate parents*," who send forth the miserable girl again, "upon the same disgusting errand."[24]

Female Drunkenness and Sexual Immorality

The foregoing anecdote highlights another aspect of the extreme anxiety about women's drinking: the association of alcohol and sexual immorality. For centuries, Anglo-American culture linked drinking to the stimulation of sexual desire. Strong drink, a Shakespearean porter observed, "provokes the desire, but it takes away the performance." While antiliquor forces agreed that liquor inflamed desire, they were less certain that it diminished performance. In reformers' minds, drinking produced both the urge toward, as well as the practice of, lewdness. In 1784, Benjamin Rush noted that drinkers commonly exhibited "certain immodest actions." Apparently Rush later discerned a closer relationship between drinking and sexuality. In a treatise on diseases of the mind, Rush counseled "temperance in drinking, or rather the total abstinence from all fermented and distilled beverages" as one remedy for "[sexual] appetite, when inordinate."[25]

As the nineteenth century unfolded, popular anxiety about alcohol's ability to inflame sexual passion intensified. Drunkenness, the Rev. Stephen Badger warned in 1811, engendered "unchaste desires, immodest language, and wantonness of behavior . . . [as] its usual effects. The passions, which were before sufficiently ungovernable and headstrong, receive additional motion and strength. The sensual appetites are kindled into an unholy flame."[26]

While recognizing that drinking motivated a variety of aggressive and immoral behaviors—"deceit, dishonesty, lying, profane swearing, cruelty . . . forgery, gambling, robbery, manslaughter, murder, suicide"—reformers seldom failed to emphasize the link between alcohol and "lewdness, fornication, [and] adultery." Antiliquor advocates conjured up an "army of libertines that is stationed at every town and city in the land," striving to entangle the unwary in immorality and intemperance. Victory could not be won until virtue defeated both intemperance and sexual immorality: "Intoxication and lewdness are always confederate. If the one dies, the other will restore it to life. They must both stand or fall together." Similarly, Nathaniel S. Prime averred that "no better fuel can you afford the lusts of the flesh than ardent spirits. Hence we find that drunkenness and lewdness usually go hand in hand." Few who drink any quantity of liquor, Prime admonished, could encounter even a "small temptation without becoming adulterers in the sight of God." By exciting the "animal spirits to preternatural action," others explained, strong drink "stupefies the conscience, fires the blood, takes off every common restraint upon the violence of passion . . . the defiled heart boils with unbridled lust, and meditates fornication and adultery." In the inebriate, remarked one minister, "fleshly lusts" overpower the fear of God; the "themes and joys which occupy the licentious revel, bear no resemblance to those of heaven. The inspiration which the intemperate feel, is earthly, sensual, and devilish." The results of this inspiration, regretted a temperance newspaper, were "violation of chastity, insensibility to shame, and indescribable degradation."[27]

Reluctantly, early nineteenth-century American reformers admitted that even women fell prey to alcohol's libidinous influence. Indeed, in estimating alcohol's effects on men and women, a long tradition in Western society has identified drunkenness in men with aggressiveness and violence and in women with lasciviousness and unbridled sexuality. The immodest actions that Benjamin Rush detected as an early sign of intoxication were, he was "sorry to say," sometimes found in "women, who, when sober are uniformly remarkable for chaste and decent manners." Given the impetus to licentious behavior provided by liquor, commentators warned against marrying a woman who drinks, for she is *"liable not to be virtuous."* Everyone conceded, O. S. Fowler reminded readers in 1842, that

> every form of alcoholic drinks excites Amativeness, which exposes any woman, when slightly exhilarated, (I do not mean intoxicated,) to be taken advantage of . . . surely the exhilaration produced . . . even by wine, exposes her . . . to be taken unawares, and robbed of her most costly jewel.

Even without the double entendre, this effect of strong drink seems to be what one poet had in mind: "Sisters, wives, and mothers too,/ He often has betrayed,/ And artless maids of beauty rare/ In deep disgrace has laid."[28]

Given the emerging middle class's dual concerns about maintaining urban order and female purity, it is not surprising that early nineteenth-century temperance literature drew a close connection between women's drinking and prostitution, the ultimate loss of female virtue. "Intemperance and prostitution," the Rev. Mr. McDowall, chaplain to the New York Magdalen Asylum averred, "like the heart, arteries and veins, are inseparably connected." The link between intemperance and prostitution became visible in houses where "chastity [was] sold at a price." Grocers rented houses to prostitutes and supplied them with liquor. Moreover, several licensed dramshops were "actually filled with profligate women." But in every "unchaste house," McDowall reported, intemperance prevailed. "Almost all impure females are intemperate, and the majority of them are drunkards." Other social critics concurred. A New Haven moral reformer noted that licentiousness and brothels had spread throughout the city. At all these "vile haunts . . . of course, intoxicating liquor is sold; and drinking and dancing are kept up far into the night." In his classic study of prostitution, William Sanger opined that his *"decided impression is that not one per cent. of the prostitutes of New York practice their calling without partaking of intoxicating drinks."* So closely did antiliquor forces associate female drinking and prostitution that temperance organizers felt it necessary to take steps to prevent backsliding among reformed women. Cincinnati's Daughters of Temperance, for example, like those elsewhere, provided in their bylaws that if any member followed "any wicked practices, or use[d] any unlawful means in procuring a livelihood . . . she shall be expelled."[29]

Opinions varied as to whether drinking caused women to fall or fallen women inclined toward intemperance. Observers advanced several variations of the former interpretation. One account had girls being deceived into brothels, given drugs and imprisoned until they at last gave themselves up to "intemperance and crime." Prostitutes, William Sanger explained, wanted to drag unsullied women down to their level and aided in men's seduction and betrayal of the "virtuous of their own sex." Sometimes, seducers even counterfeited the domestic circle to accomplish their nefarious schemes. One villain, resolved to seduce a woman who resisted his advances, took his victim to a brothel where the madam and prostitutes played the part of his family to deceive her. The confederates gave the unwitting woman a "glass of drugged wine," and as soon as "its effects were visible the villainous deed was effected." Sanger offered some cases, however, where women became prostitutes "in order to obtain liquor . . . inclination was the result solely of intemperance."[30]

Other reformers insisted to the contrary that moral degradation turned women into inebriates. John McDowall, the controversial New York moral reformer, maintained that seduction and sexual immorality led to intemperance, not the reverse, as many temperance advocates claimed. McDowall's interviews with sixty-seven prostitutes revealed, for example, that sixty-six had become drunkards only after they became prostitutes. One tract told of a licentious young girl who seduced a married man, then "stupefied her conscience . . . with unrestrained recourse to intoxicating liquor" to harden herself in her iniquity. Other women turned to prostitution for more practical reasons, such as the necessity of supporting themselves and their children if husbands abandoned them. While affirming the double standard that made women's transgression a far more serious matter than men's, sympathetic observers noted that even repentant unchaste women looked in "vain for relief" or consolation from a society that considered them pariahs. With all roads back to respectability closed to them, fallen women "rushed headlong in iniquity, to the world of woe." Tormented by guilt at their irretrievable transgression, the unfortunate wretches "drown reflection in the cup of intoxication, to smother conviction of sin, so making their case still worse." Once confirmed in their careers of vice, prostitutes deadened "remorse, if awakened," with drunkenness. After a time, despair seized "upon them; and unable to bear reflection, they hasten the termination of their earthly career of misery by the intoxicating bowl."[31]

Some reformers exhibited sympathy for prostitutes, but far more expressed alarm that degraded women would prey on men, using liquor to accomplish their unholy ends. This represented a reversal of gender roles, as man, usually the sexual predator, became the prey. Searching the streets for unsuspecting or already intoxicated men, prostitutes "roam[ed] through the city, 'seeking whom they may devour.'" Temperance fiction attested to the dangers posed by predatory prostitutes. An oft-reprinted temperance tale observed that the "stimulus of intoxication impels its youthful votary to the gaming house or the brothel." In the story, one such inebriated young man "associated himself with an abandoned woman, who was strolling purposely alone." Discovered in the back room of a dramshop by his father, the lad tried unsuccessfully to escape, while his "vile companion, and a brazen-faced Jezebel she was, had already fled." In another story, Jane, a wanton of the "wretched, abandoned" class of "females who have but one name, and by this they are only known," steals a gold watch from drunken Charles Seymour. Later, the watch, along with Charles's inability to remember the encounter, renders him vulnerable to disgrace, as proof of his association with a "female nightwalker."[32]

The spectacle of female intemperance, linked as it was to sexual immorality and prostitution, jeopardized the emerging middle-class domestic order in a number of ways. First, it imperiled men, the putative heads of households. One authority observed that many "male drunkards were coined in houses of fornication. Young men of sober habits are introduced in these craters of the bottomless pit. To please their misses, cordials are purchased," and the downward spiral to gambling, illicit sex, and intemperance began. Second, corrupted men brought the effects of vice into the domestic circle. Diseases "growing out of corrupt intercourse with depraved females," reformers warned, were among the consequences of using liquor. Moreover, the "greater number of breaches of the marriage vow are committed by men in a state of partial intoxication, by strong drink."[33] Thus the alarming intersection of intemperance and sexual immorality threatened not only the drunkard himself but the health and welfare of his wife and family and, through them, the viability of domesticity as a model for social order.

Despite men's obvious role in this threat to domestic stability—they, after all, introduced the ravages of intemperance, infidelity, and disease to the fireside—temperance literature shifted the focus to women's culpability. Commentators from both ends of the social spectrum laid the blame for men's transgressions at the feet of the women who seduced them. Simeon L. Crockett, a condemned criminal, emphasized women's role in destroying men in his "dying words," declaring that

> it is a truth that *females* use ardent spirets as mutch as men according to their privileg and dround thare delacesse, and then tha will quick form a bad character, and that as lo as the dust tha stand uppon, and then a bad house is the delight of a drunken man. Mene a promising youth has been led into sutch houses and ruined forever.

In more erudite fashion, clergyman and temperance ideologue John Marsh rehearsed the case against immoral women, noting that in the "entire ruin of young men," the "single glass was but the decoy." Marsh quoted the English poet Robert Pollok to make his point: "She urg'd him still to fill another cup;/ —— and in the dark still night,/ When God's unsleeping eye alone can see,/ He went to her adulterous bed." The woman in question "wove the winding sheet of souls, and laid/ Them in the urn of everlasting death."[34]

Female intemperance raised another hideous specter to bedevil white middle-class domesticity: the prospect of racial amalgamation. Whites, particularly in the North, feared that abolitionism might embolden African American men to pursue white women. Alcohol's emancipation of carnal appetites posed a wider amalgamationist threat, however. The potent combination of liquor and lust could lead young men or women into unspeakable degradation, which might even involve crossing racial boundaries to find debased companions. In either case, alcohol-induced racial mixing promised tragedy and mocked the sanctity of the domestic sphere. This amalgamationist scenario lent itself to the lurid sensationalism favored by some temperance fiction authors. Walt Whitman's Franklin Evans married Margaret, "a Creole," because he drunkenly succumbed to her exotic charms. When Evans sobered up and realized his error, he discarded Margaret, who committed suicide because of disappointment over his false love. In another fictional permutation of this theme, promising young heir Thomas Harvey's intemperance reduced him to haunting disorderly houses and low grogshops. When a concerned friend, the upright and respectable Andrew Sinclair, tracked him down in one such dive, Harvey's sense of disgrace made him shrink "into the utmost recess of the miserable cellar, in which congregated some dozen of the most abandoned of both sexes and colors." Concerns about intoxication leading to interracial sex were not confined to fiction, however. Mainline temperance advocates feared that real misguided youths might sink even further than their fictional counterparts through the "lower grades of intemperance" to the "filthy lazar-house of beastly drunkenness, where uproar and blasphemy are heard from the voices of half-clothed men and women, white and black, mingled in debauchery of drinking and sensuality, with an utter forgetfulness of color and sex."[35]

Female Intemperance and Gender Identity

As the foregoing suggests, female intemperance posed a number of problems for emerging ideologies of gender. Drunken women's rejection of maternal duties, wifely subordination, and sexual morality flouted both patriarchal authority and the dictates of the middle-class cult of domesticity. This alone might account for the reformers' tendency to wish that female drunkenness did not exist and to define it as the most shameful and revolting spectacle imaginable when they could not avoid acknowledging its reality. As Harry Gene Levine observed, middle-class reformers' "heavy investment in the image of women as pure and virtuous" made the topic of female intemperance an ideological minefield. Too many "examples of drunken women," Levine argued, "especially middle-class ones, could undermine the whole model of the middle-class family" envisaged by domestic ideology.[36]

Still, the vehemence of popular reaction against female intemperance suggests that something more was at play. Certainly, Americans worried that intoxicated wives defied their husbands' authority and that besotted mothers would not raise the virtuous children so necessary to the survival of the American republic. But the discomfort ran deeper, particularly among the middle class that produced and consumed the bulk of temperance literature. This should not be surprising, when one remembers the fledgling, if not embryonic state of the middle class during the early nineteenth century. It was not yet, in the words of Louis Hartz, a "triumphant middle class" that could "take itself for granted." Rather, the emerging middle class had to strive mightily to create a social identity, establish a distinctive lifestyle, and justify its values to both itself and the rest of American society.[37]

Historians who have documented those struggles have noted the centrality of domesticity, and the gender ideology that underpinned it, to middle-class formation. A wide range of domestic writers and ideologues depicted the emerging middle-class gender system that relegated women to the confines of the home while allowing men the freedom to move between home and marketplace as consonant with naturally, if not divinely, ordained binary oppositions. Women's innate qualities produced "the love of offspring, the propensity to form permanent connections, and the love of home" that suited them for a life of retirement by the middle-class fireside. Men's inherent firmness, aggressiveness, and rationality destined them for the strife of public occupations in the expanding capitalist economy. Where woman could exert a "softening and refining influence" on man's aggressive tendencies, as in the American middle class, she ranked "foremost in all human progress," and benefited the whole of society. Resisting the social imperatives imposed by "natural" gender roles produced only disaster. On the one hand, preventing women's influence from exerting itself on men produced despotism and stagnation. In "fixed or retrogressive" societies where "Woman is treated as a slave" (the examples given were usually Islamic nations), her salutary influence wanes, to the detriment of both sexes. On the other, allowing women to overstep themselves inverted proper gender relations, producing inevitably "contempt for an effeminate man, and a horror of a masculine woman." We "love woman because she is unlike us," a temperance paper observed. "She is gentle, soft, kind, fair; we are rough, in manners harsh, and in temper cruel . . . There is no attraction except between opposites, and when she simulates our nature[,] the effect is repulsive."[38] Middle-class ideology, which imbued gender roles with religious as well as secular significance, presented its recommended domestic arrangements as insurance against such unnatural deviation; as both normative and optimal. Domesticity, then, claimed to be nothing less than a social arrangement uniquely suited to the dictates of the natural order, and a large measure of middle-class identity, authority, and prestige proceeded from championing and embodying it.[39]

Not surprisingly, anything that destabilized the comforting dualisms on which domesticity depended posed serious problems for the emerging middle class. Female intemperance posed just such a threat. Women's drinking, more than other female offenses, transgressions, or irregularities, called into question fundamental assumptions about male and female nature, identity, and difference. Female drunkards displayed behaviors inconsistent with the middle-class vision of an immutable female morality: they neglected their children, engaged in promiscuous sex, and heeded the call of individual desires rather than social or familial duties. In effect, they confounded the entire supposedly "natural" patriarchal order by exposing the malleability of male and female identity, and the artificiality and performativeness of gender. Thus women's alcohol abuse threatened not just domestic ideology but the bedrock binary gender assumptions on which it was based. It was not merely that female intemperance transgressed the line between "proper" male and female behavior. Rather, because alcohol led women to display behavior that contradicted the whole notion that different and immutable natures, characters, and attributes inhered in the sexes, it hinted that no such line existed in the first place.

Intemperance bespoke appetite and aggression, character traits associated with men, not women. When properly controlled and channeled, these qualities aided men in their struggles to excel in war, politics, and business. Unleashed, they led to drunkenness and violence. In neither form could these characteristics appear in women without revealing the artificiality of the gender distinctions that domestic ideologues strove mightily to depict as natural. The attribution of appetite to women, reprising as it did earlier images of woman as a depraved, voracious creature likely to corrupt man, represented a profound challenge, both to fundamental assumptions about the immutability of male and female natures, and to the emerging middle-class domestic ideal. Women indulging a depraved appetite for liquor did not just imperil "existing power relationships between men and women," as one scholar noted. Rather, female intemperance compromised the entire gender ideology that made those power relationships conceivable and justifiable.[40]

Fundamental notions of male and female identity, then, as well as the prevailing balance of sexual power, rested on a binary gender opposition that could be defended as an immutable aspect of the natural order. Physiologists, physicians, and phrenologists attempted to trace this opposition—and the social organization that supposedly proceeded naturally from it—to physical structures. Explaining the origins of feminine characteristics, one physician and phrenologist pointed to the "superior length of the female brain," which revealed a "greater development of the organs of Philoprogenitiveness, Adhesiveness, and Inhabitativeness" (that is, love of offspring, fidelity, and domesticity). Likewise, woman's physical makeup made her less prone to sexual appetite than men. "Women," observed the same physician, "as is shown by the smallness of the upper part of the neck, have a less development of Amativeness than men." Other physicians, as discussed in a later chapter, linked women's intellect, character, and behavior to the influence of the female reproductive system. Female intemperance posed a major problem for the physiological, and ostensibly natural, explanation of masculine and feminine traits, for alcohol affected both men and women in remarkably similar ways. Whatever their views on gender, most commentators agreed that intemperance turned both sexes into subhuman brutes. Drunkenness "has found means to adapt itself," bewailed one temperance advocate: "the delicate female and the brawny backwoodsman" both succumbed to this "master vice." Even those who minimized the extent of female intemperance admitted that women "quaffing the poison 'mantled in the golden bowl'; or participating to excesses at the luscious feasts of *Circe*, would, in the language of the fable, be transformed into monsters, and revolting shapes!" Liquor deadened and ultimately destroyed the "common affections of nature," in both men and women. Such unfortunates sink "below brutality," and lose "all feeling and concern for their dearest relations and tender offspring."[41]

If intemperance revealed a common level of human brutishness to which both men and women could sink, temperance reformers had to grapple with the disturbing possibility that the putative male and female "natures" they cherished might be nothing more than veneer. The middle-class gender binary could encompass and explain man's reduction to a brute by drunkenness, for after all, appetite and aggressiveness were necessary, though dangerous, aspects of his divinely ordained character. But if the "fairest of God's creation," innately virtuous woman, could also become a "noisome pestilence, polluting heaven's sweet air with her foetid breath, and falling into an untimely grave, a loathsome mass of putrescence," how could claims for fundamental male and female difference be sustained? Consternated reformers described, with "mingled emotions of pity and disgust," drunken women in terms usually reserved for male inebriates:

> Look at her! Her hair is disheveled; her cheeks are pale and haggard; her eye is red and watery; her breath foetid; her conversation silly; her smile idiotic; her whole appearance woebegone and loathsome!—And yet she is a *woman*—belongs to the sex we call beautiful, and upon whom we are wont to bestow our admiration and love.[42]

This lament betrays equal measures of disbelief that woman could betray her true self and indignation that immutable female nature might be a mere illusion. Walt Whitman captured the impact of this gender destabilization by alcohol in his temperance novel, *Franklin Evans*. While drunk himself, the young protagonist attends a theater and sees an actress, "a wild hoyden of a girl . . . whose beauty excited my admiration to no small degree." Repairing backstage after the play, Evans finds a woman drinking beer. Her eyes, he noted had a "sickly, bleared appearance," and her complexion an "oily brown" cast. "She was my charmer," Evans realized with shock and dismay, "of the hoyden in the farce! . . . Her voice was coarse and masculine, and her manners on a par with her voice." In the revelation that the "wild hoyden" could become a crude, mannish drinker, Whitman highlighted both the artificiality and performativeness of gender and the impact on gender relations of alcohol's destabilization of seemingly natural female qualities.[43]

As might be expected, then, temperance advocates scrambled to reconceptualize female drunkenness in a way that would minimize its destabilizing tendencies, especially for the middle class. One tactic involved attributing much of women's intemperance to male drinking. Poverty and want produced by a husband's intemperance, one reformer noted, might easily lead a woman to the "same dreadful expedient, in order to drown the sorrows of her heart." Popular lecturer George Bethune echoed this sentiment, observing that a husband's drinking and abuse could make his wife so miserable that she "drinks to drown her sorrows." Other reformers too, suggested that wives' intemperance "had generally been the consequence of the same vicious and degrading propensity" in the husband. Even if wives were not rendered disconsolate by their husband's alcoholic excesses, they might succumb merely because of the bad example set by the head of the household. In a "spirit of sociability, and deference" to drinking men, women risked yielding up that "discreet reserve and subdued cheerfulness, which is at once their highest charm, and surest protection." Or, wives might simply drink to get even. As a tract remarked, if the "husband drinks abroad, the wife may take the same liberty at home."[44]

Taking a slightly different tack, some reformers presented female intemperance as the vice of groups far removed from the respectable middle class: immigrants, the working class, and African Americans. Though temperance literature warned that even women of "intellect and accomplishments" could fall prey to intemperance, most of the examples it cited did not come from the middle class. Reformers ascribed much intemperance to the working class, as did the Pennsylvania Society for Discouraging the Use of Ardent Spirits when it cautioned against following the English example of allowing factories to become "nurseries of disease and vice." "Women at the spinning wheel or spinning machine," it warned, already debilitated by confinement to cramped quarters all day, have their health further ruined by their use of "distilled and fermented liquors." Even armed with knowledge of the ills and abuses of Europe, reformers still considered immigrant women a formidable problem. Mrs. Stockton, the steward of the Philadelphia Alms House, noted that most women seeking relief were the wives of recent working-class immigrants who drank too much. Few native-born women crossed her path: "*Sober wives in general provide for themselves.*"[45]

Newspaper reports and popular accounts of public drunkenness or other alcohol-related crimes frequently identified them with African Americans or, through their surnames, the Irish. An 1841 broadside, for instance, cited the case of a "young colored female" charged with burglary, whose "unhappy present situation" resulted from intemperance. The Irish received even greater attention. One Boston pamphlet regretted that often when a husband was thrown in the house of correction for drunkenness, the wife was committed for the same offense, and the children wound up in the almshouse. "These foreigners," the author revealed, "are principally Irish." Reformers did not shrink from providing details about drunken Irishwomen. The Washingtonian Charles Woodman remembered clerking in a store where a "daughter of the Emerald Isle" called regularly to exchange corn she had earned by weaving for rum. No one rebuked her, Woodman added, though "we all knew how poor this woman was." Drunken Irishwomen found their way into temperance fiction, as well. The heroine of Henrietta Rose's *Nora Wilmot* ministers to a drunken Irish mother, managing to sober her up despite her pleas for somebody to "give me a wea throp of thrink; oh! just a wea throp." Upon hearing of Nora's exploits, her Uncle Grey expressed concern for her safety and doubted that her efforts would bear fruit:

> I have hope in almost any case where the subject is nativeborn, but our German and Irish populations, with a few very rare exceptions, are entirely hopeless. Why, do you know that one of the leading attractions, possessed of our country, to the emigrating Irishman, is the fact that whisky [*sic*] is plenty and cheap? . . . And not the least of the evil is that the women are almost as much addicted to a fondness for 'a wea throp' as the men are, and a debased woman is a far more formidable character than a debased man.[46]

Both these expedients proved unsatisfactory, however, as neither truly resolved the problem of reconciling female drunkenness with the idea of a universal female nature that rejected vice. If women drank because men did, this rendered the argument that middle-class domestic relations fostered salutary female influence on men problematic at best. Likewise, admitting of variations among female nature and character based upon race, ethnicity, or class might be superficially reassuring, but it hardly buttressed claims for immutable and universal gender difference. For this reason, a drunken woman, wherever she appeared, represented a "spectacle more hideous and mortifying" than a male inebriate. Afflictions common to alcoholic overindulgence assumed far more disturbing proportions when they appeared in women, largely because they confounded stable gender distinctions. Writing of gutta rosacea, the discolored eruptions that frequently appeared on drunkards' faces and noses, for instance, one physician noted that the "deformity is disgusting, but particularly in females."

Male and female reformers alike agreed that women who drank became "even more debased than their brutalized husbands." Even *The Pearl,* a temperance newspaper edited by a woman, could ask "What sight is so loathsome as a drunken woman? A man habituated to the glass presents an awful character, but a woman . . . presents a character far more pitiable and depraved. She seems to have lost every lineament of the Divine image—to be beyond the pale of human sympathy—and almost beyond the hope of restoration."[47]

This repugnance presented temperance advocates with a dilemma. Certainly, they could not credibly deny that women drunkards exhibited many of the gender characteristics associated with men: that was precisely *why* drunken women seemed so disgusting. But how then to explain that angelic woman could become even more depraved than worldly man without questioning the binary oppositions that underpinned so much of the gender ideology they promoted?

The Angel Woman and the Demon Rum

Reformers solved this predicament in two related ways. First, they asserted that it was woman's exalted nature that made her peculiarly prone to the abject degradation observed in female drunkards. An anonymous commentator on the moral physiology of intemperance explained: because of her nature, woman can attain a moral height that man can never reach, but the loftiness of her ascent means that she has farther to fall. Woman "soars higher into purer realms, and falls lower into darker abysses. She is the most divinely beautiful, or the most hideously ugly of the last and highest of creation of God." Thus, this moral physiologist noted, one usually finds besotted women among the "most extreme forms of this disease [intemperance]." The largest number, "by a vast majority is found in the lowest form, the animal drunkard, only it is still far worse, the drunken harlot."[48] In this formulation, alcohol transformed women into mannish brutes because the sublime morality posited as innate in females by prevailing gender ideology rendered them vulnerable to such a precipitous fall. This cast the contradiction to stable male and female natures as more apparent than real. Women were different from men; the monster alcohol exploited those very differences to compromise woman's moral nature and transmogrify her into a horrible creature that resembled but outstripped the most degraded male drunkard. By the 1860s, these "long familiar sentiments" were well established. A physician and professor who spent years treating female inebriates summed it up thus: "A debauched woman is always, everywhere, a more terrible object to behold than a brutish man. We look to see them a little nearer to the angels than ourselves, and so their fall seems greater."[49]

The second strategy to resolve this seeming contradiction supported the first while furthering the temperance movement's efforts to demonize alcohol and those who trafficked in it. Though women could fall so low as to become drunken harlots, temperance literature averred, their inherent morality and religiosity afforded near invulnerability against all but the most powerful and insidious foes. Alcohol proved to be such an enemy, an unmitigated evil masquerading as an innocent article of commerce. "Nothing else in nature, but rum," insisted a temperance newspaper, "can cause a woman to so degrade herself," as to appear in public "reeling under beastly intoxication. . . . Debase her, steep her in guilt, and in her sober senses no such public shame can approach." Alcohol's fell power could even sunder the strongest of bonds, that between mother and child.

> Is there another influence under heaven . . . strong enough to drag a mother from the side of a dear, sick, suffering child, and lead her, while she can stand up or move, to abandon it to the united power of disease, biting cold, and utter loneliness . . . except the accursed influence of the intoxicating cup? . . . I have never witnessed the operation of any other power than that of alcoholic drinks which was capable of conquering *a mother's love*.[50]

Certainly, no other means of altering consciousness produced results so distinctly at odds with what gender ideologues believed women were or should be. Other intoxicants produced results consonant with approved gender roles. Nitrous oxide, for example, the effects of which were often exhibited to the public in the 1840s, purportedly revealed the "true self" of the user, or so enthusiasts claimed. For female participants in nitrous oxide demonstrations, this generally meant "demonstrations of moral virtue. Most recited scripture, broke into song, or lapsed into poetic verse." Nor did opiates, whose use was widespread, pose undue problems for the emerging gender ideology. Though physicians, reformers, and social critics decried the misuse of opiates such as laudanum, they were not as troubled by women's use of the drug as they were by their drinking. Women's fragile constitutions and difficulties with menstruation, pregnancy, and childbirth made it understandable that they might resort, often on doctors' orders, to this seeming panacea. Since opiates produced lassitude, it was easy to reconcile their abuse with, or mistake it for, gender norms that stressed female passivity and retirement into the domestic sphere. Not surprisingly, the majority of opium addicts during the latter half of the nineteenth-century were middle-class white women. Even altered states of consciousness not produced by drugs, such as spiritualist trances, seemed to fit the prevailing image of women. Most spiritualists considered women to be better mediums than men, supposedly because of the innate sensitivity of the female nature. Only alcohol, it seemed, undermined fundamental understandings of gender.[51]

This twofold account of how women could become more degraded drunkards than men fit well with the larger program for alcohol reform outlined in temperance literature. It reaffirmed gender roles implicit in the middle-class ideology of domesticity on which temperance was in large measure based. In addition, explaining women's drunkenness in this manner heightened public awareness of the dangers of alcohol and provided a rationale for why women had to be protected from the ravages of liquor. To further exploit public sentiment in favor of protecting women, however, temperance advocates shifted their focus away from women seduced by liquor to those whose misfortunes sprang not from their own intemperance but from that of the men who surrounded them. As the next chapter demonstrates, drunken hags could not mobilize public support for the battle against liquor as well as respectable women who were victimized by men's intemperance.

Victims and Exemplars

Promoting Gender Ideology in

Temperance Literature

With the notion of angelic women seduced by demon rum, which preyed on the very delicacy that defined woman's nature, temperance advocates rationalized the contradiction to middle-class gender ideology posed by female intemperance. Explaining away drunken women was only half the equation, however. To win popular support for reform, and to harmonize with middle-class avowals of female virtue, temperance ideologues needed to devise positive, affirming roles for women in the battle against drink. They supplied this need by populating temperance literature with two kinds of women: pitiful though sympathetic victims of male drunkenness whose suffering goaded the indifferent into action; and moral exemplars whose goodness and righteousness encouraged the temperate and reformed the inebriate. These two archetypes, or a combination of them, encompassed the overwhelming majority of women encountered in temperance literature. Each served, in a variety of ways, the related goals of promoting the temperance cause and affirming middle-class notions of gender. Not surprisingly, the ideological work done by promoting these two models of female participation in temperance reform had significant implications and consequences for women's status in American society and culture. This chapter examines temperance literature's deployment of these two roles for women and explores their larger ramifications.

Women as Victims of Male Intemperance

Writing in 1813, temperance advocate John Watson lamented the victimization of women by male drunkards. "The variety of sufferings of the female sex," he observed, "arising from the use of spirits and consequent drunkenness among the men, claims a considerable space in a portraiture of the subject; they are too great and extensive to admit of enumeration, too serious and impressive to be tolerated, and also, too frequent and general to need a description." Despite Watson's denial that the dire effects of male intemperance on women required further elaboration, such enumeration and description became an omnipresent and indispensable weapon in the temperance movement's rhetorical arsenal during the following decades. Woman as the victim of male drunkenness proved a powerful image for temperance reformers of all stripes, for it seldom failed to evoke interest in the cause, sympathy for beleaguered women, and anger at the purveyors and consumers of alcohol. For the middle class in particular, though, casting woman as victim recommended itself for two reasons. First, male drunkenness afflicted women in all the relationships central to domestic life. As drunkard's wife Mrs. Frances B. Norris put it, intemperance "hast cursed/ Woman in every sphere of life;/ Thou'st given her griefs and woes the worst,/ As mother, daughter, sister, wife."[1] Second, victimized women offered a means of working through class as well as gender issues. In both style and substance, pathetic accounts of the violence and fear endured by women betrayed middle-class anxieties during a period of social and economic uncertainty. Industrial and commercial expansion in the antebellum United States elevated many to the middle class, but prosperity could not alleviate the gnawing uncertainty that the latest economic bust might, however worthy a family might be, capriciously reduce it to penury and disgrace. Stories of women's victimization provided a metaphor for larger concerns, employing the sentimental language and literary conventions so beloved of the middle class to work through fear and indignation at the possibility of being denied the comforts of economic security and social position by forces beyond an individual's control.[2]

Hence while middle-class reformers urged that intemperance injured all women in some way, they emphasized certain images of victimized woman more than others. Conceiving of male drunkards as the potential or actual heads of households, they focused concern on female roles that contributed most directly to the maintenance of the middle-class home as a refuge from the outside world and nursery for succeeding generations. "Alcohol, the foe of humanity, is the demon curse of the domestic sphere," asserted Lorenzo Dow Johnson, "the murderer of countless thousands of wives and mothers." Wives, mothers, and to a lesser extent, daughters, were essential to the functioning of the middle-class domestic sphere in ways that sisters were not. Thus while reformers acknowledged that liquor caused "many a . . . gentle sister's tears," they paid the sisters of drunkards the least attention by far in temperance literature. Only occasionally did tracts, songs, or sermons mention the sisters who "hung their heads in shame for one they loved so well," or exhorted women to persuade "husbands and sons and brothers" to support temperance measures.[3]

Opponents of alcohol lavished somewhat more attention on the plight of the daughters of intemperate men, who required paternal care and protection even more than did sons. The "drunkard's daughter" became a stock character in temperance writings, reflecting middle-class anxiety about perpetuating social status through advantageous marital alliances. A father's drunkenness compromised a family's propriety, casting doubt on the suitability of its female offspring for connection with respectable middle-class families. Temperance fiction often noted the shame and stigma visited upon innocent maidens by paternal inebriety. In Mrs. Henrietta Rose's *Nora Wilmot*, for instance, the heroine loses social position and wealth when her politician father becomes a drunkard. Mrs. J. Thayer's *The Drunkard's Daughter* reminded readers that being the child of an inebriate compromised a young woman's marital prospects. From respect for social convention and concern for the reputation of her suitor, Thayer's heroine, Alice Ray, declines to marry the wealthy Charles Mortimer "while disgrace attaches to my name," insisting that the couple wait until her father reforms.[4]

Most discussions of the drunkard's daughter went beyond mere social embarrassment to highlight the abuse, hunger, and poverty produced by her father's drinking.

> Go feel what I have felt,
> > Go bear what I have borne—
> Sink 'neath a blow a father dealt.
> > And the cold world's proud scorn;
> Then suffer on from year to year ...
> Thy sole relief the scorching tear.
>
> Go weep as I have wept
> > O'er a loved father's fall—
> See every promised blessing swept—
> > Youth's sweetness turned to gall;
> Life's fading flowers strew'd all the way—
> That brought me up to woman's day.

Experiencing these travails, often at a tender age, marked daughters for life. No gladness resided in the "young bosom" of a typical drunkard's daughter, for she "had learned in early childhood, the lessons of care and forethought that belong to maturer years." Were she to aspire to a better life by bringing "such garlands for that young brow as others wore, the ruthless hand of a drunken father tore away the wreath and hope departed!" Other accounts took pathos to even greater heights. One "Affecting Incident" found fourteen-year-old Ellen on her deathbed, disturbed by her father's drunken ranting. Raising her "little skeleton head," Ellen implored her mother, *"why don't you ask pa to be still, while I am dying?"* The last words "were in vain. With the last sigh of her gentle spirit there went up to Heaven also the inhuman ravings of the drunken father."[5]

Often, temperance literature depicted a daughter not only having to suffer "starvation" and the "harsh treatment of her father," but also to participate actively in his addiction to liquor. A recurring image had the bedraggled and ashamed daughter sent to fetch liquor for her brutal father. Lucius M. Sargent's story, "The Cranberry Meadow," for example, contrasted the "glowing cheeks and merry voices" of children on their way to school with the "pale, soiled face, tattered dress, and bare feet" of Mary Milman, who was on the way to procure liquor. Or, in a widely circulated tract, the Rev. John Marsh portrayed Hannah Hawkins, the daughter of reformed drunkard and celebrated Washingtonian lecturer John Hawkins, begging her father, "don't send me after whiskey today!" More harrowing still, some writers depicted daughters helping subdue delirious fathers. One songster recounted a case of delirium tremens:

> In stern defence he fiercely stands
> With ghastly eyes and firm clenched hands;
> His little children sob and cry,
> Instinctive from their father fly;
> The wife and elder daughters try
> The raving maniac to tie,
> The wife and elder daughters try
> The raving maniac to tie.[6]

Similarly horrific scenarios suffused the elaboration of another more prominent image of woman in temperance literature: the mother. Here the emotional impact often derived from the contrast, explicit or implied, between prescribed standards of middle-class mothering and the reality of maternal helplessness in a drunkard's household. Temperance advocates emphasized the terrible spectacle of dutiful mothers unable to protect and care for their beloved children in the face of poverty, violence, and abuse from drunken fathers. On the death of a drunkard from delirium tremens, for example, a physician noted that his bride, "and too, the infant by her side," had long since been laid "beneath the weeping willow's shade." Raising the emotional pitch, a temperance almanac described a drunkard's home, in which the "poor mother and her babes are cowering over a few decaying embers, blue and shivering with the cold . . . the mother weeps as she hugs still firmer in her embrace the little one which is striving to draw nourishment from her bosom." Even this imagery paled before the efforts of other temperance writers. A correspondent for *The Lily* conjured up for readers the portrait of a drunken suicide, "ghastly in death . . . and there, mute in helpless innocency, lies the corpse of his little daughter," the two-year-old strangled by the father's "murderous" hand with "a cord that had cut quite through the skin, and nearly seperated [*sic*] the head from the body." This occurred while the mother was attending to another ill daughter. The article left its middle-class female readers with a vision with which they could identify: the mother sitting and holding the dead baby, anxiously awaiting the "magic of the daguerreotype. 'Oh give me at least this,' she said, 'all that will soon remain of my child.'"[7]

Temperance reformers also sympathized with mothers who lost children to intemperance. Though they trusted that the "lessons of virtue and temperance, taught by the tender eloquence of maternal lips, and enforced by the sad contemplation of maternal wrongs" might save children from the "corrupting influence of their father's example," experience often belied these hopes. Mothers beseeched rumsellers to spare their sons, fearing that "even now he neareth, the drunkard's awful grave." "'Tis over—all my task is done, My world forever past," lamented another heartbroken mother whose son had died of drunkenness.

> The panders of thy vice have fled,
> But I have held thy aching head,
> And watched and wept and prayed,
> And sure, I think, had'st thou but known
> What my poor heart has undergone,
> Thou wouldst not thus have strayed.

When invoking the image of disconsolate mothers, temperance writers had few scruples about manipulating their readers' emotions. *The Appeal of a Wife and Mother*, a widely circulated tract, presented its audience with a veritable horror show of alcoholic abuse and devastation. The female protagonist endures the curses and blows of her husband and is eventually removed from affluent surroundings to a "rude-built and low thatched cottage" by the shore. There her woes grew worse: three sons die of their father's neglect and abuse, and she "was here destined to see two of my boys become the victims of intemperance . . . the most profligate and abandoned sailors in the navy." The unremitting gloom and desolation of this and similar tales left readers with no doubts about the baleful influence of male intemperance on mothers.[8]

Implausible as it might seem that temperance writers could surpass this level of pathos and sensationalism, they took the morbid and lachrymose to new lows in their embellishment of the most common image of victimized woman: the brokenhearted and tormented wife.

Wives, whom contemporary opinion invested with the greatest share of responsibility for maintaining the middle-class domestic sphere, figured more prominently than any other female figure in temperance literature. Many tracts, stories, and sermons emphasized the constant shame and anxiety to which a husband's intemperance subjected women. Even husbands who avoided chronic drunkenness but continued to drink could destroy a wife's peace of mind. Julia Cunningham, the heroine of Mrs. R. S. Harvey's "A Single Glass of Wine," for example, married William Russell, who indulged to excess on occasion but never became "a confirmed inebriate." His lack of "moral strength" to forswear forever the intoxicating cup, however, left Julia in constant fear and trepidation: "could you but see Julia Cunningham now, . . . her finely rounded form so thin and wasted; her brilliant eyes shaded with unceasing anxiety; her step tremulous with sad foreboding when absence is too lengthened."[9]

Other authors addressed the plight of wives whose husbands did become drunkards, often using themes or language that resonated with middle-class experiences, expectations, or values. Playing off the importance of transmitting property and providing for widows, a facetious "Drunkard's Will," for instance, left only "shame, poverty, and a broken heart" to his "beloved wife, who has cheered me so far in the path of life." Most commentators, however, treated the unfortunate women married to drunkards with deadly seriousness, portraying them in relation to their husbands as "a weeping wife to mock, 'till all her hopes in anguish end." A Richmond, Virginia, temperance society's annual report went so far as to compare the treatment of women in "pagan" nations favorably with that of the "enlightened" and "refined" woman afflicted with a drunken husband.

> To the female who has tasted the ecstasies of friendship, who has known the flattery of hope, and enjoyed the pleasures of an enlightened intellect and refined taste; when she sees the object of her deepest, fondest affection, despised by himself and loathed by others; when she sees her hopes and her happiness at once going down with the sunset of her companion's reason; — nay, when she perceives her fondness returned with abuse, and her devotion recompensed with malice and cruelty; tell me, to a female thus situated, must not the swinging hook of Hindostan, be a cradle of delight? Yes; compared with the mental agony of such a spirit, the flame from the pyre of her husband would come on her frame like the bland zephyrs of the Spring.[10]

Nineteenth-century American society attributed enormous importance to the marriage contract and recognized the tremendous sacrifice of identity and personal autonomy women made upon entering it. This explains the repeated emergence in temperance writing of the injustice of men's failure to keep their part of the bargain by cherishing, protecting, and providing for their wives. Here, too, it is easy to detect a more general obsession with contractual obligations and their fulfillment, understandable consid-ering the importance of such agreements to antebellum middle-class sta-tus and prosperity. "Woman, silent-suffering, devoted woman," bemoaned one orator, "here bends to her direst affliction." Who will protect her, he asked, "when *he* is her insulter, her oppressor? What shall delight her, when she shrinks from the sight of *his* face, and trembles at the sound of *his* voice?" In a variety of temperance publications, friends regretted the helplessness of drunkards' wives to ameliorate their pitiful condition. Af-ter the "demon Alcohol" had crushed the "fond hopes" of one such wife, her friend bewailed that his "disappointed and broken hearted companion could only mourn over her blasted hopes, as she saw her husband violat-ing his solemn vows to her and becoming a slave to alcohol." If broken marriage vows elicited sorrow from some, they provoked indignation in oth-ers, especially female temperance advocates. One wife upbraided the "icy-hearted rumseller" for stealing her husband and leaving her alone. "Alone in-deed, for he who shares my lowly dwelling now/ Is not the same to whom I pledged the sacred marriage vow./ I did not wed that tremulous, and weak, and blasted thing,/ Nay, woman's early love could ne'er to such an idol cling." A writer for *The Lily* minced even fewer words:

> I heard that a friend of my youth was in deep distress, mourning over the degradation of him whom she had chosen to be her companion through life, and who had vowed to God to love and cherish her so long as he should live. Alas! for the weakness or wickedness of man, that temptation can so easily induce him to break such holy vows, and lead him to treat with cruelty and neglect, a loving wife and children. But so it is.[11]

Broken promises and shattered dreams were bad enough, but temper-ance advocates reminded their audiences that drunkards' betrayal of their marriage vows had material consequences as well. The economic uncer-tainty—and the prospect of falling from comfortable circumstances to poverty and want with which the drunkard's wife constantly contended—resonated with an anxious middle class that had not yet solidified its so-cial or economic position in American life. When men did not fulfill their responsibility to support their families, wives had to scramble to make ends meet and maintain at least a semblance of respectability. Frequently this involved an inversion of the emerging middle-class domestic econ-omy: wives, rather than husbands, working for wages to support the fam-ily. "How many wives of such men," demanded Theodore Lyman, "are obliged to toil hard and late for the support of a family—to suffer re-proach, rebuke, and self-denial, and domestic weariness and want!" Worse still, even when women managed to eke out a living for themselves and their children, the absence of legislation protecting a wife's wages allowed a drunken husband to pilfer with impunity her meager earnings to buy liquor. In *Confessions of a Reformed Inebriate*, for example, the drunkard Charles's idleness forces his wife, Harriet, to make artificial flowers to buy food for their children. Desperate for liquor, Charles breaks into her band box in her absence and exchanges a week's work for alcohol. In situations like this, wives had few legal options and little recourse but to apply for poor relief, the ultimate degradation for a respectable middle-class woman. This humiliating step often meant confinement and the threat of losing her children. *The Lily* cited one case of the wife of a "degraded sot" who, in dire need with winter coming on, applied to the Poor Master, "vainly hoping to obtain such relief as should enable her to withstand the winter and keep her family together." All the Poor Master could offer was to bring her and the children to the poorhouse. The distressed woman pleaded "for a little relief without being subjected to so degrading a step. It was all useless—she must got to the poor house, or shift for herself as best she could."[12] These and similar tales of women victimized by male idleness and profligacy lent weight and substance to the charges the men's breach of faith produced more than mere disappointment and mental anguish.

Affecting as these images of shame, poverty, and degradation were, they did not match the emotional impact of the most potent weapon in temperance reformers' arsenal: scenes of men victimizing women with brutal violence. Drunkards' wives, the movement scolded, encountered blows from the men supposed to be their protectors. At the slightest pretext, drunkards beat children, servants, and "melancholy to tell, he does not refrain his hand from *her*, the wife of his bosom! Nay, perhaps, grasping some convenient piece of furniture, he approaches her with curses in his mouth, and menaces her with instant death." Tracts, sermons, newspapers, and books arrayed similar incidents with equal anger. A woman who had once shared the purest pleasure with her husband, thundered one minister, became the "true thermometer of his stormiest passions, now quivering, shrieking, fainting from his fury, is belabored with a walking stick, or cloven down with a fire shovel." Frequently wife abuse occurred in view of the couple's children. A tract described a man "driving his wife out of the house in the cold, dark night. See how he cruelly beats her. Hear the wind whistle. See how the snow flies. See the poor children wringing their hands and crying out 'Oh, father, do not drive mother away! Do not drive mother away!' And then he turns and curses them." So prevalent was the image of battered wives that it became familiar enough to joke about. A newspaper item recounted how a lady asked a beggar girl what her mother did. "'Does jobs and takes in washing,'" the girl replies. Inquiring what her father did, the lady learned that he "'Drinks rum and licks mother.'"[13]

Here, as well as in discussion of the poverty visited upon wives by drunken husbands, commentators pointed out the limited options available for preventing or responding to drunken male violence, given the state of marriage law. Sometimes separation and alimony could be obtained if a drunken husband became too violent. Legal authorities noted with alarm the frequency with which drunken violence against women compelled them to interfere in familial and domestic relations. A South Carolina judge estimated in 1829 that "two thirds of the cases [of alimony] tried in the last fifteen years may be fairly attributed to Intemperance." A prosecutor went further, arguing that "every single case of alimony within my experience at the bar" originated from intemperance. Frequently, the level of violence required even more drastic measures. In Providence, Rhode Island, an 1841 broadside on crime and intemperance reported that many jailed men had been "confined on complaint of their wives, who felt their lives or the lives of their children to be in danger." Despite some concern for women's safety, the legal system stacked the deck in men's favor, leaving women few viable options. Chiding legislators for continuing to laud the "majesty of law," William B. M'Clure remarked indignantly that it "guarantees to the husband the privilege, drunk or sober, of belaboring his wife with a cudgel, provided it be no thicker than his thumb. Let maidens therefore take the measure of their future husband's thumbs, in order that they may calculate with some certainty upon the size of the weapon and the severity of the blow."[14]

Within the temperance movement's discussion of violence against women, three sub-themes recurred: the wife anxiously awaiting her husband's nightly return; the wife being thrown out of doors by her drunken spouse; and the wife's murder by her husband, usually with a weapon. All three contrasted sharply with the portrait of marital and familial felicity that domestic and sentimental writers ascribed to the middle class and offered as a model for the rest of American society. Temperance writers delighted in portraying the drunkard's wife, sitting "in pensive silence, waiting the return of her unnatural and unfaithful husband, tortured by the mingled emotions of hope and fear." The "miserable wife listens" to hear the "steps which she longs yet dreads to hear," of the man who once brought gladness but now "staggers to his wretched home, the brutal tyrant of his desolate household." In the "loneliness of midnight, she has anxiously awaited his return from some nocturnal revelry." Instead of receiving "tokens of affection" she is often "met with cold indifference, or even repulsed with fiendish cruelty."[15]

In many accounts, the fiendish cruelty manifested itself in another inversion of prescribed middle-class norms. Rather than maintaining and protecting woman in the domestic sphere, drunken men ejected her forcibly from her natural orbit, turning wife and children out of the house, usually in the dead of winter. The family's health had already been undermined by insufficient food and warmth, their wardrobe reduced to rags by the drunkard's spending his wages on liquor so that being exposed to the elements was no small inconvenience. One version has the besotted husband returning home raving and swearing at his terrified wife, "perhaps dragging the partner of his bosom by her hair, and throwing her out the door, there to perish if another shelter cannot be obtained for herself, and, perhaps, for her dear infant babe." John Marsh, one of the temperance movement's most skilled ideologues, also employed this imagery to great effect, deploring the "want, and wo, and wounds" that the drunkard's wife endures, "till she is dragged by the hair of her head and cast out with her babes to the pitiless storm." Shock and dismay at this brutal expulsion of woman from her proper sphere, the home, reverberated through all types of temperance writing. One letter to *The Olive Plant* chronicled the hardships produced by a particularly spiteful drunkard. His wife and family were

> often . . . turned out of the house in the middle of a winter's night, and cold water thrown over the fire, my hard labor had gained, so that when he was at length exhausted with his passions, and we were enabled to get an entrance into the house, not a spark of fire were we able to procure; and shivering with the piercing cold, we would have to go to bed, benumbed, and often with clothes frozen upon us.

Likewise, a widely circulated temperance tract related one drunkard's reaction to his wife's rebuke at not providing food for the family. Smashing the dishes laid before him, he seized her "roughly by the arm," opened the door and forced her through it, bidding her to enter again, if she dared. "The night was cold and windy. I was thinly-dressed, and even ill. But I forbore to take refuge under a neighbor's roof. My heart was too sad and desolate to admit of human consolation." Man's brutalization of woman, reformers urged, knew no bounds of cruelty.[16]

But an even more harrowing story of female victimization remained for them to deploy. Once the brutish husband returned, harsh words and temporary eviction might be the least of a wife's dangers. Temperance advocates highlighted the murder of wives by drunken husbands as the ultimate and likely end of female victimization by male intemperance. Wife murder represented the complete negation of the ideal of companionate marriage and affectionate family life then being articulated by the middle class. Sometimes the wife and mother gave her life to protect her children. In one account the drunkard "staggers across the room," inadvertently knocking down "that little toddling thing on her way to meet him." His alarmed wife rushes to save her baby from harm: "See! The drunken wretch has thrust her angrily aside with his strong arm; and she has fallen—fallen with her head across a chair," and sustained a fatal wound. A clergyman reported being entreated by a ragged, shivering boy, "whose sobs and tears almost prevented my understanding him, to visit his mother." The boy's father "had split open her head with a stick of wood," and her life was despaired of. Upon visiting the unfortunate victim, the cleric learned that the husband insisted on taking wood she had begged "to make her and her child more comfortable," to trade for rum. When she resisted, "she received the wound in her head from his hand!" Here the murderous blow results from a specific disagreement. For the most part, though, temperance writers depicted wife murder as the logical consequence of male intoxication and barbarity. As one would-be poet put it: "The LIQUID FIEND reigned in his heart; the bride/ He once ador'd lies murder'd at his side!"[17]

Most stories of wife murder portrayed the violence as purposeful and calculated rather than inadvertent or accidental. A temperance newspaper told of one inebriate who followed his wife around their house with a knife "to take her life. . . . Not unfrequently, ere he lay down at night, he sharpened the knife, placed it beside his bed, or his pillow, and swore 'by the Holy God that he would cut her throat before morning.'" Significantly, drunkards nearly always used weapons, rather than clenched fists, to inflict their homicidal wrath on their spouses. We have already encountered tales of wives being assaulted with firewood, pieces of furniture, and fire shovels. But the drunkard's armory contained a wide range of additional weapons for use against innocent wives. The besotted husband of "an unoffending wife," for instance, used a heavy stick to send her "immortal spirit to its last and final account." One brute "caught up a mallet" and dealt his wife a blow that "drove reason from its throne, and in three days . . . the spirit from its tenement." Another shot his wife with a pistol, the "ball enter[ing] her back and lodg[ing] in her abdomen." Making tangible the unmitigated evil of alcoholic beverages, a popular temperance story chose a liquor bottle itself as the murder weapon.[18]

Indeed, the temperance movement's fixation on the details and accoutrements of wife murder became so graphic as to resemble the lurid accounts of crimes published in the penny press. Here, as elsewhere, the misogynist current that ran through temperance discourse expressed itself, linked, however, to an ostensibly sympathetic treatment of women. Drunkards routinely "tortured [their] wives and children, hewed them down and left their bleeding trunks headless" in their houses, or "inhumanly murder[ed] their wives with axes and bludgeons—seizing them by the dishevelled hair of their bruised heads—throwing their mangled bodies here and there in their wretched habitations."[19] While the intent was doubtless to condemn the effects of alcohol on women's lives, the execution placed a positive value on female victimization by emphasizing its didactic usefulness. This becomes especially clear in discussions of women's deaths caused by their execrable treatment at the hands of drunken men. When they succumbed to male mistreatment, women's deaths appeared almost advantageous as a testament to the evils of liquor. Celebrated temperance lecturer and entertainer John Gough, for instance, sang the following to numerous audiences:

> Sally my wife bowed her beautiful head—
>> Oh how I wept when I knew she was dead—
> She was my angel, my love, and my guide—
>> Vainly to save me from ruin she tried;
> Poor broken heart! It was well that she died,
>> Long, long ago—long ago.

One must wonder if it was well that Sally died because death alleviated her torment or because her demise provided an object lesson for the edification of erring men. Here as elsewhere, a woman's death served as an opportunity to urge her husband to reform. In another rendition, the dying wife begs her husband not to leave her deathbed and children to go drinking. Selfless to the end, the woman offers the "tattered rags . . . which clad my freezing form," to comfort her children while she "will brave the storm." Perishing at last from "slow torture," the woman's last "gasping breath was spent in prayer for him whose cruel strokes her chords of life had rent!"[20]

As the foregoing suggests, temperance reformers praised—almost without exception—drunkard's wives who endured their cheerless and difficult lives with stolid resignation. Many accounts had wives wishing to die but struggling on out of a sense of womanly duty. As children flee from their brutish father's wrath, Nathan Beman observed,

> The wife, as one that has become wo-hardened, or who expects no refuge but the grave, and no protection from a drunkard's *tender mercies* this side of heaven, remains and receives the curses, and then, perhaps, the blows of that man who, in the days of her espousals, led her away from a father's sheltering roof and from a mother's cheering kindness, and who took the oath of God upon him to love and protect her.

Similarly, a wife beset by her drunken husband testified that he had "often threatened my life, and were it not for my little ones which my husband often beats and kicks when drunk, how thankful I should be to lay down and die." When drunkards "rave and storm," their wives, "with patient assiduity," put forth "all those little tendernesses which woman is capable of exercising, to soothe and calm him to repose." Her solicitude requited with blows and curses, "how readily would she lay her aching head in the grave," but her "strong affection" for her children makes her persevere. "They have need of her, for they are worse than fatherless, and for their sakes she is willing to bear and struggle a little longer." As another commentator put it:

> She would like to die. Often has the thought thrilled through her soul like a frightful vision, but how can she die? Are not her children clinging around her for hope and protection? Is she to abandon them, to deliver them to the

savage mercy of a brutal father? Oh no! she must pursue her task of devotion faithful to her duties; she must shield them from the blows which will become her share. To her, life will be a protraction of human agony; but how long since has it ceased to be a joy![21]

In simultaneously lamenting and extolling the plight of these women, temperance reformers articulated a conception of the ideal wife. Deploring male drunkenness and praising female perseverance, they depicted the women sufferers whose treatment they deprecated as the epitome of femininity and womanly virtue. Wives could endure the most atrocious treatment by their husbands, they urged, because of woman's constitutional inability to withdraw her love once it had been given in marriage. Like her piety and morality, woman's loving fortitude was, in this view, innate. Conversely, any woman who ceased to love and obey her drunken husband appeared as less than a true woman. Having given their husbands at marriage "a woman's heart, and a love that many waters can not drown," drunkards' wives could be expected to accept, even embrace, their cheerless and difficult lives with imperturbable stoicism, attempting to protect their children and reclaim their husbands against all odds.[22]

Remarkably both male and female temperance advocates considered a wife's endurance to male abuse a cardinal female virtue. One woman vowed adamantly to endure long enough to save her fallen husband for the sake of cherished memories that her "bosom can ne'er forget," and the "strength of a love that can never die": "I will save him yet, I will save him yet!" Another female author discoursed on how perseverance and adversity defined "Woman's Love":

> Man's love lives but with hope; while woman's heart
> Still echoes to the music of the past.
> A love all sacrifice and suffering; a star
> That gathers lustre from the gloom of night;
> A martyr's fond idolatry; a faith
> Baptized in tears, to sorrows consecrate.[23]

Male commentators, too, spoke respectfully of woman's fidelity, moral strength, and, especially, capacity for suffering. An admiring physician related how a wife's "intense affection . . . and solicitude for his recovery" had eclipsed the disgust occasioned by the "stench of sour wine and half digested food plastered over" her drunken husband's unshaven beard. When an outraged friend counseled "less sensibility on such an occasion, saying that her husband was a beast of intemperance," the wife in question retorted, "'[B]ut sir, he is my husband still.'" This affecting scene, and others like it, which did generate support for temperance, also established a high standard of female piety and devotion that wives would be expected to meet.[24]

Not all temperance reformers shared this vision of the good wife or placed much confidence in men's attempts to protect women. Amelia Bloomer, Elizabeth Cady Stanton, Susan B. Anthony, and others in the more radical, women's rights wing of the temperance movement rejected the notion that women should be expected to stay with degraded, abusive husbands at the cost of their and their children's lives. They recognized that the mainstream temperance movement's gender ideology exacerbated rather than ameliorated the problem of male drunkenness. Amelia Bloomer, for example, noted that the standard advice given to a drunkard's wife on her duty, along with the examples of "angelic wives which she has been exhorted to follow," had perpetuated the "vices and crimes of society" that stemmed from intemperance. Similarly, Susan B. Anthony called for a different kind of female influence that followed not "in the wake of sin," but acted to prevent it. Espousing firm belief in the "all powerful" influence of woman over man, Anthony suggested that if a man knew that his drunkenness would cause his "pure minded and virtuous" wife "assuredly [to] leave him, and take with her the property and the children," it would influence him to lead an upright life. Consequently radical feminists advocated expanded property rights for married women and increased access to divorce and child custody in cases of drunkenness, abuse, or abandonment. Elizabeth Cady Stanton went so far as to press for women's "right and duty" to divorce drunken husbands, thereby sparing themselves and their children the debasing life of a drunkard's family. For these radicals, men's unwillingness to redress the imbalance of power within marriage rendered ineffective male solutions to the problems of drunkards' wives. Only expanded women's rights could enable wives to defend themselves, rather than relying on men to champion their interests.[25]

If they prescribed different remedies than more conservative temperance advocates, radical feminists—most of them products of the middle class—shared in the general celebration of womanly fortitude in adversity. Even *The Lily* spoke admiringly of the long-suffering drunkard's wife as the epitome of womanly virtue. One article told of a wife who, "with the affection that never dies in the soul of a true woman, is preparing coarse food which poverty sparingly deals out," while her husband beat her. Another related the story of a "guardian angel," the wife of a "miserable, loathsome drunkard" whose refusal to desert her husband "beautifully verified," as in a thousand other cases, that "Woman's love all change will meet,/ And like the ivy round the oak,/ Cling closest to the storm." This admiration for a wife's staunch love and devotion characterized even the writing of those who advocated separation or divorce. Mary C. Vaughn's poem "The Drunkard's Wife and Home," for example, depicted a self-reliant woman who took her son and left an abusive, drunken husband. But this momentous step could only be justified after she had "loved, and striven, and hoped, and prayed,/ Through years of woe, till love in tears

was quenched,/ and hope died out, and naught but faith remained."[26]
Thus men and women, radicals and conservatives, subscribed to a gender
ideology that found the suffering and victimization of drunkards' wives
both useful rhetorically and admirable morally.

Critics did not censure temperance supporters, as they did advocates of
moral reform, for disseminating lurid and salacious material that threatened to further, rather than combat, vice.[27] Considering the uses to which
temperance reformers put female victimization, however, one might easily
conclude that a similar cultural dynamic obtained. Antiliquor advocates
lauded women's ability to endure suffering, arguing that womanly virtue
never manifested itself so well as in the adversity produced by male abuse.
Here two conflicting messages intertwined: woman must be saved from
male intemperance, but male intemperance brought out all the finest
qualities of woman. A "lost inebriate" who had sunk "even lower than the
most degraded of his species," but was cared for nonetheless by the "very
being whose hopes and aspirations he had forever crushed," led one reformer to apostrophize: "Woman! thou art indeed an enigma! All weakness when danger approaches, but indomitable in the hour of trial?"[28]
Thus indignation against strong drink coexisted with, perhaps even depended upon, a perverse pleasure in seeing women victimized so that in
affliction they could display their abundant femininity. In essence, middle-
class temperance reformers made a virtue of victimization.

Women as Moral Exemplars

Temperance writers alleviated this bleak picture of female victimization
by supplementing it with another role for women in temperance reform—
that of moral exemplar to encourage men to reform. As moral exemplars,
women exhibited the purity, morality, and religiosity that middle-class
gender ideology asserted were their innate characteristics. Women's ability
to exert moral influence on men, temperance literature claimed, made
them effective and essential warriors in the struggle for a sober America.
Indeed, when reformers personified temperance, they did so as a woman.
An 1852 edition of the *American Temperance Magazine,* for instance, shows
Temperance holding an overflowing goblet of pure water as she tramples the
demonic figure of intemperance (Figure 1). Another periodical, the *Temperance Recorder,* pictured Temperance as an angelic female figure killing the hydra, Intemperance, by pouring cold water on its heads (Figure 2).[29]

Being temperate themselves, the argument went, women could provide
a powerful example of virtue and sobriety for men to emulate. Philadelphia's Female Total Abstinence Society, for instance, aimed "by our example and precept" to "hold the firm, establish the wavering, reclaim the
fallen and degraded, [and] shelter the distressed, among our own sex." Reformers commended this role of moral exemplar for women, arguing that

Figure 1—The Goddess Temperance tramples the Demon Intemperance.
Source: *American Temperance Magazine and Sons of Temperance Offering* (New York) 3, no. 1 (1852). Courtesy of Swem Library, College of William and Mary.

Figure 2—The Goddess Temperance slays the Hydra Intemperance.
Source: *Temperance Recorder* (Albany) 2, no. 9 (1833): 70. Courtesy of the Huntington Library.

they were singularly suited to fill it. Setting a "moral example in this world is of the greatest importance," opined one temperance writer, for in the companionship of the "virtuous and pure minded," the wavering find "a shield to guard them against danger." Woman, he continued, not only protects the innocent but "teaches the love of virtue to the fallen, by showing them the horror of vice, and in the last struggles of her stupefied husband, between honor and degradation, she opposes the buckler of love to stay the last blow."[30]

Though moral exhortation suggested a more dynamic role for women than did abject victimization, it did nothing to threaten the prevailing middle-class gender binary that cast men as active and women as passive. In serving as moral examples, women eschewed the audacity and forcefulness more appropriate to male opponents of alcohol. "Not by harsh and seemingly coercive measures, but by the force of example and persuasion," the *New York Washingtonian* assured its readers, did women exercise their moral power. Commentators likened women to "beacon lights to point the unwary youth to the paths of piety, humility, and virtue," reminding them that this complemented man's more combative function in the battle against alcohol. Frequently women who embraced what might otherwise seem a secondary role conceived of it in religious terms that assigned them a special position based on their innate morality. One Daughters of Temperance Union exhorted women to rejoice along with men to "see the foe recede, And let her in the 'still small voice,' The cause of temperance plead; And while the thunder tone of eloquence is stirr'd, Her whisper'd warning God may own, His voice through her's be heard." Another woman affirmed that the

> clear, tho' slender light, whose purity and brightness diffuses comfort through the humble dwelling . . . is not less useful in proportion to its "little spheres," than the splendid and costly lamp, designed to illuminate some vast building, devoted to purposes of great public utility; and if trimmed and fed with equal care, will doubtless be equal [sic] acceptable in the view of the great "Father of Lights."[31]

Indeed, temperance advocates believed that woman's moral example redounded to the benefit of the movement in the most mundane of ways. The very presence of virtuous women at social occasions, they argued, elevated the moral tone and promoted temperance. One temperance paper suggested that a "union of the sexes" at a Fourth of July celebration would "check all improper tendencies, increase the enjoyment, and extend the usefulness of the occasion to its utmost limit." Similarly a Massachusetts temperance convention proposed that "all alcoholic drinks be banished from public festivals, and their places at the table be supplanted by the *Ladies*." Temperance literature asserted that if her mere presence failed to suffice, a woman's timely rebuke, or willingness to resist social convention in the service of temperance would be most efficacious. When a liquor dealer offered a bouquet to a young lady who was admiring his flowers, for instance, she demurred. "'No sir,' she answered with severity, 'I accept no compliments or presents purchased with the money which is the price of souls.'" The newspaper reporting this anecdote wished that "God's blessing [may] rest on that sweet but firm and conscientious girl." Not even the clergy were immune from feminine reproof in the temperance cause. Upon asking a Daughter of Temperance if it was wrong to buy alcohol to make pickles, a "minister of the gospel" received an unhesitating yes as his reply. "'I do not wish to be the judge of your conscience,' she continued, 'but it would be wrong for *me* to make pickles with alcohol.'" Even when the nonplussed cleric appealed to a fellow clergyman to uphold his opinion, the Daughter remained adamant. "'Most assuredly it is wrong,' said the lady, 'and in buying alcohol for such purposes [you] give your influence to the Rumseller.'"[32]

As this story suggests, even the relatively passive role of moral example might bring women into conflict with middle-class notions of propriety. To uphold their moral duty, women even ignored conventional notions of respectability and weathered the disapproval of friends and family. Signing the total abstinence pledge, for example, seemed to many an unfeminine admission that a woman needed help staying sober. Dedicated temperance adherents knew differently. Some ladies have the "queer notion," a temperance paper remarked, that they "are insulted when asked to sign the Pledge. What! a Lady drink?" Acknowledging that some ladies did in fact drink, the article solicited female support for the pledge for moral, rather than personal reasons:

> Ladies, do not be offended at our observations, we only wish to persuade you to join us. If you sign the pledge, you are with us, we can the better succeed in routing our adversaries, as you possess such a sweet, irresistible influence over mankind. We are engaged in a glorious battle; will you enlist under our banner? There is no neutrality; you are either for or against us!

Temperance fiction explored this dilemma as well. In Osgood Bradbury's *The Distiller's Daughter: Or, The Power of Woman,* heroine Adaline Phillips braves her family's displeasure and informs them that she signed the pledge "before hundreds of witnesses" at a Washingtonian meeting. *"'Signed the pledge!'* all repeated at once in much surprise. *'Signed the pledge!'"* Despite her mother's scolding that she is a "very foolish girl to mix in such company," Adaline stands her ground, insisting, in a rebuke to her parents, that if the "higher classes" would sign and keep the pledge, "I believe it would prevent a good deal of trouble in many families in the city."[33]

Women exercised their power of moral example through the agency of what reformers of both sexes called "female influence." Temperance advocates understood this term to mean the operation on society generally—and men more particularly—of qualities that middle-class gender ideology depicted as inherent in women: religiosity, morality, compassion, and propriety. "It is not enough that our mechanics, our laborers, our strong men, our gifted and our youth, are engaged in the great work," John Neal told a Portland audience. *"Our women must be with us, or we cannot hope to prevail—* our mothers, our wives, and our daughters—the other half, and in such matters, by far the most influential half of our whole population." All over the United States temperance advocates agreed. "Female influence," the *New York Organ* opined, "is not only a useful auxiliary in every moral and social reform, but a necessary co-adjutant." Without it, no "great moral or social revolution was or ever will be accomplished." In Virginia, a temperance orator assured his audience that women are always ready to "lend their influence when the interest of man requires it . . . we know too that the ladies (like truth) are powerful and must prevail." Along similar lines, the 1843 *Temperance Almanac* reprinted a Philadelphia convention's resolution:

> That the influence of the female sex, in favor of the temperance cause, has
> had a highly salutary effect upon all classes in the community, and especially
> upon those who are the hope of future generations, the *children and youth,*
> and that should the influence to which they are so justly entitled, be unit-
> edly and universally exerted in favor of this cause, they would do much to
> perfect and to perpetuate the moral renovation of the whole human family.[34]

Temperance literature employed art, music, and poetry as well as prose
to laud female influence. Pictorial representations highlighted female
virtue in the service of temperance. The cover of the inaugural issue of the
American Temperance Magazine, for instance, depicts a woman distributing
cups of pure water drawn from a nearby waterfall to men and children
(Figure 3). In its January 1843 issue, the *Journal of the American Temperance
Union* shows mothers leading their children to the table to affix signatures
to the promise of lifelong abstinence from strong drink (Figure 4).[35] Like
pictorial illustrations, poetry and music emphasized religious themes and
remarked upon woman's divine warrant to minister to men.

> She binds all broken, bleeding hearts with Love's
> sweet silken tie—
> A soothing, healing balm imparts in words of
> sympathy.
> She warns the drunkard of his fate—the poison
> cup she stays,
> And places him within the reach of brighter,
> happier days.
>
> Oh, what can match with woman's love, in this sad
> world of care!
> Without her aid and influence, Man ever
> would despair.
> But heaven has placed her here on earth, with
> virtues more refined,
> To cheer the pathway, and to guide the
> footsteps of mankind.

Or consider "Female Aid Required," a temperance hymn:

> Ye Sarah's [*sic*] now arise,
> Ye Miriams all come forth;
> While Hannahs, truly wise,
> Now prove your genuine worth.
> No power like yours—save that above
> To teach sobriety and love.[36]

Figure 3—Woman offers cold water to men and children. Source: *American Temperance Magazine* 1, no. 1 (1851). Courtesy of Swem Library, College of William and Mary.

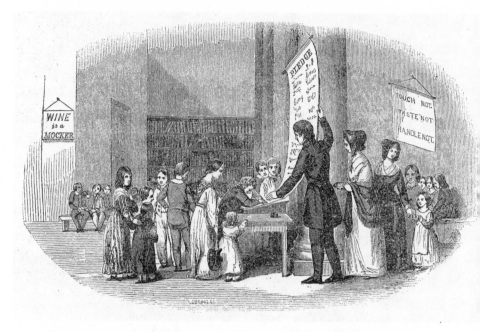

Figure 4—A Sunday School Signing the Pledge. Source: *Journal of the American Temperance Union* 7, no. 1 (1843): 9. Courtesy of Swem Library, College of William and Mary.

In accordance with middle-class precepts, temperance literature encouraged an interpretation of female duty that emphasized moral example and influence, usually exercised among family, friends, and acquaintances, rather than in more public venues. A Son of Temperance professed "utmost respect for the female character" but declined to admit women to the fraternity so as not to "subject ladies to the taunts and reproaches of a jealous and suspicious world" that often distrusted secret societies. If they had to have a society, this Son recommended establishing a Daughters of Temperance union so that they could "go to work and initiate each other as fast as you please." But far better, he urged, was to extend their blessings to the Sons: "On whatever thou frownest, it withers! On whatever thou smilest, it blossoms! May we not hope for thy smiles upon our fraternity? For thy blessings on our Order?" Though men excluded females from the most visible temperance organizations, they nonetheless celebrated the importance and efficacy of women's efforts. Neither intemperance nor any other evil, they averred, could long withstand women's united efforts. Once a majority of the "Daughters of America" have "enrolled their names in favor of 'Virtue, Love and Temperance,'" the *New York Organ* maintained, they will "bid the tyrant Alcohol, depart forever! and be obeyed." Though prevented by bodily weakness and a becoming timidity from pressing their claims in soldierly fashion, women would nonetheless win the day. As the "arbitress of manners" and "censor of morals," woman "reassures virtue" and checks vice. Acting together, with the "gentle weapons of filial, maternal and conjugal persuasion, [could not woman] accomplish more than man, even if clad in a panoply of steel?"[37]

Female influence seemed an ideal avenue for women's temperance efforts because it did not require them to step outside of the roles and relationships prescribed by middle-class gender ideology. Indeed, female influence depended on the sway that close ties to men gave wives, mothers, daughters, sisters, and sweethearts over their male relatives and friends. Through her loving concern and gentle rebukes, for example, a sister might alert her brother to the danger of social drinking. Adeline Whiteman, the heroine of a T. S. Arthur short story, provided a model for sororal influence. After chiding her brother for drinking wine, Adeline begs him not to be angry with a "sister who loves you tenderly, and whose very love makes her perception of danger tenfold more acute. . . . You may be unconscious of it, but I have too frequently seen you under its influence in company not to fear and tremble for you." Edward leaves in a snit but returns later to thank his sister for putting him on the road to reform. With such a success under her belt, a young woman might extend her influence into other relationships. *The Temperance Offering* commented approvingly of Ellen Murphy, an "Irish maiden" who, after reforming her brother, convinced her beau to give up drinking as a condition of marriage.[38]

Mothers also exerted their share of influence in temperance literature. In a variant of the ideology of republican motherhood, temperance reformers expected the first line of defense against alcohol to be erected during childhood by maternal influence. In this vein, an 1843 temperance almanac offered readers an illustrated dialogue in which a mother instructs her son in the evils of drinking and selling liquor. For "the sake of a few cents," she tells him, a rumseller has "turned this man out more degraded than any beast, to go home and abuse his family . . . if this man ever commits murder, the man who sold him the liquor will be, in the eye of . . . God, guilty as an accessory." Sometimes temperance literature depicted mothers prevailing on adult sons to abstain from alcohol. In one narrative, Mrs. Harris endures years of her son Wendall's intemperance, ever cherishing the hope of his reform. When a Washingtonian meeting comes to town, she prevails on Wendall to attend with her. Hearing the "kind words, persuasive eloquence over minds which had become spell-bound to intemperance," Wendall signs the pledge. He embarks on a "virtuous and sober life," much to the delight and relief of his "now honored and rewarded" mother.[39]

Daughters' influence on their drunken fathers provided material for much temperance literature. Here daughters pleaded, cajoled, and otherwise induced fathers to abandon drink and depravity for a respectable middle-class family life. In the best-known example, John Marsh related how Hannah Hawkins, the daughter of celebrated Washingtonian lecturer John Hawkins, helped reform her father. Little Hannah, who was in the habit of placing a pillow under her father's head and sleeping on the floor next to him when he passed out, one day begged her father not to send her out to buy rum. After fleeing from her father's anger, Hannah crept back into the room. Seeing his fearful daughter, Hawkins thought of his "past life; my degradation; misery of friends; and felt bad enough. So I called to her and said, 'Hannah, I am not angry with you, and I shall not drink any more.' She cried, and so did I."[40] The Hawkins soon enjoyed again the comforts of economic security and domestic bliss.

Grown daughters as well as little girls brought their fathers back from the brink of death and alcoholic disgrace. One daughter saved her intemperate father from losing his house for nonpayment of bills. The daughter extracted a promise to sign the pledge if the mortgage got paid; it did, the father signed and departed "home with a happy heart . . . the daughter had saved the $1100 by working in a factory." Another daughter feared that her father, her only living relative, would become intemperate. "But would he receive advice from a child?" she fretted. Appealing to his tender side, and to memories of his wife, the young woman confided her fears that the "worm of the still" was beginning to "prey upon our happiness." Perchance, the account goes, "the stern brow of that proud man was blanched, and his lip quivered," but he thanked his daughter: "Blessings on you, my child, you have saved your father."[41]

As might be expected, the undying filial devotion of daughters to their besotted fathers provided ample fodder for sentimental fiction. Frequently temperance fiction demonstrated how female characters could use their victimization as a means of moral influence. Alice Ray, the heroine of a temperance novella, won the admiration of her peers for her deportment, good sense, and virtue, despite laboring under the social stigma of being a drunkard's daughter. Leaving boarding school to nurse her ailing father, who was injured when a tavern keeper threw him into the street, Alice performed "every act of kindness and attention" possible, bearing with equanimity his "irritable complaints" and "the caprices of his wayward fancy." Despite his entreaties and demands, Alice refused to give her father liquor, believing that it would kill him. In the course of her father's ensuing harangue, the old man learned that Alice has declined an offer of marriage because she did not wish to disgrace her lover with a drunken father-in-law. Nonetheless, Alice cares for her father, hoping and praying for his reform. "She's a noble girl, she prays for her father, too," muses Ray, "well, it's well to have someone pray for me." Inspired by his daughter's self-abnegation, Ray reforms. Alice later attributes his sobriety to his illness, but Ray insists that it "was herself, her own goodness, that made her father a man again."[42]

An even more heartrending tale found Kate Franklin, another drunk-ard's daughter, reading the Book of Job as her father returns home. She convinced him that he has "but to make one effort" to "be free once more. Chains, strong as adamant, cannot bind the soul to sin, unless it is a willing captive." Her father repented, but in his distressed state inadver-tently causes a fire that burns the family's home. Kate's courageous efforts to save her mother and sister rendered her left hand useless, its sinews "contracted by the fires she smothered." Still, the story ends happily. Kate married and "in the hands of God, had been made the instrument" of her father's salvation. He remained sober, and though she carries "on her youthful and lovely person a sad memento of her father's sin," her disabil-ity became a "witness of filial heroism and devotion."[43]

Wives, like daughters, garnered a share of praise for their salutary influ-ence over wavering or intemperate husbands. Making home the cheerful, welcoming place that sentimental and domestic writers described, temper-ance literature insisted, would encourage men to stay by their firesides rather than go to taverns. "The aim of a wife," editorialized the *New York Organ*, "is to become the friend, the partner, the consolation of her hus-band, to educate her children, to direct all the household affairs." An ami-able, cheerful wife made the "domestic circle" the most "perfect of terres-trial states," a "heaven here" and a "foretaste of a heaven hereafter." Some wives aided their husbands through ingenuity and common sense, as well as vivacity and kindness. One reformed man's wife had surreptitiously "obtrude[d] something in my way, either a lunch or some sweet thing, just before my usual period of drinking." After a week of sobriety, the wife shared her "fearful apprehensions of my growing habit" and convinced him to reform. In another example of womanly wisdom particularly suited to a status-conscious middle class, fictional wife Julia Goodwin pro-posed consigning her husband's liquor to the scrap heap along with some camphene lamps that pose a fire hazard. If he promised to cease drinking and "banish all intoxicating drinks from your house," Julia pledged that "at the end of one year, your parlors shall be lighted with gas, and you shall not complain of the expense." Reflecting on the dangers of alcohol, Mr. Goodwin consented: "My resolution is taken. *You* have helped me to make it, and I trust that with the help of God I shall be enabled to keep it." Free from the expense of alcohol, Julia kept her pledge, making her home safe from fire and intemperance.[44]

When burdened with a confirmed drunkard, women exerted influence through unremitting kindness and support, caring for their husbands and praying for their reform, even in the face of poor treatment. Cases such as these illustrated the often symbiotic relationship between the two pre-scribed female roles, victim and moral exemplar. If women persevered in their adversity, their example of constancy and love might eventually re-claim their inebriate husbands. A physician recounted the experiences of a "worthy Christian woman, the wife of one of the most notorious drunkards I have ever known." Toiling for years "apparently without hope, abused, insulted, but never despairing," the woman eventually effected her husband's reform, helping him live a "temperate and upright" life. Many temperance narratives, apocryphal or otherwise, attested to the efficacy of a wife's devotion and constancy. An 1843 almanac related the story of Caroline Carleton, whose husband, William, becomes a "bloated, filthy and brutish" drunkard after their marriage. Instead of greeting William with "frowns and reproaches," or repulsing him "as a scourge and an outcast," Caroline "extended to the lost inebriate the hand of affection and kindness." After years of degradation, William reformed, and the "rich glow" on Caroline's cheeks "indicated that all was now right, both within and without." Similar stories abound. The "once happy" Idella Pemberton "murmured not . . . amid the want that poured upon her and the reproaches of her husband," William. Petitioning God for her husband's reform, Idella endured until her prayers were answered, and William signed the pledge. Drawing a moral from Idella's story, its clergyman author asked, "Is your husband a drunkard? Be gentle with him and pray for him." A similar lesson emerged from the account of Maria and her husband, another drunken William. Urged by her mother to take the children and leave her abusive mate, Maria refused. "I will never desert him . . . the only reward I ask, mother, is an approving conscience." Maria's "meek uncomplaining ways" reformed William at last. "To you alone belongs all the credit of my reformation," he asserted. Her "meekness and forbearance" were the means of changing a "worthless inebriate into a worthy member of society."[45]

Typically, temperance literature exhorted women to exert moral influence humbly and gently, avoiding criticism of or action against an intemperate husband. Assertiveness, anger, or dissatisfaction did not comport with the gender roles then being limned by middle-class ideologues. Moreover, temperance literature averred, unfeminine conduct, such as berating an inebriated mate or threatening consequences for continued misbehavior, usually backfired. The *New York Washingtonian,* for instance, told of Biddy, an Irish wife who attempted to shame her husband, Barkhum, into sobriety by getting drunk whenever he did. This female audacity failed, and Biddy resolved to treat Barkhum kindly and be an example by joining the temperance society herself. This approach bore fruit; Barkhum repented and realized that hard work and sobriety will "put potatoes into the bin—dollars into the purse—and rason [*sic*] into the head." Native-born wives who took an aggressive stance fared little better in the temperance press. In a "Domestic Incident," a Mrs. Peters declared that she would leave a drunken husband and advise others to do so, too. She has not a "spark of sympathy," she maintained, for drunkards' wives, who live with "disgusting brutes, the very sight of whom ought to turn a woman's stomach." One night, when Mr. Peters came home drunk and collapsed, she evinced only worry and solicitude. Mr. Peters whispers, "If my husband were to do so," with a "roguish twinkle in his eyes" and a barely suppressed "merry smile." Mr. Peters's joke chastened his wife, who behaved more circumspectly from then on.[46]

As was the case with opposition to the celebration of female victimization, the admonition to exert influence on men despite the cost did not go unchallenged. Radical temperance advocates, mostly those also committed to expanding women's rights, proposed that wives might have to leave an abusive drunkard and exert their moral influence from afar. Susan B. Anthony argued that society should regard it a "sin for any woman to live with the drunkard in the relation of wife." Women could not change confirmed drunkards, Anthony claimed, and persisting risked moral contagion. If husbands refused to change, she warned, wives sunk to their level, and the "clean are made filthy, and the filthy no less vile. . . . [T]he wife of the drunkard *always* . . . feels degraded, and is so." Another radical, Mary C. Vaughn, created a poetic model for the assertive, independent wife:

> She had resolved—she never more would share
> The drunkard's home. She vowed in sight of God
> No fealty to the wretch whose broken vows
> Had made her worse than widowed, many a year.
> She would go forth and seek new friends, and earn
> By labor of her toil-brown hands—those tiny hands
> That once had swept the harp-strings, and had gleamed
> With light of flashing gems—bread, and a home!

Vaughn's wife lives happily alone, eventually forgiving her husband when he returns to her years later to beg her pardon before dying.[47]

For the most part, however, the conventional wisdom then emerging in the American middle class held that reproof or separation reflected badly on a woman's constancy, fidelity, and femininity. Harsh words or actions might drive a husband deeper into the slough of intemperance, as one repentant wife found. Had she but known that her "murmurings" would drive her husband to the tavern, she would have repressed them. "Painfully" did she remember "that woman's province was to cheer and raise, to bear and forbear, to meet the storm of adversity with a soul-cheering smile, that might inspire with hope and strength," the man to whom she had been given as a "helpmeet." Tough love, it seems, had no place in a woman's moral arsenal. Temperance fiction drove home this point, chastising those wives who separated from drunken husbands. One heroine left her drunken husband, then learned that he has been accused of murder. She blamed herself for his predicament; without her guidance and moral example, she believed, he went to pieces. "'Oh, sir,' sobbed she, 'if he is guilty and must die, it is I who have murdered him! I deserted him, when all the world cast him out!'" Wracked with guilt, she returned to her husband's side, and her selfless devotion reformed him. In this case, the story ended happily: the now sober husband is proved innocent, and his wife gets a second chance to repent her desertion and resume her proper meek deportment. Some temperance fiction took a much more punishing turn. Fictional heroine Sidney Percy's story parallels that of the woman in Mary Vaughn's poem, cited above, but with a very different outcome. Having left her husband, Alfred, because of his chronic drunkenness and abuse, Sidney set out on her own. "You have made the final choice between the selfish enjoyment of 'a glass of brandy,' and the happiness of your wife and children," she told him in a farewell note. Unlike Mary Vaughn's heroine, who prospers, Sidney proved unable to make her own way. "Ignorant of business, or the ordinary means to which females in her situation usually resort for occupation and support," Sidney spent her savings and fell ill. The story concluded with her death among strangers, leaving "her two boys, at an almost infantine age, to the protection and charity of strangers to them and their unfortunate parents." Though tales of successful separations from drunken husbands did emerge from time to time, most temperance literature depicted the fate of Sidney Percy as the most likely and, perhaps, deserved outcome of a woman's failure to remain with her husband and exert a salutary moral influence for reform.[48]

The dual roles sketched for women in temperance literature, victim and moral exemplar, overlapped and supported each other. The affliction of wives, mothers, and daughters made temperance a woman's issue and paved the way for expanded female participation in alcohol reform. Female influence, the form that participation was supposed to take, gained authority from female distress and provided a rationale for women to persist in their suffering. Conceiving women as victims and moral exemplars also reinforced and shaped the emerging middle class's assumptions, values, and predilections about female (and by implication, male) attributes. In both guises, women could, at least in theory, remain squarely within the domestic sphere and acceptable bounds of female deportment, exhibiting fidelity, tenderness, delicacy, and womanly virtue. Prescribing and celebrating these roles for women revealed the fears and anxieties of a class not yet fully formed or completely confident of its place in American society. The heartrending tales of travail and redemption in which women figured prominently reflected larger anxieties about middle-class morality, downward mobility, and the viability of a domestic sphere that could shelter families from the vagaries and depravities of the market. After all, the blissful realm from which drunkards and their families were ejected and to which angelic, long-suffering women strove to restore them was the comfortable and prosperous middle-class home. Assuaging these fears required, among other things, casting the domestic arrangements and gender roles endorsed by the middle class as natural rather than contrived. For reasons that should be obvious by now, temperance literature constituted a primary venue for this ideological project. As the next chapter shows, the clerics, reformers, and domestic writers engaged in this work found their efforts abetted in significant ways by developments in the medical profession. The professionalization of American medicine, which occurred contemporaneously with, and in many ways depended upon, antebellum class formation, provided a powerful impetus to middle-class efforts to portray its vision of women and gender as both natural and desirable.

3

The Suffering Woman

Physicians and Gender Ideology

In a pioneering work on women's health published in 1848, Philadelphia physician Charles D. Meigs discoursed not only on the emerging medical fields of obstetrics and gynecology but on the social influence of what he took to be innate female characteristics. Woman's intellectual nature, he asserted, differed from man's and was unsuitable for politics, administration, or leadership. Still, woman exerted enormous power for the good of society through her salutary influence over men. Doctors, above all others, Meigs observed, "ought to be best able to appreciate the influence of the sex in the social compact." Rather than exercising power as do men in the marketplace or political arena, however, woman "reigns in the heart; her seat and throne are by the hearthstone." In Meigs's view, woman's ability to soothe and nurture imparted to her the capacity to "assuage the rage of her master" and reduce "the furious tide that boils in his veins" to a gentle flow. By the "mere contrast of her gentleness, her docility, her submissiveness and patience," woman holds sway over man and finds the "best rewards for the pains, hazards and toils of existence . . . within the narrow circle of her domestic reign."[1]

To illustrate his vision of female character, Meigs did not choose a figure from history or literature, despite his intimate knowledge of both. Rather, he focused on a temperance print, "The Intemperate" (Figure 5), which circulated widely during the 1830s. The print, engraved by Philadelphian William E. Tucker, capitalized on the popularity of a short story of the same name by sentimental writer Lydia H. Sigourney.[2]

Figure 5—The Intemperate. Source: *Remarks on the Utility and Necessity of Asylums or Retreats for the Victims of Intemperance* (Philadelphia: Brown, Bickering & Guilbert, 1840). Courtesy of the Historical Society of Pennsylvania.

The story recounts the sufferings of Jane Harwood, whose husband's intemperance forces her family to move from their comfortable home and set out for a new start in the wilds of Ohio. During the arduous journey, James Harwood "gradually abstracted and sold" the "few utensils and comforts they carried with them" to purchase liquor, the consumption of which produced "overbearing and arbitrary" behavior. When their horse dies from James's neglect and mistreatment, the Harwoods are forced to abandon their wagon and continue on foot. Dreading that her husband's anger would be directed at their feeble four-year-old son who lagged behind, Jane, "after in vain soliciting aid and compassion from her husband," carried the boy while their infant daughter clung to her shoulders. Bearing up under this burden, sustained by "the strength that nerves a mother's frame, toiling for her sick child, [that] is from God," Jane hurries along, fearing that if she fell behind, "her husband would tear the sufferer from her arms, in some paroxysm of his savage intemperance."[3] Tucker's print depicts this scene. Contemplating the graphic representation of this scene,

Meigs remarked what "a beautiful picture is that engraving of the 'Intemperate!' which you see everywhere in the print shops." He paid particular attention to the inspiring countenance of the woman, "as she bears on her bosom the youngest child, while she leads a sick boy by the hand, and is clutched by a timid older girl." The woman, Meigs observed, struggled on, uncomplaining, though the entire family was "barefooted, houseless, hopeless, homeless," leaving behind their "pretty cottage" to "pursue, along a rugged way, the uncertain, drunken footsteps of the husband and father."[4]

Meigs's reading of the print revealed his familiarity with and embrace of a middle-class ideology of gender then being articulated in temperance literature. The denomination of intemperance as a male vice, the depiction of the afflictions that men's drunkenness visited upon their wives and families, and the assurance that drinking would result in the destruction or loss of house and home all recapitulated themes then current in temperance writing. Meigs's reference to the print also points to the importance of doctors and medical writing to the development of gender ideology in temperance literature. Physicians, like other middle-class Americans, imbibed the gender ideologies being promulgated in sentimental fiction and temperance literature and incorporated them into their own writings. But medical doctors, in contrast to other temperance writers, played a unique role in the creation and elaboration of gender ideology. For unlike other antiliquor advocates, doctors could claim a scientific imprimatur based upon medical knowledge and clinical observation for their assertions about male and female characteristics. Thus during the first few decades of the nineteenth century, medical writing became an important venue within temperance literature for thinking about gender.

Doctors, Temperance, and the American Middle Class

Physicians owed their increasing intervention and importance in temperance reform, as well as their investment in particular ideologies of gender, to a number of historical circumstances specific to the antebellum era. Their embrace of temperance principles coincided with the medical profession's efforts to solidify the respectability and middle-class status of its members. Beginning around 1830, American doctors set about constructing a professional "character," with "the purpose of raising doctors in public esteem and creating solidarity within the profession." During the antebellum era, when popular respect for doctors was "at its lowest point, and mistrust of medicine at its highest," medical educators and advocates deemed it essential that doctors embody the virtues and qualities that elevated professions such as law and the ministry in public estimation. Prominent physicians and medical school professors urged their colleagues and students to cultivate earnestness, temperance, classical education, and industry in order to protect and extend the good reputation of their profession. All these traits, but particularly temperance, figured prominently in the advice books that proliferated during the 1830s and were aimed at young men who inhabited, or aspired to, the middle class.[5]

Participating in temperance reform recommended itself to doctors for several reasons. First, it promoted competence and allayed public fears of medical blundering by inebriated doctors. By the early 1840s, for example, prominent physician and reformer Daniel Drake noted proudly that the "reproach of intemperance can no longer be laid to the door of physicians" and that the refrain "'he is an excellent doctor if called when sober'" was no longer heard.[6] Second, assuming leadership positions in temperance societies allied doctors with the respectable middle class, whence came the bulk of support for the reform movement. Since the beginning of the century, medical men had played leading roles in the establishment and support of temperance societies and institutions. A doctor was among the three founders of one of the earliest documented temperance societies, which was established in upstate New York in the early nineteenth century. Physicians figured prominently in the establishment of the more elitist Massachusetts Society for the Suppression of Intemperance as well. A meeting of concerned citizens in 1811, which included respected doctors R. D. Mussey and Joseph Torrey, led to the founding of the MSSI, which became the Massachusetts Temperance Society in 1833. A warm relationship between physicians and the MSSI continued over the years: in 1827, the Society's annual report noted approvingly of the "ground being taken by several medical societies in different parts of the country" regarding temperance, reserving special praise for the Massachusetts Medical Society. In Pennsylvania, too, physicians assumed leadership positions in temperance organizations. In 1831, for instance, one of four vice presidents and eleven of thirty-six managers of the Pennsylvania Society for Discouraging the Use of Ardent Spirits were medical doctors.[7]

Women, Gender, and Medical Science

When doctors engaged in temperance work, and particularly when they cautioned against the dangers of drink in print, they confronted questions about women and gender. As aspirants to or members of the middle class, most American doctors, like their British counterparts, shared a belief in innate feminine virtue, sobriety, and religiosity. In medical writings on temperance that circulated throughout the Anglo-American world, physicians hastened to aver that of the "two sexes, there can be no doubt that men are much more addicted to all sorts of intemperance." Some provided quantitative measures of the differential proclivity for inebriation. Attributing the bulk of crime to intemperance, British physician Dr. William Carpenter argued that the ratio of male to female criminals in Britain was "100 to 21.25, the ratio of deaths from intemperance at the age of 20 and upwards is . . . 100 to 21.78—an accordance which can scarcely be accidental." This nearly five-to-one ratio suggested that female intemperance represented a relatively rare aberration from the natural order of things. Some considered it so unusual as to obviate the need to consider it at all, a tendency that also reflected women's secondary status in American society. In his study of drinking patterns in Mississippi, for example, Samuel Cartwright enumerated 790 "male adults of Natchez and vicinity. As the women are all temperate, no notice was taken of them in collecting statistics; nor of the minors, but only the people proper, the true sovereigns."[8]

Medical dismissal of female intemperance as a singular deviation from naturally ordained female behavior both reflected and shaped popular attitudes about gender. Middle-class domestic ideology, based as it was on a vision of home as refuge presided over by pure and faithful woman, could not encompass widespread female drunkenness. Doctors shared the popular aversion to women's inebriety, depicting it, when infrequently encountered, as especially appalling. Dr. Charles Jewett, for instance, recounted his observation of a waiter carrying "three glasses of a compound of which intoxicating poison is the principal ingredient" into the back room of a public house. "I sincerely hope, ladies," he added icily, addressing his female readers, "for the honor of your sex, that ladies constituted no part of the company." Similarly, William Sweetser excused his "rather ungallantly" alluding to females by denying that intemperance "is even so common among them as in our sex." He mentioned female intemperance, he continued, because "when it does occur it forms a more shocking picture." Sweetser's mild reproof paled in comparison to other medical animadversions. "A man addicted to intemperance is," one physician avowed, "until cured of his infirmity, a curse indeed to those about him. A drunken woman would have made purgatory of Eden: she would make such of heaven."[9]

Still, for all their allegiance to middle-class notions of gender and womanhood, doctors were also scientists and healers. In these roles, they could not ignore the relatively widespread incidence of female intemperance. Their early interest in the physiological effects of alcohol on women stemmed in part from the desire to reconcile their class interests with their professional experience. This interest might also have sprung from the uncomfortable suspicion that they themselves were responsible for many of the "unnatural" cases of female inebriety. In the early 1790s, Dr. J. C. Lettsom, a British physician whose work circulated in the United States, charged that physicians produced female intemperance by prescribing alcohol for a variety of women's ailments. Lettsom noted that some victims of alcohol "are often those of the most delicate part of the female sex, whose habits of intemperance are not unfrequently introduced by those who should have been the guardians of their health." American temperance crusaders picked up this theme. "Vast mischief has resulted to mankind," the Baltimore Temperance Society scolded from the employment of certain cordial medicines in the form of tinctures. They are often prescribed by physicians when the system being exhausted by disease, both body and mind are puerile and capricious, and hence the easy victims of a vicious habit. This is apt to occur especially to delicate, nervous females, whose unpleasant sensations are always temporarily relieved by the excitement which is produced.

Dr. Harvey Lindsly echoed this sentiment, urging that "more female drunkards are made by this means than by any other." She is "only taking medicine, and this too by the advice of her physician! Her conscience is pacified, and she does not know, for she does not reflect, that she is drinking ardent spirit—the bare idea of which would probably fill her with apprehension and alarm."[10]

Lindsly's fear that incompetent doctors would turn unsuspecting women into drunkards circulated beyond medical literature, finding its way into popular temperance fiction. In 1842's "Confessions of a Female Inebriate," the unfortunate protagonist begins drinking wine on a doctor's advice as she recovers from "great debility" occasioned by a previous disease. The wine relieved the "sensations of weariness, languor, and faintness at the stomach," under which she had long labored, but became a necessity even after her health improved. "Yet I did not dream of discontinuing my medicine; on the contrary, I was gradually increasing the quantity, . . . as its effects were less perceptible." Predictably, disaster follows, as the unnamed woman attempts to stop but cannot. Her husband leaves her after she accidentally kills her young daughter with an overdose of laudanum administered while she is drunk. The story ends with her discovery that her husband has died in Europe, leaving her desolate and alone. In a variation on this plot line, another 1842 temperance tale, *The Drunkard's Daughter,* relates the destruction of a family when a doctor prescribes wine for an ailing wife whose husband falls off the wagon because of the presence of alcohol in the house.[11]

These medical writings concerning women's vulnerability to iatrogenic addiction to alcohol and the fictional representations they generated bear the imprint of middle-class ideas about gender. In the course of their medical practice and temperance activism, doctors recognized that alcohol abuse seemed to follow a different etiology and produce somewhat dissimilar physical consequences in men and women. This discrepancy allowed them to explore the moral and physiological differences between the sexes at precisely the historical moment when gender ideology assumed enormous significance for the class from which they sought recognition and acceptance. In an era before physicians and other scientists had devised control groups, scientific samples, and other techniques of systematized medical research, doctors relied on observations of their patients to arrive at conclusions about physiology, anatomy, and etiology. But they did not perform this intellectual and scientific work in a cultural vacuum: many of their conclusions about female moral, intellectual, and physical attributes rested on middle-class assumptions about the nature of the sexes. That is, the requirements of middle-class gender ideology shaped many of the questions they asked and the answers they found. But this relationship was reciprocal rather than one-sided. When physicians published their findings in medical and temperance literature, they both directed conventional wisdom into specific cultural channels amenable to the middle class and gave it the appearance of scientific truth, seemingly arrived at dispassionately and objectively. In this way, using the vehicle of temperance literature, medical science intensified and legitimated certain class-based notions of gender.

"The Reproductive Organs are Preeminent"

Consider, for example, how doctors explained women's susceptibility to iatrogenic addiction by reference to their reproductive physiology. Like many of their contemporaries in the nascent American middle class, physicians took for granted female mental and physical fragility, attributing it to the otherwise salutary delicacy of the sex. "The female character," Dr. Thomas L. Nichols explained, "differs from that of the male, as the constitutions of the sexes differ. Their actions must be judged by different standards."

> Love, with woman, seems the absorbing passion of her soul. Honor, glory, riches and power are leading motives with men—in women we find love, friendship and maternity. We regard in men the qualities which favor these objects of their ambition, while in women we place the highest estimate upon the delicacy, purity and fidelity, which give their greatest charm to their predominant qualities.[12]

But doctors went further than their nonmedical counterparts, finding the cause of these characteristics in the close connection between women's reproductive organs and other parts of their bodies. In determining woman's character, physician John Wiltbank observed

> the reproductive organs are preeminent. They exercise a controlling influence upon her entire system, and entail upon her many painful and dangerous diseases. They are the source of her peculiarities, the centre of her sympathies, and the seat of her diseases. Everything that is peculiar to her, springs from her sexual organization.

Female sexual organization, Wiltbank continued, "planted in the heart of woman" an instinct for fidelity and love of her family both "powerful and absorbing," because it promised to "keep up an uninterrupted succession of generations."[13]

For physicians, this happy state of affairs helped explain both why few women became drunkards and what physiological causes underpinned the rare cases of female intemperance they did observe. Woman's reproductive functions disinclined her to want alcoholic stimulation, but the strain imposed on her system by those functions could sometimes produce intemperance. Doctors believed that the risk of intemperance was particularly great during childbirth and nursing, when women had to "bear up under the new drain now established in the system." Prescribing ale, porter, or wine to strengthen nursing women's milk might lead to the mother's intemperance and the child's debility as well. Considering the danger at this critical juncture, doctors believed that they could not "too strongly reprobate the pernicious practice, still but too common, of nursing women employing habitual brandy and other alcoholic stimulants."[14]

Medical writers drew upon female delicacy and fragility, staples of middle-class gender ideology, to further explain the seemingly incongruous existence of female drunkards. Given the frequent debility and nervousness produced by menstruation, pregnancy, nursing, and other feminine vicissitudes, women could be "sometimes insidiously seduced" into intemperance by using

> tinctures, stomachic elixirs, & c. Their nerves are weak, their stomachs feel faint, and unpleasantly, perhaps from improper diet and want of exercise, from keeping late hours, or from other causes; or they may be subject to hysterical affections, for all which complaints spirituous tinctures are likely to be advised. . . . They are taking *medicines* for their *nervous weaknesses,* or some other *weaknesses,* taking them, very likely, under the direction of their physician.

Thus intemperance might easily occur if physicians prescribed liquor for delicate, nervous women who sought temporary relief from their chronic medical difficulties. Unfortunately that very delicacy of constitution that made them so attractive to men also put them at risk of intemperance, a vice that "destroys females more certainly and in a shorter time than males."[15]

The prevailing assumption that women possessed more innate sensitivity and emotional volubility than men also helped physicians explain sexual differences in the etiology and physical consequences of intemperance. Doctors agreed, for instance, that female drunkards became hysterical much more often than males. Females, "possessing more nervous irritability and sensibility than males," William Sweetser declared, are more "liable to neuropathic disease, under the influence of intemperance. Hysterics often come on." Robert Macnish attributed the prevalence of hysterics to a "delicacy of fibre in women, and a susceptibility of mind, which makes them feel more acutely than the other sex all external influences." Thus while intoxicated, a woman's "whole system is often violently affected with hysterics" and other varieties of "nervous weakness."

Harvey Lindsly agreed, holding that women's mental and physical "delicacy" places them "peculiarly under the control of external excitements. Hence the exhilaration produced by wine and ardent spirits, not unfrequently [sic] ends in a violent hysteric fit."[16]

Doctors also detected the influence of female delicacy in the differential incidence between men and women of peripheral neuritis, or neuropathy, a neurological disorder sometimes occasioned by chronic alcohol abuse. The symptoms of this disease include pain, numbness, or paralysis in the limbs. As Dr. J. C. Lettsom described it in 1791, neuropathy produced a "palsied state" in the arms and legs of some drunkards, frequently accompanied by terrible pain: a cramp in the "lower extremities" causes "involuntary motions [that] draw up the legs, and produce the most piercing shrieks; and the features of the face, altered by convulsive twitchings, excite pain in a spectator." Though Lettsom recognized that this neural disorder afflicted both men and women, he concluded that it "is in general more frequently the attendant of the female sex." Other physicians confirmed Lettsom's diagnosis. Writing in the *New England Journal of Medicine and Surgery,* Dr. James Jackson described the identical syndrome, naming it *arthrodynia a potu,* while noting regretfully that most of the cases he saw "have been mostly among females." William Sweetser cited Jackson's article, repeating that the disorder "has most frequently been met with among females."[17]

How did physicians explain the differential incidence of neuropathy? In large measure, they accepted Lettsom's reasoning, which conformed to middle-class notions of gender. Persons of "delicate habits" who attempted to overcome "nervous debility" by using alcohol, Lettsom believed, represented the likeliest victims. The temporary relief accorded by recourse to spirits led to their frequent use, until they became "as necessary as food." Women, the frequent sufferers from nervous disorders, became addicted to liquor slowly due to "natural delicacy." The "poison being admitted in small doses," Lettsom added ruefully, "is slow in its operations, but not less painful in its effects." Though formulated in the late eighteenth century, Lettsom's account affirmed nineteenth-century physicians' observations and assumptions about gender.[18]

Medical Misogyny

In hastening to explain away the rare instances and peculiar etiology of female intemperance as unfortunate consequences of woman's "delicacy, purity and fidelity," doctors affirmed the gender ideology then being formulated by the American middle class. Yet even while praising the feminine qualities so admired by men, doctors could not escape the misogynist tendencies inextricably linked in Anglo-American thought to more positive portrayals of women. Sometimes medical misogyny emerged in offhand comments, as when one doctor attempted to deflect criticism of physicians' role in iatrogenically induced intemperance among women by attributing the persistence of using alcohol to fortify mother's milk to the "well-meant but mistaken motives" of "female attendants."[19] Or, it might be manifested by more sustained discussions of female intemperance. Medical men generally agreed that for male drunkards, appeals to self-respect and familial duty, perhaps by aggrieved wives and children, might foment reform. In women, however, exploiting female contrariness and conceit seemed a better course than invoking the tender emotions. Though medical opinion on female physiology and character would seem to have precluded the existence of a prideful, recalcitrant woman, doctors apparently saw no contradiction in recounting in medical writings on alcohol an oft-repeated tale about the travails of a man whose wife became intemperate. The unfortunate husband consulted a doctor, informing him that everything had been tried but to no avail. The physician, doubting that reformation was possible, advised the hapless man to "place a hogshead of brandy before her, and let her drink until she *gave up the ghost!*" The wife in question eavesdropped on this exchange, however, and Thomas Trotter related the result:

> her pride was wounded, and her resentment roused to the highest pitch imaginable. In the whirlwind of passion the chain of the habit was broke in an instant; female delicacy resumed its ascendancy over her actions; and from that moment she abjured the intoxicating charm. I am sorry to add, my honest friend was never after beheld with complaisance by the fair convert, though he had proved her best benefactor.

Most of the major medical writers on alcohol repeated this story, affirming the "spirit of perversity" and "mere principle of contradiction" that might cure the "fair sex" of inebriety even as they extolled the natural delicacy that unfortunately exposed women to disease and intemperance.[20]

The most glaring example of misogyny, however, can be found in medical discussions of a bizarre, allegedly alcohol-related phenomenon, spontaneous human combustion. Nineteenth-century physicians on both sides of the Atlantic seemed fascinated by reports that inveterate drunkards sometimes spontaneously caught fire and burned, quite literally, to a crisp. As R. D. Mussey explained the process, "the bodies of some few drinkers have been so thoroughly steeped in spirit, as literally to take fire and consume to ashes." Mussey speculated that an "inflammable air" exhaled from the "lungs or skin, or both" took fire from the "too near approach of a lighted taper, or some ignited substance." When discussing spontaneous combustion, doctors noted that females fell victim either predominantly or exclusively. In 1822, for example, *The Medical Repository* reprinted the findings of a Dr. Charpentier of Guerigny on two "interesting cases of spontaneous combustion, occurring during the extreme cold weather in two aged females, both addicted to intoxication." Robert Macnish reported more female than male cases, and Daniel Drake appended to his *Discourse on Intemperance* a thirteen-page translation of a French paper by Pierre-Aime Lair on the topic, which concluded that the "combustion took place only in women."[21]

When they conjectured on why this horrific consequence of intemperance affected only women, physicians relied on commonly held ideas about gender. Thomas Trotter lifted passages from Lair verbatim for his explanation, urging that women's bodies are "in general more delicate than [those] of the other sex." Women's "solids [are] more relaxed; their fibres are more fragile and of a weaker structure, and therefore their texture more easily hurt." Further, their sedentary lifestyle inclined women toward corpulency, especially in old age. This, in connection with the female body being more "spungy [sic]" than the male, made for greater absorption of imbibed spirits into the tissues. Trotter, like Lair, opined that old women were most susceptible, for "love, departing with youth, leaves a vacuum in the mind" that old women often fill with intoxication, particularly when they can "indulge it without restraint."[22]

In the medical discussion of spontaneous combustion, gender figures prominently and in complex ways. As in other temperance literature, writers ambivalently affirm their admiration for womanly virtue while manifesting fear and distrust of women. Thus Trotter and others attributed women's susceptibility to combustion to their delicacy and fragility, much in keeping with nineteenth-century gender norms. But they did so in a way that conjured up earlier images of women, particularly older women beyond their childbearing years, as dissolute hags who endangered those around them. Though Americans no longer feared witchcraft, they did harbor suspicions about the corrupt bodies of old women and thus were drawn to "stories in which hags burned to death in a manner as horrific as it was convenient."[23]

Physicians partook of the curious admixture of panegyric and contumely that characterized middle-class attitudes toward women. But doctors did more than merely reflect popular notions about gender; they influenced them in turn. As the middle class shifted its gaze during the 1820s and 1830s from women as potential drunkards to women as victims of male drunkards, doctors obliged by assuring their nonmedical peers of the acuity of their gendered vision. Medical affirmation of middle-class gender ideology lent scientific weight to the popular opinion that female drunkenness was not only rare but disgusting and unnatural as well. Thus doctors buttressed the notion that women, or at least the "true" women created in the middle-class mind during the antebellum years, did not abandon themselves to the ravages of liquor. So effective was medical affirmation of the abnormality and rarity of female intemperance that it became the conventional wisdom, obscuring the class and domestic ideology that underpinned it. It convinced even feminist opponents of the emerging domestic order and helped define intemperance as a male vice imposed upon suffering women. The inaugural issue of Amelia Bloomer's radical newspaper *The Lily,* for instance, related an incident in which a physician was called to attend a sick woman. The doctor concluded that she would recover on her own, as the cause of her "sudden and alarming illness" was partaking "too freely of a legalized poison obtained through the aid of our Board of Excise. . . . In plain words, (and we have the doctor's word for it,) the woman was drunk, *dead drunk!*" This "startling fact" occasioned an indignant peroration: "We are well aware that there are *gentlemen* (!) in our village who are frequently bereft of reason and sunk to the level of the brute by using this fatal poison, but we were not prepared for the intelligence that there were those of our own sex who had become so degraded."[24]

Thus physicians shaped and intensified the gender ideology they borrowed from their middle-class compatriots in important and, for women, sometimes ominous ways. Physicians and their lay counterparts in the temperance movement considered women the primary sufferers from male intemperance. Daniel Drake asserted bitterly that "of all on whom the dreadful effects of this vice can fall, none are so injured as a wife and children: the wife especially, for whose situation, when the habit is confirmed, there is, in general, no remedy." Images of the "deserted wife" left to "grieve over her blighted prospects" and become the "victim of brutal violence, from the cruelty of inflamed and unrestrained passion," abounded in physicians' writings and speeches, reflecting the temperance movement's contention that women "have been the greatest sufferers from Alcohol. . . . [Y]ou have seen your homes made desolate and wretched, by the intemperance of those you loved."[25] But physicians also adopted middle-class notions of wifely duty in the face of adversity and oppression, contributing the weight of medical authority to an ideology that celebrated female suffering.

Female Suffering in Domestic Thought

From the sentimental and domestic writers so beloved of the middle class physicians took the conviction that women should cleave to their intemperate husbands no matter how dreadful the abuse and misfortune this fidelity occasioned. In this respect, the temperance writing and domestic fiction of Lydia Sigourney provided a primer in the necessity of female fortitude and suffering. Her story "The Intemperate," which inspired the print so admired by Charles Meigs, offers a number of excellent examples. Her heroine, Jane Harwood, embodied feminine submissiveness and sacrifice. Brokenhearted though she was at leaving her home, Jane could

not forget her marital obligations: "when the hills that encircled her native village faded into the faint, blue outline of the horizon, there came
over her such a desolation of spirit, such a foreboding of evil, as she had
never before experienced. She blamed herself for these feelings, and repressed their indulgence."[26]

Eventually the Harwoods reach their destination and are received
warmly by their new neighbors. Despite the prospect of a fresh start,
James continues drinking, even finding a new way to distress Jane by mis-
treating their son and thereby opening "a direct avenue to her heart-
strings." On the pretext of hardening the boy, James takes him "more
than once" from "the little bed that maternal care had provided for him,
and forced him to go forth in the cold of the winter storm."[27] Predictably,
the boy sickens from this treatment and eventually dies. Though it seems
at first that the boy's death will motivate James to reform, he soon returns
to his evil ways. On one of his many forays for liquor, James drowns during a violent storm, leaving Jane an impoverished widow. Through all
these trials, Jane remains true to her wifely duties:

> She could not forget the love he had once manifested for her, nor prevent the
> chilling contrast from filling her soul with anguish. . . . So faithful was she in
> the discharge of the difficult duties that devolved upon her, —so careful not to
> irritate her husband, by reproach or gloom, —that to a casual observer, she
> might have appeared to be confirming the doctrine . . . that happiness is in ex-
> act proportion to virtue . . . [no one could deny that] virtue is the source of all
> that happiness which depends on ourselves. . . . But to a woman, —a wife, —a
> mother, how small is the portion of independent happiness![28]

Despite the bleak ending, Sigourney conveys a pathetic, if not perverse,
satisfaction with Jane. After the "widowed mourner" left town to live with
a relative, the local residents "remembered her example of uniform patience and piety, and the saint-like manner in which she has sustained her
burdens, and cherished their sympathies," and "felt as though a tutelary
spirit had departed from among them." For Jane, Sigourney allowed the
comforts of family but noted that "in the cherished sadness of her perpet-
ual widowhood, in the bursting sighs of her nightly orison, might be
traced a sacred, deep-rooted sorrow, —the memory of her erring husband
and the miseries of unreclaimed intemperance."[29]

Sigourney, the doyenne of domestic writers, expanded on the theme of
female duty in her popular *Water-drops* (1848), containing a number of
tales in which drunken sons and husbands ruin the lives and trample the
dreams of their mothers and wives. As Ann Douglas noted, the message of
Water-drops is "overwhelmingly that man's brutality has no function but
the torture of woman."[30] Still, Sigourney counseled wives to support their
husbands and pray for their reformation, whatever the personal cost. In

her widely read "Letters to Females," for instance, she exhorted women to shoulder their duty to promote temperance, reserving a stern apostrophe for her married readers:

> Wife! —who by solemn vows, before men and angels, hast entered into a union that death alone can dissolve, has it been your fate to see the vice of intemperance casting [a] deadly shadow over your heart, where your highest earthly confidence reposed? . . . [W]ere you careful not to upbraid, not to provoke, not to argue reproachfully; but to repress your own sense of suffering, . . . to revivify those affections, which are the foundations of purity and joy? . . . Then, though the harvest of your toils may have perished, —though the desolation of your peace nothing earthly can solace, —still, you will have escaped the rankling torture of the reflection, that you are verily guilty concerning him who was 'your more than brother, and your next to God.'[31]

The same message emerged in a purportedly real incident that mirrored the plot of Sigourney's story "The Intemperate," which inspired the print of the same name (see Figure 5). An 1842 publication, *The Afflicted Family*, recounted the ordeal of the Ellison family. Like Sigourney's Jane Harwood, Mrs. Ellison removed to the West "much against [her] own inclination," at the insistence of a husband "much addicted to habits of intemperance." The Ellisons soon lost their way and found themselves stranded in the wilderness with no food or shelter from the winter cold. Mr. Ellison left his family in the forest in order to seek food and aid. Regrettably, he brought a gallon of whiskey with him on this errand and, "having drunk too freely of the poisoned cup" on the first day, got lost again. When he finally brought aid to his unfortunate family thirteen days later, three of his five children had perished from hunger and exposure, and the others teetered on the brink of death. Reflecting on the meaning of this ghastly tale, the anonymous author regretted the torments experienced by Mrs. Ellison, admitting that a woman's best efforts cannot always reclaim a "confirmed sot." Still, the "wretched wife" should never abandon her husband, though she suffered more "than those martyrs who sealed by a life of persecution and death of torture, the fidelity of their hearts to the true faith, she must not forsake her husband—no, let her watch over him, weep over him, pray over him—it is her lot—a bitter and terrible one, yet she must endure it."[32]

Physicians imbibed and endorsed this rhetoric, finding biological imperatives for what domestic ideologues like Lydia Sigourney and the anonymous chronicler of the Ellisons' trials considered the "proper" women's reactions to male intemperance and abuse. Further, by invoking their expertise in female anatomy and physiology, physicians bestowed a scientific imprimatur on these gendered imaginings. In the process of this reciprocal exchange between medical science and temperance literature, physicians shaped broader notions of gender by placing a positive value on—and finding a physiological basis for—women's capacity to endure suffering at the hands of men. The career and writings of physician Charles D. Meigs illustrate in high relief the intersection and reciprocal interaction of medical science, temperance reform, and gender ideology.

Charles D. Meigs and His "germiferous gestative[s]"

Meigs, the son of a Yale mathematics professor, attended the University of Georgia, where his father had become president in 1801. After graduation Meigs apprenticed with a prominent physician for three years, then enrolled in the medical course at the University of Pennsylvania. In 1817 he graduated with a thesis on *Prolapsis uteri,* a topic that presaged the later focus of Meigs's future career: obstetrics, gynecology, and the diseases of women.[33]

One of the many remarkable men of affairs produced by early nineteenth-century America, Meigs pursued a variety of intellectual and professional interests. He mastered Latin, Greek, French, German, and Italian and participated avidly in the activities of the American Philosophical Society, the College of Physicians of Philadelphia, and other learned societies. The doctor also manifested an interest in temperance reform. In 1829 Meigs contributed to a committee report published by the Philadelphia Medical Society intended to dissuade physicians from prescribing medications containing ardent spirits. Two years later, Meigs's name appeared among the managers of the Pennsylvania Society for Discouraging the Use of Ardent Spirits.[34]

Meigs devoted most of his attention, however, to furthering his medical knowledge and professional standing. His dedication and skill earned him a thriving Philadelphia practice and a reputation as one of the most respected and successful physicians in the city. Meigs also found time to make a name for himself as an author and educator. Between 1826 and 1831, he served as one of the editors of the *North American Medical and Surgical Journal* and in 1830 began a series of lectures on midwifery. In 1831 Meigs published his first work, a translation from the French of A. A. L. M. Velpau's disquisition on obstetrics entitled *Elementary Treatise on Midwifery*. Meigs followed this with a work of his own in 1838, *The Philadelphia Practice of Midwifery,* which went through several editions and cemented his reputation as a medical author and educator. In recognition of his accomplishments, the Jefferson Medical College appointed him professor of obstetrics and diseases of women and children in 1841. Before his retirement in 1861, Meigs had authored or translated five other books and numerous articles on obstetrics and gynecology, making himself "the acknowledged leader in the branch, not only in Philadelphia, but in the United States."[35]

As one of the pioneers of American obstetrics and gynecology, Meigs contributed through his writings on women's health and physiology to the reappraisal of gender roles that took place during the early nineteenth century. Unlike many other writers' opinions, Meigs's pronouncements on female qualities and characteristics carried the authority of science. As the preeminent expert on pregnancy, childbirth, and female diseases, Meigs would presumably be in a unique position to determine what biological and anatomical factors differentiated women from men. Combining medical knowledge with keen observation, Meigs might also discern if and how these physiological features translated into intellectual and moral differences between the sexes. Of interest here is the striking similarity between Meigs's conclusions about female nature and gender difference to those articulated in two genres beloved by middle-class readers: sentimental fiction and temperance literature.

Like other physicians, Meigs attributed enormous importance to the influence of woman's reproductive physiology, which rendered her a "moral, a sexual germiferous gestative, and parturient creature." Female sexual nature, Meigs averred, gave the female "physical, intellectual, and moral attributes, a bias different from that of the male . . . [her organs] require a . . . more complex system of innervations, more expensive to the nerve centers" than is the case for men, "more delicate, sensitive, impressible than his." The clear implication of all this, in Meigs's view, was a natural "dependence and physical disability as compared to him; a reliance and trusting to his power; and in fact, all the peculiarities that mark her as a creature of the feminine and gentle sex." Pursuing this theme, the doctor reserved his most rhapsodic prose for describing that "miraculous" organ, the ovary. Meigs challenged his readers to ask themselves "whether *she* was not made, in order that *it* should be made." The answer was clearly affirmative, "if you know that her ovary is her sex—and that she is peculiar because of, and in order that she might have this great, this dominant organ concealed within the recesses of her body."[36]

Exactly what moral and intellectual attributes did Meigs assign to the influence of a woman's sexual organs? Predictably, he identified the same characteristics and traits then being articulated by middle-class ideologues and temperance writers as the hallmarks of domesticity. Meigs lauded the modesty, religiosity, and capacity for love that he believed inhered in the female character. Woman is "naturally prone to be religious," he insisted, for hers "is a pious mind. . . . If an undevout astronomer is mad, what shall we say of an irreligious woman?" Unlike other writers, Meigs linked these qualities directly to the operation and influence of woman's physiology, giving his observations the authority of medical science. Modesty, for instance, one of woman's "most charming attributes," sprang from the "natural timidity and sense of dependence" produced by the "debility" imposed upon women by their sexual organs.

Or in discussing woman's tenderness, Meigs noted that the female heart is, "the seat of tenderer and gentler emotions than those of her mate . . . her susceptible soul is alive to the human charities and trembling sympathies that spring spontaneously in the delicate innervations of her feminine constitution." These "tenderer emotions" manifested themselves in a woman's relationships with her husband and children. "For woman," Meigs opined, "man's love is the moving spring of all her actions. This is at the foundation even of her vanity." This fountainhead of female activity paled, perhaps, only in comparison to woman's devotion to her children, which, Meigs believed, exceeded man's capacity for cherishing his offspring. "Why does she love her child more than its father does[?] Why, he grew to her."[37]

It is here, in Meigs's ascription of what he took to be natural and proper female qualities to physiological structures, that the ominous implications for women, particularly regarding their reactions to male drunkenness, become clear. Women, physicians and the lay public agreed, suffered the consequences of drunkenness, a vice that they defined as occurring almost exclusively in men. But despite the misfortune visited upon innocent women by intemperate men, middle-class temperance reformers did not recommend that beleaguered wives leave their husbands, nor did they stridently protest wives' ill treatment. Meigs's reading of "The Intemperate," incorporates completely this rhetoric of female suffering and self-abnegation.[38] In particular, Meigs focused on the "immortal fidelity [that] is depicted by the artist in the face of that woman! A face beautiful in its expression of resignation, and of pride in her own faithfulness and truthfulness." Meigs noted too her fortitude in the face of the loss of the "homestead she had brought as her dower, in that blessed morn when in the village church she gave herself away *for him*." While acknowledging the bitter reward for her trust and love, Meigs praised the woman's apparent resignation and fidelity as emblems of true womanliness. Despite the husband's dreadful abuse, the dutiful wife "will cling to him until the death of the drunkard shall have broken the bond; and after that, go weep on his discreditable grave, and forgive him too. Such pictures are from life. There are thousands of such."[39]

This middle-class ideology of gender, which conceived of women as submissive, long-suffering, and loving to a fault, emerged in the short stories, tracts, sermons, songs, reports, and other literary products of the temperance movement. As a temperance advocate himself, Charles D. Meigs would doubtless have been familiar with this material, even if he had never read Lydia Sigourney's harrowing tale of Jane Harwood, which inspired the print. His immediate identification of this vision of womanly virtue in his gloss on "The Intemperate" demonstrates the pervasiveness and influence of middle-class notions of gender. Yet Meigs and other physicians did not merely receive passively this vision of womanhood but contributed to the gender ideology on which it was based by offering scientific evidence of the "naturalness" of the characteristics attributed to women. Temperance writers remarked upon woman's capacity to endure suffering in the interest of preserving home and family; Meigs provided a biological reason for this quality that was, once again, grounded in female reproductive functioning. The pains of childbirth accustomed women to torment, Meigs concluded, saying: "Men cannot suffer the same pains as woman. *What* do you call the pain of parturition? There is no name for it but *Agony.*" Meigs apparently viewed this agony as natural, if not desirable. In medical history, he is remembered less for his pioneering work in obstetrics than for his ferocious opposition to the administration of anesthetics to women during childbirth.[40] If woman's greatest accomplishment and defining quality, the ability to bear children, involved agony that necessarily must be endured, it was a short leap to conclude that withstanding other forms of torment related to her womanly duties as wife and mother was no more than should be expected. Perhaps most ominous, this paean in both temperance literature and medical writing to female fortitude, submissiveness, and endurance as the touchstone of womanhood might easily promote the belief that women demonstrated their femininity and attractiveness precisely by being oppressed and afflicted by men.

What resulted from this medical intervention in temperance literature and gender ideology? Our answers can be suggestive at best, but it seems clear that medical revelations about female delicacy, in conjunction with acknowledgment of the distress caused by male intemperance, prompted interest in protective legal measures such as prohibition. But the denomination of female submissiveness, fidelity, and endurance as both normative and "natural" in the scientific sense may have forged a double-edged sword. One cannot view the spirited resistance met by proposals to liberalize divorce, allow married women to own property, or permit greater female participation in civic affairs without reflecting on how these measures would have violated the standards for female deportment set out in temperance writing and legitimized in medical literature.

For women to abandon their husbands, for example, however justified the provocation or excuse, meant relinquishing those qualities identified as inherently female: fortitude, loyalty, loving tenderness, and the desire to exert religious and moral influence over men. A married woman's claim to an independent existence would be immodest, contradicting the natural dependence on man that Meigs denominated as a hallmark of femininity. Dire consequences ensued from this type of complaint or similar "rude, boisterous, or immodest speech or action," Meigs insisted. Immodesty "unsexes and disgraces [woman]. This modesty is one of the strongest of her attractions; and she sometimes, perhaps, affects to possess it for the purpose of riveting her chains on conqueror man."[41] In this regard, one might also consider how the feminine ideal engendered in the temperance movement and affirmed by Charles D. Meigs influenced physicians who built upon his pioneering work in gynecology. As historians of medicine

Figure 6—The Bad Husband. Source: Currier and Ives, 1870. Courtesy of the Library of Congress.

have demonstrated, by the late nineteenth century American gynecologists viewed female behavior that deviated from the norms popularized by temperance literature as evidence of a derangement of the sexual organs that determined women's moral and intellectual life. Their prescription, in many cases, was the removal of the ovaries, that "dominant organ" to which Meigs traced the sources of the female character.[42]

Whatever our other speculations, one thing is certain, however: the image of the suffering drunkard's wife that captivated Charles D. Meigs continued to fascinate American society. In 1870 Currier and Ives appropriated it to produce a lithograph nearly identical in subject and composition to "The Intemperate" (see Figure 6). In contrast to earlier renditions, in which the tortured wife is a central, if not the primary, figure, the Currier and Ives version shifts focus to the brutish husband. The 1870 print places him further in the foreground, slightly increasing the distance to his lagging wife, emphasizing that he, and not she, is the focal point. Moreover, the Currier and Ives wife is more of a cipher than the expressive woman of the "Intemperate." The latter gazes longingly over her shoulder, perhaps at the life and comforts left behind; the former turns her seemingly crossed eyes distractedly toward the heavens. The (sym)pathetic but very human heroine of the early nineteenth-century had been transformed to a generic figure representing female suffering, the mate of "The Bad Husband."[43]

Female Moral Suasion

Manipulative Belles and Undutiful Wives

> The influence of woman is irresistible, and I invoke the mothers
> and daughters of this country to contend earnestly for their
> "homebred, fireside nights," which have in so many
> instances been cruelly invaded by the liquor-sellers.
> —John Tappan, 1838[1]

Temperance literature attributed enormous power and importance to women's influence over men as wives, mothers, daughters, and sisters. Proponents of the emerging ideology of domesticity claimed that women possessed moral and religious sensibilities inherently superior to those of men.[2] The female sex, they argued, should employ these proclivities in the home to influence men and children to lead upright and virtuous lives within the domestic sphere and beyond it. "The domestic circle indeed forms the primary department for the exhibition of female talents and virtues," Congregational minister Benjamin Wadsworth told his Danvers, Massachusetts, audience in 1817. "The good effects of female influence," he added, "are not however confined to such narrow limits. They often extend through the whole sphere of their connexions [*sic*] and acquaintance, through all their social walks, and indeed through the community." Every woman wielded this far-reaching moral influence, regardless of her station. "Even a single female, born in obscurity, brought up in retirement, and spending her days in private life," Justin Edwards told a Boston "Penitent Female's Refuge Society" in 1825, "exerts an influence that may operate on thousands, ages after she is dead."[3]

Reformers prophesied great things if female influence could be harnessed for the temperance cause. Let young women but extract a promise of temperance from their beaus, the *Temperance Recorder* opined, "and intemperance will soon be put to flight; and the wife, mourning over the ruin of all her hopes, by reason of the drunkenness of him she loved, will not be seen in our land." Let every "lady persuade one of her female friends to sign the temperance pledge," a temperance almanac insisted in 1845, "and the country would soon be clear of drunkenness." These and similar pronouncements reflected enormous confidence in womanly sensibility and influence. The "instincts of women are right," William B. M'Clure declared in 1852. "They decide in an instant, where a man must reason for an hour. She is omnipotent in any good work she undertakes. If women once set their hearts upon a thing, it is done. All arguments and impediments vanish into smoke before the fire of their zeal." Even Susan B. Anthony shared in this optimism. In her first address as a Daughter of Temperance, Anthony ventured that in her "humble opinion, all that is needed to produce a complete Temperance and Social reform in this age of Moral Suasion, is for our Sex to cast their United influences into the balance."[4]

Some temperance advocates employed martial rhetoric to praise female influence, perhaps acknowledging unconsciously the importance of military valor in claims to citizenship and public authority and attempting to attach it to women. "The influence—the power—the weapon is in your hands," declared a clergyman, "and if you dare wield it, you are competent . . . to strike a blow that shall shiver to atoms every temple of pollution in the land." Given the "mighty consequence and responsibility" of wielding this potent weapon, reformers urged women not to "slumber and sleep at our posts, when the enemy to destroy souls is in our midst." In a particularly pronounced use of martial rhetoric and buoyant optimism, one temperance periodical praised the efforts of the Daughters of Temperance.

> The Daughters are coming to the rescue—and the day is not distant when the distillers' fires will be extinguished—when a drunkard will be a wonder in the community—and the rumsellers will have emptied their . . . demijohns of death into the sea, to tempt no more the simple and unwary . . . Woman marshalled [*sic*] for the field and the invader fled![5]

Doubts about Female Influence

Along with these spirited endorsements, however, were doubts. Temperance advocates came to see that female influence was not a panacea for the ideological ills of the middle class. In voicing their qualms they revealed, once again, the strand of misogyny woven into the fabric of domestic ideology's praise of women. Female influence, many commentators worried, could be a potent force for good, but in the wrong hands, it possessed an equally powerful potential for evil. Woman wields a moral energy, *The American Quarterly Temperance Magazine* observed in 1834, which proved "resistless whenever virtue and virtuous principles sway her mind; or, which makes her a fiend incarnate, wherever principle is wanting." Similar misgivings surfaced frequently. Woman's influence is "either of the most exalted or of the most debasing character," argued Nathaniel W. Chittenden. In the female character, he explained, "there is no mid-region; it must exist in spotless innocence, or else in hopeless vice." In every "civilized" country, another writer affirmed, women's influence for good or evil was much more potent than many recognized. Wives especially, because of their intimate and constant contact with men, exerted a power for "good or evil [that] is altogether irresistible." So potent was female influence for "good or ill," an anonymous pamphlet insisted, that an "angel from above, or beneath, can neither use nor counteract" it.[6]

Much of the concern about misapplied female influence betrayed male discomfort with the sources and nature of woman's power over men. Domestic writers emphasized innate female piety and morality as the source of influence, but more practical-minded commentators recognized that physical beauty, personal charm, and sexual attractiveness accounted for a large share of men's fascination with women. One temperance paper, for instance, recommended that women unite to "discountenance" intemperance, expressing certainty that the "force of [female] example and persuasion" would prevail when coercion failed. The accompanying illustration of how this might work in practice, however, revealed the true nature of female influence. The author recounted the story of a young man who signed the total abstinence pledge because his pretty cousin Kate had "laid a tariff amounting to an entire prohibition upon her sweet lips, and insists upon keeping it up till I become teetotal." As this example suggests, temperance advocates considered courtship an ideal time to exercise female influence. In the early stages of drinking, before the liquor habit became ingrained in their characters, the argument went, young men would "prefer to sacrifice the *cup,* rather than the society of ladies." Using their youthful allure as leverage, some women gave men little choice: one tent of the Daughters of Rechab, the female wing of the Independent Order of Rechabites, a temperance society from the 1840s, marched in a Fourth of July celebration under a banner reading "Temperance or No Husbands!"[7]

Courtship offered an effective venue for female influence, largely because the women involved were usually young and at the height of their attractiveness to men. Young women's influence over men, noted *The Pearl,* "commencing at precisely the period of life, when that of the mother, in a great degree, ceases, is all powerful for good or evil." Though woman inspired men's "gentler and nobler sentiments" in general, admitted another reformer, her influence soared when she "burst into early womanhood, encompassed by bright hopes and fond heart, —when the Creator adorns you with graces and charms that draw towards you the dullest souls." The "power of fascination" that these youthful charms afforded could thus be used to seduce men to virtue. If Eve could tempt an innocent man to sin, William B. M'Clure queried, surely her "fair daughters" will not admit "such waning influence, dimmed lustre, and faded charms, that they cannot even tempt and persuade men to do what God has not forbidden but enjoined?"[8]

The problem with enlisting baser motives in the service of higher ends was that the "wizard power" with which women ruled over "man's sterner nature" might be perverted or exploited by the immoral and unscrupulous. If a beautiful woman could entice men to abstain, she might also inveigle them to drink. Hence the alarm with which commentators reported the use of women, some of whom looked like they might otherwise grace middle-class parlors, to attract men to drinking establishments. A few, like an 1835 temperance almanac, preferred to see this use of female influence as a foreign practice. In England, for example, attractive women served gin in surroundings of "dazzling grandeur":

> Ay, and the presiding goddess, (*deceiving fiend* we might call her) who mixes and serves out these noxious libations, appears under the guise of a *beautiful female*, with graceful and fascinating manners! What a mockery is this! and what a contrast is presented between the . . . joyous, smiling, attentive appearance of the beauty who presides . . . and the miserable, wretched, beggarly appearance of her customers![9]

Another reformer told of a New Haven confectionery run by a "foreigner" who catered to young men and boys: one might find ten to twelve apparently respectable lads "in familiar conversation with the very pleasant woman who commonly attends." Conjuring up images of malignant European decadence that might infect America, he warned that this shop threatened "to scatter among us, to a fearful extent, the worst vices of the French metropolis." But before long, Americans had to admit that using sex to sell liquor had become a thoroughly American practice, however much the acknowledgment pained them. More than a few respectable drinking houses, lamented Presbyterian minister Albert Barnes, "—tell not this, lest the daughters of the Philistines triumph—not a few are under the direction of females—dispensing death and ruin to the souls and bodies of men." Others expressed similar dismay. It was not so much the use of cheap strumpets as advertisements for liquor that concerned middle-class reformers, for respectable men would reject their overtures; rather, they

Figure 7—Love, Purity & Fidelity. *A Son of Temperance chooses between female influences*. Source: Nathaniel Currier, 1851. Courtesy of the Library of Congress (Prints and Photos Division, LC-USZC2-586).

worried that women with some pretense and appearance of refinement would consent to tempt men. The *New York Organ* marveled that "fashionable, genteel and beautiful ladies can be found to add their charms to the fascination of liquor and cigars, in alluring men to dissipation," but so it was.[10]

Temperance reformers' discomfort with women's sexual power over men, as well as their misogynistic suspicion that women would use that power for evil, emerge forcefully in a striking 1851 lithograph by Nathaniel Currier, "Grand, National Temperance Banner." The print depicts a Son of Temperance torn between temperance and drunkenness, each represented by a woman vying for his attention (see Figure 7). A virtuous Daughter of Temperance, clad primly in a white dress that largely hides the outline of her body, stares blankly ahead while demurely offering the Son a crystal goblet of water with one hand and holding her other hand over her heart. She makes no physical contact with the male figure but waits for him to take the proffered glass. Her opposite number presents a stark contrast. The female embodiment of intemperance, arrayed in a more sensual dark gown that reveals the outline of thigh and breast, stands much closer to the discomfited Son, tugging at his arm and directing his gaze to a table laden with liquor, cards, and other implements of vice. She, too, offers him a goblet, but hers is filled with spirits from a decanter on the table. The scene appears to depict the precise moment when the beleaguered Son is poised to choose sobriety and virtue but hesitates when distracted by the allurements of the dark-clad temptress. Though he leans toward temperance and appears to be touching, though not holding, the water goblet, he gazes almost wistfully backward toward vice, his outstretched arm and open hand in an ambivalent gesture of either rejecting or reaching. Recognizing the danger in this defining moment, the virtuous maid presses hand to heart in apparent trepidation that he may choose unwisely.

Currier's lithograph encapsulates much of the middle-class ideology of gender and temperance. Conflicted and contradictory visions of woman's nature as well as a misogynistic distrust of female power emerge clearly. The picture attests to the force of female influence and the indecisiveness of man when faced with such potent sway. Here women use their influence for good and evil, and the results for men are far from certain. What is certain, however, is the temperance movement's discomfort with the erotic nature of women's power over men. Currier might have depicted intemperance as an ugly woman but chose not to, for that would have failed to resonate with his middle-class audience. After all, a wizened hag would hardly appeal to the well-dressed youth in the lithograph or to the promising young men of affairs temperance workers hoped to safeguard. Rather, Currier portrayed both women as attractive, reflecting middle-class anxiety over the preponderant role of beauty and sexual desirability in women's interaction with men. Thus while ostensibly championing temperance and virtue against the enticements of evil, the lithograph also betrays the deeply ambivalent feelings many middle-class reformers harbored about women's moral capacity and the abuse of female influence.

Few reformers expressed these doubts or evinced more indignation at the misuse of female influence than middle-class women themselves. Half of the champagne sold in New York City, *The Pearl* regretted, was "sold by women and bought and drunk by men at their solicitation." By the mid-1840s, the author noted, a new class of grogshops, run by attractive females, lured the unwary to perdition. Young men in particular could not withstand the "fascinations" of the "pretty barmaids" who ran the establishments. They drank too much, often only as an excuse to speak to the "divinity of chalk and rouge" who tended bar. These unwitting youngsters risked becoming drunkards "while ogling the pretty painted creature mixing toddies . . . and fancying they are making an impression upon her heart—a heart as open as day to their sixpences, but of much better proof than her brandy against the ardent glances of these verdant youths." This, *The Pearl* bemoaned, was "female influence . . . acting directly, on a scale of vast extravagance, and making drunkards of thousands!"[11]

The Misuse of Female Influence
Sloth, Thoughtlessness, and Malevolence

Dire pronouncements such as this betokened a deep ambivalence about women's commitment to the temperance cause. They also reflected a society and culture in which emerging positive valuations of women's moral and domestic nature wrestled with older, less complimentary portrayals. Though middle-class domesticity rested on depicting women as pillars of morality and sobriety, domestic writers, clergymen, and other assorted ideologues could not always convince themselves, let alone their audiences, that such was the case. Their failures bespoke the resurgence of an Anglo-American tradition of misogyny that periodically appeared in public discourse before and since the antebellum era. Like a persistent virus, it might become dormant as more complimentary or sympathetic views of women came to the fore, only to flair up at the hint of any fundamental change in the sexual division of power in society. This appears to have been the case during the antebellum era, when, in the service of domestic ideology, middle-class reformers pointed out both the wrongs perpetrated against women by men and women's capacity to influence men in a cause that stood to benefit them and curtail male prerogatives.

The problem with female influence, many feared, stemmed not from a small number of "divinities of rouge and chalk," but from the sloth, thoughtlessness, or outright malevolence of most women. Reformers charged, for example, that female vanity and blind allegiance to fashion often interfered with moral obligations and temperance work. Thoughtless young women, William R. DeWitt warned in 1840, spent too much time "studying the fashions, and before their mirrors . . . adorning themselves outwardly with costly apparel (often too costly for their means, or the means of those on whom they are dependent)." Their inattention to religion and morality, he scolded, rendered them unfit to "fill the elevated sphere allotted to them in society." The *Temperance Recorder* also took fashionable ladies to task, chiding them for refusing to subscribe to temperance publications, despite their habit of "spending fifty dollars per annum for periodicals, the moral tendency of which is even doubtful." *The Pearl* struck a similar chord in 1846, when it fumed that membership in female temperance societies had declined, largely because New York's young ladies had become unwilling to "spend a moiety of the time they waste promenading Broadway and reading useless books." As if to jar women from their fashionable torpor, a temperance almanac shrilled that "ON YOU CHIEFLY DEPENDS THE ONWARD PROGRESS OF THE TEMPERANCE REFORMATION." Intemperance, the anonymous writer urged, was assembling all its forces "outside the state prison, house of correction, poor houses and insane hospitals for one last death-struggle. . . . Let then every lady be aware that she has something to do."[12]

Even more than female sloth, temperance advocates feared women's complicity in, or even active promotion of, male drinking. This danger loomed large and seemed most egregious in middle-class households, where entertaining served a number of social, familial, and business functions. To appear fashionable and hospitable, thoughtless women permitted liquor to be served in their homes and even encouraged men to drink it. "Depend upon it," Nathan Beman declared in 1829, "female hospitality has done much to deluge the world with drunkenness; and it is time that female decision should do something to stay the burning waves!" Female reformers agreed. Women, *The Olive Plant* opined, had "betrayed the sacred trust" by serving alcohol to family and guests and thereby assisted in making the "wine cup fashionable . . . often has her hands [sic] tendered it to many who now fill a drunkard's grave." Distrust of their own sex explains why mothers voiced fears when their sons attended social gatherings, lest they receive the "wine cup from *female friends*."[13]

Attributing such enormous power to female influence led many reformers to blame women for the bulk of male intemperance. It was bad enough that women failed to perform their moral duty to promote sobriety, but misusing female influence to induce men to drink, it seemed, increased dramatically intemperance's toll. "Alas! alas!" wailed one orator, "could the grave give up its secrets, what tales of horror would it not reveal of woman's perverted influence, —of woman thoughtlessly leading men, through the intoxicating cup, to the brink of utter and hopeless ruin!" Whatever their virtues, John Neal insisted, women were "chargeable, with perhaps a chief part of our present degradation, guilt, and sorrow." How can men remain sober, he demanded, when women made "every sociable coming together, every fire-side interview, every joyous event . . . our very homes a snare to us?" Female approval threw a "more bewitching enchantment" around the already seductive poisoned chalice, and through their persuasions and entreaties, "millions had learned to sip the cup, who, in the bitterness of a *Drunkard's Death,* have drunk it to its dregs."[14]

The Manipulative Belle and the Undutiful Wife

Concerned observers noted with alarm that some female promotion of intemperance stemmed not from thoughtlessness or vanity but from outright malevolence. To demonstrate their power over men, women enticed or commanded them to drink, even though this risked turning them into drunkards. Here again temperance advocates expressed misogynistic dismay over the sexual component of female influence. Typically women used their feminine allure to coerce men to drink. A reformed drunkard, for example, withstood the "fascination" of wine at a dinner party until a "young lady, whom he desired to please, challenged him to drink." With "banter and ridicule" she "cheated him out of all his noble purposes," and he drank, only to reawaken the demon of intemperance and die in delirium tremens ten days later.[15] This concern that women might use their feminine wiles for evil rather than good crystallized into two stock characters: the manipulative belle and the undutiful wife, who inhabited much of temperance literature. Both betray their middle-class origins, for each represents a nightmare vision of women's proper role within the household perverted by a selfishness or lust for power that domestic ideology denied could even exist in the fair sex.

The manipulative belle attempted to induce men to drink to demonstrate her power over them and to make them prove their devotion to her. Helen More, the protagonist of Maria Lamas's *The Glass,* might serve as the apotheosis of this character. Headstrong and beautiful, Helen resolved to make three male suitors, all of whom abstained from alcohol, not only drink but become "intoxicated before a month had passed." When her fashionable mother scoffed, Helen became "determined to show her the power I possessed." Helen succeeded, and the three got drunk at a party, to the "great mystification of their friends, my mother's delight and my own triumph." One of the Helen's unfortunate victims eventually died of delirium tremens, cursing her as "Satan in woman's shape—she tempted me and I fell!"[16]

In another fictional telling of this scenario, Charles Hastings returned home after embarking on a promising career as a lawyer and state legislator. Soon after his arrival home, Charles squired childhood sweetheart Helen at a ball. There, Charles's friends importuned him to drink. Having been abstinent for four years, he refused. The party then enlisted Helen's aid, but still Charles demurred. Finally, Helen coaxed: "Charles," she said, "just one glass for Auld Lang Syne." He at last complied and got drunk, loosing a "stream of appetite" that "rolled on like the pent up stream." Charles sank quickly, especially after Helen informed him that she would never marry an intemperate person (!). Charles eventually killed himself but not before leaving a note to Helen: "Who made me what I am? What jewelled hand held out the poisoned chalice to my lips, and bade me drain it to the dregs? that hand was *your own*. It robbed me of character, . . . honor . . . [and] life. Adieu!"[17]

A common variation of the manipulative belle motif had a young bride enticing her groom or a wedding guest to drink. In "The First Glass," an 1834 temperance story, promising youth Frank Hayford resisted repeated entreaties to drink at the wedding of his friends Harriet and Wendoll. Finally he succumbed to a toast: "At that moment the beautiful face of Harriet shone out upon him from a bevy of maidens, and a smile and an inclination of the head, as for '*a health*', met his eye at the instant. The glass was lifted and drained, and the face had disappeared." A variety of horrific consequences ensued, and before dropping dead at the end of the tale, a debilitated and degraded Frank confronted Harriet and Wendoll:

'Your bridal, Wendoll, has decided my fate; and you Harriet,' continued he, in a low tone, and looking her suddenly in the face with a heated cheek and an unsettled eye, 'must account for this, and for my blood! . . . do you forget, Harriet, that smile, and your nod, and your '*health*'! yes, *your* solicitations, your plot brought me to the first drop of drink, and that drop has brought me to this.'[18]

Tales of bridal feasts abounded in which a new husband, wanting to avoid being a "poltroon . . . who drains not the whole" in "drinking long life to his lovely bride," allowed her to press "the poison to those lips/ That had refused so long."[19] The "bridegroom often died a drunkard," a book devoted to the dangers of wet weddings noted ominously, "and the bride broken-hearted, from wounds received on the bridal day!" The problem arose largely because women, the votaries of fashion, used their beauty and feminine wiles to entice abstaining guests to drink to the bride. Likening the seduction of teetotalers to Delilah's conquest of Samson, the work exhorted women to remember their power to weaken men's strength of conviction: "O! if woman only knew, or rather would remember this, for she does know it, how many would it save from the beginning of ruin's ways!"[20]

Domestic life, as well as the sexually charged atmosphere of courtship and weddings, provided opportunities for the malevolent misuse of female influence. Another familiar figure in temperance literature, the undutiful wife, also threatened male sobriety. Sometimes she resembled her manipulative unmarried counterpart. In one temperance story, a young bride, "in a coaxing voice, turning her eye upon her husband as she spoke," enticed her reformed husband to try some of her aunt's brandied peaches, scuttling his hard-won sobriety.[21] In most cases, however, the undutiful wife drove her husband to drink with bad behavior. Once again, middle-class values, perspectives, and anxieties concerning the gendered division between the domestic and public spheres came to the fore. By not making the family fireside a welcoming retreat from the rigors of the marketplace, undutiful women might easily drive men to the tavern and gambling hall. In T. S. Arthur's "A Story for Wives," for instance, Edward Nichols avoided home because of his wife Margaret's "fretful, moody, unhappy states," finding solace in the "gay companions and the choicest things to tempt his appetite" offered by fashionable drinking establishments. Despite moral qualms, Edward found frequenting barrooms better than "moping at home with a wife in the dumps! Liked home best—that is, home when the good lady is in a good humor." Never one to miss an opportunity to belabor his point, Arthur concluded: "Does our little story need a word to enforce the lesson to wives that we would teach! Let wives who have good home-loving, temperate husbands . . . not fail to repress a peevish, fretful, fault-finding temper, if inclined thereto, for nothing will so surely estrange a man from home as this."[22]

Another variation of the undutiful wife critiqued women who forgot their subordinate role in the household. Harsh words or actions might drive a husband deeper into the slough of drunkenness. Temperance writers urged sisters, aunts, and other women who ran households for male relatives to heed this advice as well. One story recounted the travails of Cordelia and William Gleason, a brother and sister. Cordelia indulged her "foolish temper" and felt herself "superior," thereby making the Gleason household unpleasant for William, who shunned "his home as he would a pest house." William fled to the tavern for solace, becoming a drunkard and blaming his sister for his "downfall." Even though the story ended with William's reform and Cordelia's contrition, it offered an object lesson for women who could not control their tempers: "think for a moment on the many years of suffering of poor William Gleason, and resolve to yield to its influence no more."[23]

Blaming Women for Male Intemperance

By the 1840s and 1850s, as the antiliquor movement shifted its focus from moral suasion to prohibitory legislation, negative rhetoric about women became more pronounced. Increasingly critics blamed women and misapplied female influence for male intemperance. Some harsh criticism came from women, both radical feminists and more conservative activists, who considered non-temperance women as traitors to their sex and allies of the liquor trade. *The Olive Plant,* for instance, insisted that women should feel a primary responsibility for ending intemperance since women had contributed to the problem by permitting liquor to be served in their homes. *The Lily* went further, conjuring up images of Eve tempting Adam not with forbidden fruit but with the poisoned cup. One correspondent expressed pity for the latter-day Adam but reserved "a feeling nearer akin to loathing, and disgust, for the woman who can thus lead him on to ruin." Such women, an indignant editorial charged, were "in league with the bloated drunken keeper of the vilest groggery." Did not women who countenance drinking realize that their own "destiny will be linked for life with a disgusting drunkard[?]"[24]

But this censure seemed mild compared to that leveled by men in the mainline temperance movement. Here again sympathetic portrayals of women coexisted with, even facilitated, misogynist pronouncements. Often in the same breath in which they lamented female suffering at the hands of male drunkards, middle-class men blamed women for male intemperance. John Marsh, for example, praised female influence in his 1851 survey of the temperance movement but added a stern rebuke that betrayed hostility and a readiness to blame:

> Who drinks to the dregs the cup of bitterness like the drunkard's wife? and who is often the drunkard's wife, but the delicately-reared daughter of her who controlled the fashion and would have wine at her parties? There is not a lady who sets before young men the intoxicating cup, concerning who we may not say, Father forgive her, who knows not what she does. O when the destinies of men are unfolded in the final day, how many of the lost will reflect with anguish on female influence.

Marsh went beyond merely blaming women for male intemperance by suggesting that drunkards' wives deserved the abuse they endured for their role in creating the vice. Others concurred. "Who can know," Thomas P. Hunt said, "what woman has suffered from her impudence and cruel tender mercy in offering her husband a glass of wine." At bottom, Hunt and Marsh said what others before them had only hinted at: if women did not do their moral duty by upholding temperance, they deserved all the heartache and abuse they got.[25]

The Failure of Female Influence

If women's alleged misapplication of their influence posed a grave problem for middle-class temperance advocates and supporters of domestic ideology, the failure of female influence to effect reform represented a more serious challenge. Even when conscientiously and consistently applied, female influence too often failed to win men's hearts and change their destructive behavior. Women deluded themselves who thought that after marriage, when the "dances, and musters, and merry meetings were all over," intemperate swains would succumb to their influence and "settle down at home, and become right steady men." Foolish maidens who believed this, candid reformers warned, would get either their hearts or their "heads *broke* . . . by a drunken husband," or wind up in "the poorhouse, or insane hospital." In some cases, men rejected women's appeal outright, proving entirely immune to, or even resentful of, women's attempts at reforming. "Her kindness pleads in vain—/," lamented a temperance songster, "His heart is sear'd and hard;/ And tauntings loud, and cruel blows/ Are that fond wife's reward."[26]

Even Lydia Sigourney, the doyenne of American sentimental and domestic writers, recognized that male stubbornness frequently defeated female influence. This recognition emerges clearly in "The Intemperate" (discussed in Chapter 3); it also informs her short story "The Widow and her Son." Despite the best efforts of his widowed mother and his sister, Margaret, to reform him, Richard Jones "liked the society of idle boys. He was known to be addicted to his own way, and had been heard to express contempt for the authority of women." Margaret's warnings curbed Richard's bad behavior only temporarily. When she upbraided her mother for not being harder on Richard, Mrs. Jones replied that all "that was in my power to do, has been faithfully done. I have not spared him. But he revolted. He despised my woman's voice, my motherly love." After a last desperate effort by Margaret to save her brother, Richard lashed out against female influence: "Is there to be no end to these women's tongues? So has it been for three years: preach, preach, till I have prayed for deafness. I have had no rest, for Mrs. Jones' eternal sermons, and now you must help her, with your everlasting gab." In a fit of spiteful vengeance, Richard went to sea, playing on his mother's fear that he would become a dissipated sailor. This he proceeded to do, putting an ocean between him and female influence in the process.[27]

Though intended to build support for temperance, the prevalence of horrific stories of wife murder, family disgrace, and male brutishness (see Chapter 2) also attested to the ineffectiveness of female influence. Reluctantly temperance advocates admitted that female influence could not stem the tide of drunkenness. In families with drunken fathers and husbands, Elisha Mitchell acknowledged dolefully, the wife and mother "can in part only and not entirely remedy the evil." Nor did wives' appeals to liquor vendors work. In Fall River, Massachusetts, for instance, temperance women visited a liquor dealer and "earnestly besought [him] to relinquish his business." Despite their pleadings, the dealer dismissed them callously and peremptorily: "I know it is a bad business, ladies, but I have bought a large estate and have no other means of paying for it, and if I *do* kill one of your husbands now and then, I can't help it." Indeed, *The Pearl* declared indignantly that female influence might even worsen matters: "Your suasion only stimulates the rumseller's appetite for his accursed gains."[28]

So insidious and tenacious was intemperance, reformers warned, that it might reverse the course and character of moral influence within the household. Sober wives might not only be unable to reform their drunken husbands but could themselves fall victim to intemperance through the example set by their mates. In part this admission reflected a candid estimate of gendered power relations in the home. Though clerics, reformers, and sentimental writers lauded the domestic sphere as woman's empire, physician and temperance reformer Daniel Drake allowed that husbands, "in general, exert more influence over wives, than wives can exercise over them." This being the case, drunken husbands posed two different threats to womanly virtue. First, the "lords of creation" influence women by playing on their "spirit of sociability, and deference" to induce them to drink. In the "evening circle," a medical journal averred, women yield a "dangerous compliance with men's love of drink, when they allow the sweet luscious cordial to be handed to them, whilst the stronger nerves of the others are stimulated by wine." Or, as another physician put it, husbands "sometimes teach their wives to be drunkards by indulging them in toddys and such fluids, every time they themselves sit down to their libations." This motif surfaced in the many temperance works inspired by George Cruikshank's "The Bottle," a series of engravings depicting the ravages of alcohol on a family. In one rendition, James Latimer coaxes his wife into drinking against her better judgment. After repeated refusals, Latimer urges:

> "Yes, try it. If it's good for me, it's good for you. Drink it off. It's nothing but cordial."
>
> "No —no. I don't want it."
>
> "Nonsense! You must drink some. You don't know how good it is. Here, just take a drop!" And he continued to hold out the glass.
>
> Mrs. Latimer, thus urged, took the glass and sipped a little of the pleasant compound.
>
> "Isn't it good?" enquired her husband.
>
> "Yes, it is good," she replied.
>
> "Then drink it all down." An invitation with which the wife did not refuse to comply.[29]

In the second scenario, male intemperance and its dire consequences compromised even female virtue and perseverance. An American Temperance Society report told of a young drinker who worried that his wife, "anxious for her salvation, was in danger of becoming pious." He opposed her religious leanings, striving by all "means in his power, to banish serious impressions from her mind." After succeeding in stifling his wife's budding religiosity, the drinker himself repented, found God, and appealed to her to follow him. But she remained "as he once wished to have her," thereby opening a "great gulph [*sic*] . . . between them" that may last for all eternity. Or, through weariness and despair, women might fall prey to the ill that beset their partners. One reformer told of a woman whose husband's drunkenness "broke down her spirits, until at length she ran to the same dreadful expedient, . . . the cares of family and house were all extinguished by recourse to the bottle." Too often, lecturer George Bethune agreed, a drunkard's wife would "follow in his ruin. The wife drinks to drown her sorrows." Or, a wife might drink out of spite. "Excessive drinking is contagious," a tract cautioned its readers. "If the husband drinks abroad, the wife may take the same liberty at home."[30]

When men did become abstainers, it was often male fellowship and intervention, not female influence, that effected reform. One story told of an inveterate drunkard whose mistreatment and neglect eventually caused his wife's death. Even the loss of his wife and the difficulty of caring for his children unaided did not convince him to quit drinking. Though encouraged by his oldest daughter—"the image of her mother"—it took the impassioned preaching of an aged clergyman, "a prophetic soul," to win the drunkard's heart. The preacher's appeal was "no regular discourse, but an exhortation of unspeakable fervor—it was Christian love wrestling in strong agony to break the bonds of the drunkard—love still pitiful and entreating." In a resolution that would be repeated in many tracts, news items, and stories, this fervent male plea induced the inebriate to sign the pledge and reform. Especially after the advent of the Washingtonian movement in the early 1840s, men rather than women provided the impetus to sobriety. Many temperance narratives have women playing a secondary role, praying for their men's redemption and persevering in the worst of conditions. In Lydia Sigourney's "The Widow and her Son," mentioned above, Richard Jones reformed not through the earnest pleadings of his mother and sister but through the intervention of a kindly Quaker man and employment on a temperance ship, on which the crew received no rum rations. In another story, a distraught mother could prevail on her son only to attend a Washingtonian meeting, though not to sign the pledge. Not her beseeching but the "influence of the living voice of a reformed man" finally led the errant son to a sober life.[31]

Temperance drama, as well as fiction, conveyed the impotence of female influence when compared to other forms of intervention. Stage drunkards, having reached the nadir of their drinking careers, frequently reformed through the efforts of a "close friend . . . co-worker" or "stranger introduced into the plot at the last minute to effect a solution, much in the manner of the classic *deus ex machina*," rather than those of a female

relative or acquaintance. Concerning the nineteenth-century stage, theater historian John Frick noted that temperance playwrights "reinforced
one message: a lone woman whose sole weapon was her 'moral authority'
was virtually powerless against the combined forces of the liquor industry, her husband's coterie of bar-room companions, and the drunkard
himself." This pattern emerged clearly in one of the most popular and
widely performed temperance plays, W. H. Smith's *The Drunkard* (1844).
This stage play, which aimed at translating the "raw, unmediated emotionalism of the Washingtonian experience speech" into an aesthetic
form suitable for middle-class consumption, raised doubts about
"women's capacity to exert moral influence over their husbands."
Though the drama stressed the "tactical validity of moral suasion if prac-
ticed by a male," it portrayed the efforts of the protagonist's wife as completely fruitless. In the end, "male intervention, not female moral suasion," redeems the unfortunate inebriate.[32]

The difficulty with employing female influence effectively, temperance
activists realized, lay in the tenacity of intemperate habits once acquired.
One drunkard, for instance, listened sympathetically to his wife's entreaties to stop drinking but was powerless to heed them: "Alas, it was already too late! Even HER persuasive appeal could not save me. I was under
the influence of a fascination so powerful, that although I felt the force of
the appeal, it was only a temporary check." Once men left women's physical presence, their moral sway proved fleeting indeed when men encountered alcoholic temptation. In one account, young Charles Morton assured his future wife, Louisa Staples, that business called him from her
side one evening; he promised to avoid evil companions and return to her
soon. Morton went but failed to fulfill his promise. "In the whirl of dissipation, Louisa, who alone possessed his heart, was forgotten, and so was
his promise to return."[33]

The Dynamics of Female Influence in *Edith Moreton*

Female influence, in most accounts, succeeded far better at affirming
the conduct of sober men than improving the behavior of drinkers. In
theory, female suasion could reform the world, but in practice, it worked
only when preaching to the choir. This message emerges forcefully from a
popular temperance novella, Maria L. Buckley's *Edith Moreton* (1852).
Buckley's tale contrasted the fortunes of three young couples, each posi-
tioned differently with regard to temperance principles. The first couple,
Frank Malvern and Sophia Delmaine, represented the male and female varieties of full-blown moral decay. Frank, one of the "B'hoys of fashionable
life and society," inclined toward drinking and gambling in his search for
financial gain without hard work. He proved himself an arrant scoundrel
by plying others with alcohol to make fleecing them in gambling halls

easier. At the end of the story, Frank and an accomplice land in Sing Sing after a conviction for forgery. If Frank personified the perversion of manly virtue, his wife, Sophia, presented a portrait of misapplied female education and influence. Afflicted with a "pride and love of show," Sophia suffered from an inferior education provided by a miserly uncle. At a cheap country boarding school, she mastered none of the "useful branches" of education that would prepare her to be a wife and mother. Rather, she acquired the "refinements of fashionable life," learning only to "thrum the piano" and "to gabble a little French and Italian. . . . She was, from the force of education, a coquette, and no efforts could prove effectual in reclaiming her." Sophia demonstrated her moral turpitude in the course of the narrative as well by blackmailing her husband, Frank, and her wealthy uncle for their role in perjured testimony during a trial. Sophia's wickedness eventually backfired when the uncle she had been blackmailing beggared her by leaving his fortune to a "fashionable church" in his will. Sophia, unable to work, died an impoverished wretch.[34]

Charles Sinclair and Emily Wallbridge, the story's second couple, provide a striking contrast, even an inversion of the moral flaws of Malvern and Delmaine. Both Charles and Emily sprang from wealthy families but remained humble and virtuous. Charles excelled in school, later emerging as a promising attorney. Emily grew into a beautiful and moral young woman. Significantly, both shunned alcohol. Their shared moral qualities drew the lovers together. Recognizing that "never was there a holier love than that of Charles and Emily," her father agreed to their marriage. Buckley contrasted explicitly the Sinclair and Malvern marriages: one "was a union of love and virtue, the other a union of gain." Charles prospered financially and advanced in his profession, returning home every night to a "doating [sic] wife [who] received him with endearing embraces." Emily exerted female influence in exemplary fashion, supporting her husband and strengthening the moral home they had established. Her "cup of earthly happiness full," she also continued the charitable work she had pursued in single life. "While thus engaged, the young bride looked even more lovely. She received, wherever they went, the blessings of the 'poor and lowly,' to whom she had always been a ministering angel." At the story's conclusion, Buckley rhapsodized the Sinclairs' happy home. None of the "volatile and fashionable 'fops' of the day, who sneeringly alluded" to Charles's domestic habits could appreciate their happiness. They "looked for happiness in another quarter—in another sphere—but they found it not." People like Frank and Sophia, "blind to every passion but that of folly and dissipation," could not fathom the "pleasures, the joys of domestic bliss."[35]

Buckley used the Malverns and Sinclairs to exemplify opposite poles on a moral spectrum. On one end, avarice, dishonesty, and intemperance made the Malverns irretrievably immoral, while on the other, selflessness, humility, and temperance rendered the Sinclairs above moral reproach. The dramatic focus of the tale, however, resides not in these polarities but in the middle ground occupied by the title character, Edith Moreton, and her lover, Thomas Harvey. Buckley describes Edith as "one of those angelic creatures, whom to know is to love." In many respects, Edith resembled Sophia: she was a moral, sensitive, beautiful young woman. Her problems stemmed not from her own shortcomings but from those of her beau, Thomas. Like Charles Sinclair, Thomas showed academic promise and enjoyed a comfortable inheritance, which would increase when his wealthy uncle died. In contrast to Charles, who buckled down to exploit his advantages through hard work, Thomas toured Europe, picking up Continental vices along the way. Upon his return to America, Thomas "dove headlong into the vortex of fashionable dissipation," engaging in heavy gambling and drinking. Edith, who had fallen for Thomas before his disastrous grand tour, pined for him when he returned a changed man. As would be the case for any faithful woman who inhabited sentimental fiction or temperance literature, Edith could not withdraw her love once she had bestowed it, even though her heart ached to learn that Thomas "had taken up the vice of fashionable 'moderate dissipation.'"[36]

Late in the tale, Frank Malvern and a confederate lured Thomas into a life of further dissipation to deprive him of his inheritance. After a night of drinking and gambling, Thomas got arrested and beaten by the night watch, who threw him in jail. Though bailed out by his school chum Charles, Thomas required nursing after his beating. Edith fell ill upon hearing of Thomas's disgrace but rushed to his side nonetheless to "administer to his want";

> but alas! not that Edith he had known in happier days, emaciated by long and acute suffering, a canker-worm preying on her heart, and his desertion the cause. . . . Did he deserve this attention? How many weary days and more weary nights did that loving girl pine over his desertion—while he was reveling in dissipation and riot. Edith's voice, though feeble, retained all that musical sweetness that so often captivated the young man, and now when those silver notes were spoken to cheer him and compose his mind, they were daggers to his heart, so painful was the monitor conscience working within him.[37]

Ruined financially by Malvern's use of suborned testimony in court, Thomas resolved to reform. While Edith embarked on a Southern trip to recover her health, Thomas realized that his renunciation of drinking and gambling "might be the means to restore her to her former vivacity." Neither his love for Edith nor solemn resolutions to conquer his "love of dissipation" and "live a steady and sober man" availed anything: "How futile his promises—how false his pledge—a taste once acquired for 'the bowl' can rarely be eradicated. . . . So it was with Harvey—he loved Edith—but he loved his *glass* more—he forgot her in her absence, he forgot her in what is falsely termed the 'social hour.'"[38] Finding Thomas a drunkard upon her return, Edith died rapidly from a broken heart.

Buckley's novella vividly illustrated antebellum attitudes about female influence. Woman's persuasive power could be perverted, as it was in Sophia Delmaine, to lead men astray and hasten the already depraved to perdition. Or, as in the case of Emily Wallbridge, it might bolster the resolve and reward the integrity of constitutionally moral men. What it could not do, as the fates of Edith Moreton and Thomas Harvey revealed, was to lead men in a moral direction they were not already headed. In an important sense, Emily succeeded where Edith failed because her female influence was superfluous; Charles would have lived a sober, moral, and upright life with or without it. Despite possessing all the same moral qualities and personal charms as Emily, Edith proved entirely incapable of reforming Thomas. The inefficacy of female influence for changing men's behavior, except perhaps for the worse, could hardly have been lost on Buckley's readers.[39]

Women's inability to use their moral and religious proclivities to reform drunkards posed serious ideological problems for middle-class reformers. Why, if the middle-class vision of gender was correct, did female influence not work in practice? And if incorrect, how could the emerging bourgeois distinctions based on that vision—between home and marketplace, public and private, male and female—be sustained? During the antebellum era, when middling Americans anxiously attempted to solidify their social and economic status and coalesce into a middle class, these questions assumed more than merely academic importance. Temperance advocates pondering these questions found themselves forced to examine the relationship between middle-class gender ideology, alcohol reform, and the expanding American marketplace. Their deliberations, as expressed in temperance literature, comprise the subject of the next chapter.

5

Toward Legislation

Temperance Reform and Free-market Capitalism

The doubts expressed by critics and supporters about the misuse or ineffectiveness of female influence, as well as the larger ideological problems to which they pointed, reflected the pressure of changing social conditions and drinking patterns on the temperance movement. In an important sense, the ideological difficulties occasioned by the failure of female influence resulted from middle-class temperance enthusiasts being victims of their own success. Alcohol consumption decreased by more than half between 1830 and 1840, due in large measure to temperance agitation. The middle class in particular seems to have embraced abstinence or moderation as temperance became a hallmark of bourgeois respectability. As one reformer reported smugly, the salubrity of middle-class life militated against drunkenness: "The inestimable comforts of home, b exercise of domestic affections, and the natural and healthful exhilaration of body and mind consequent upon regular industry and rewards, do much for this class in abating inordinate desires for artificial excitement."[1]

Still, by the 1840s many reformers feared that, for all its success, temperance reform had reached a crisis. Though drinking had been reduced in middle-class families and homes, the sources of the alcohol problem remained. Most drunkards did not begin their destructive course at the fireside, where female influence could operate, but at taverns and dramshops. "Where do the habits begin which fester and gangrene the soul? Not at home—Not at home!" an indignant temperance advocate thundered.

Rather, both individual and societal intemperance took root beyond the domestic sphere, where the salutary and restraining effects of female influence and familial bliss could not reach. "It appears from extended investigation," a crestfallen reformer admitted, "that while the consumption of ardent spirits in families . . . is greatly diminished, the consumption in dram-shops is dreadfully increased." Worse still, new and destructive patterns of consumption emerged even as the overall amount of drinking decreased. As William J. Rorabaugh has demonstrated, the early decades of the nineteenth century witnessed a decline in customary habits of drinking small amounts steadily throughout the day but a sharp rise in binge drinking, both solo and communal. Demographic change in the 1840s intensified the anxieties produced by these developments. Immigration posed a serious challenge to the reform efforts of the native-born middle class who dominated the temperance movement. The burgeoning Irish and German populations proved resistant, if not hostile, to the exhortation and influence that fostered wholesome and sober behavior in middle-class households. Temperance reformers interpreted these developments as ominous signs that the battle with alcohol was far from over.[2]

By the 1830s, antiliquor forces insisted that even moderate drinking would eventually lead a person to succumb to intemperance. The temperance movement's transition from advocating moderation to insisting that only total abstinence would prevent moral decay contributed to fears that hard-won gains could easily disappear with the onslaught of a new wave of drunkenness. This faith in total abstinence as the only safe course also contained a social component: if American society would protect itself from drunkenness and ruin, all intemperance had to be eliminated lest it spread to the sober community. Throughout the early nineteenth century, temperance advocates likened drunkenness to a moral epidemic that threatened to infect the whole population. "Who is himself secure of life in the midst of such a contagion," asked a New York minister in 1813. "And what evidence have we," he continued, "that the plague will not break out into our own families, and that our children may not be among the victims. . . . " Where intemperance exists in an individual, another reformer warned, "it usually spreads itself to other members of the community." Intemperance's seeming omnipresence worried its enemies. "In every direction, in every department of society, the destroyer walks, and is heard," an orator observed ominously. Liquor adapted itself to assault all strata of society, sparing "neither the bond or the free, the high or the low, the rich or the poor, the priest or the layman, nor age, nor sex, nor condition." The temperance movement's stance during the 1830s that any drinking at all imperiled an individual intensified these images of contagion as concerned citizens began to worry that intractable pockets of intemperance could contaminate the whole of American society, even reinfecting the newly abstinent middle class.[3]

Moreover, by the 1840s it seemed certain that female influence would not stem the tide of intemperance, grandiose expectations and pronouncements to the contrary notwithstanding. This failure posed serious problems for the temperance movement and its middle-class supporters. Admitting women's inability to use effectively their putatively superior morality and religiosity weakened domestic ideology at its very foundation. If women could not use their domestic authority and moral influence to make their homes havens for men returning from the market, bedrock notions of class, gender, and separate spheres seemed in jeopardy. This ideological problem had ramifications beyond reform. Numerous scholars have noted the American middle class's need to separate the female home and the male marketplace as, in the words of one recent commentator, a "central anchoring point of middle-class formation." Separate spheres legitimated a "bourgeois identity in which moral status and the amoral pursuit of success might be intertwined."[4] Women's inability or unwillingness to use female influence in the temperance cause jeopardized this identity and left middle-class temperance ideologues few viable options. Emphasizing misogynist blame of women for not doing their part would hardly help, for it would throw the home, women's sphere for exercising morality, further into the shadows. Nor would admitting female ineptitude serve much better. For separate spheres to make sense, both men and women had to exercise real and efficacious power and authority within their respective orbits.

Temperance advocates and domestic ideologues resolved this difficulty by recognizing the permeability of the boundaries separating home and market. Women could not be expected to exercise authority in their sphere, reformers reasoned, if it could not be safeguarded from the withering and polluting influences of the other. Liquor, unlike other vices or moral problems, crossed the boundaries of home and market easily in ways that no woman, however scrupulous or vigilant, could prevent. Drunken men returned from taverns to the fireside, heartless rumsellers seduced innocent children sent abroad on errands with their infernal wares, guests expected to be entertained with ardent spirits, and thoughtless physicians prescribed alcohol for a variety of complaints. In short, liquor, an "enemy to the best interests of man," violated the "sanctuary of domestic peace" with near impunity. From the "tavern, the tippling shop, its native haunts; it has found its way, into the convivial party, the gay assembly, the grave meeting for business, the circle about the parlor fire, the retirement of the bed-chamber." Even the most watchful women could not prevent liquor's infiltration of their families. "Under the disguise of friends," a temperance almanac revealed, liquor's "emissaries had entered every house. They had been, in many cases regarded with caution, but if rejected in one form, they were sure of success in another." Often temperance literature presented this assault on home and family as an invasion by an army of implacable foes, a theme that would continue to resonate throughout the nineteenth century. The "demon" alcohol came in many forms—drunken fathers, ruined children, incompetent physicians—and "invade[d] the peace, and blast[ed] the hopes of the domestic circle."[5]

Rather than seeing the permeability of boundaries between home and market as proof of the artificiality of separate spheres, as would many modern historians of the period, temperance advocates construed it as a perversion of the natural, divinely ordained order. That human beings could resist what God had decreed was best for them did not invalidate the divine plan; it merely acknowledged the reality of evil in the world. Writers conjured up images of paradise lost to make their point. The "curse of intemperance" had "defiled the domestic sanctuary," a particularly grievous offense, considering that if "there is a spot . . . that can remind us of the Eden we have lost, it is to be found alone at the family altar." But the "unhallowed step" of intemperance invaded this blissful abode; now the "fountains of the heart have been broken up, and agony unspeakable and unmitigated, is felt at every throb." One temperance tract had an aggrieved woman wailing, "Oh that wine! that wine! How like the serpent it stole into the Eden of our bliss, and stamped a curse upon me and mine, unutterable and indescribable."[6]

Under such circumstances, one could hardly expect female influence to function as it should. As early as 1815, Benjamin Wadsworth observed indignantly:

> The baleful effects of strong drink in families are truly deplorable. Those young nurseries of virtue, social affection, and conjugal happiness, become transformed into schools of vice and the dreary abodes of discord, anarchy and contention. Instead of the domestic altar, and the friendly circle collected around for morning and evening devotions, what is heard but reproaches and recriminations? When heads of families exceed the bounds of sobriety, how can it be expected that religious order, instruction, and government should be maintained?[7]

Later commentators elaborated on this theme, detailing the ways in which intemperance thwarted female influence, particularly a wife's moral sway over her husband. Alcohol and its attendant vices inured men to the pleasures of home in two major ways, making them unwilling even to listen to their wives' earnest pleas and gentle admonitions. First, the stigma attached to drunkenness impelled many inebriates to leave their homes to drink, rather than expose their families to "the exhibition of their infamy." The presence of children would "enforce the appearance of integrity, long after virtue has departed," and drunken husbands would shun to the "last moment of tottering reason," drinking before "her, who suffers from it indescribable misery." In general, guilt over their moral transgressions would likely induce drinkers to avoid the "society of refined and virtuous females." Respectable women, they knew, would not wish their parlors "fumigated with the smoke of tobacco or the exhalations of alcohol," or their ears assaulted by the "silly talk and indelicate innuendos produced by alcohol." Such a "separation between the sexes," warned Edward Hitchcock, inclined men to seek venues for indulging their "grossest manners and inclinations." Shunning the companionship of women prevented female influence from operating; it could be nothing but "injurious to our social condition."[8]

Second, liquor created a "depraved appetite" whose "cravings" supplanted the "charms of domestic and social enjoyments." Once upon the path of intemperance, the "winning attentions of his wife, the prattle of his babes . . . are insufficient to recover him from his ruinous course." Moreover, once accustomed to the "boisterous revelry" of the "club room, or the dram shop," men no longer relished the "quiet scenes of domestic duty and purity." Gambling dens often featured liquor and fine food to entice their patrons to stay, but those whose appetites were "pampered" found that the "plain fair of the homestead becomes tasteless and vapid if laid before the returning wanderer, and the fondest care of wife and mother in preparing the daily meals fails to satisfy." Through no fault of women, the pervasiveness of liquor, combined with the drunkard's ability to cross the boundary between market and home, rendered female influence inoperable.[9]

Anxieties about the Market

The difficulties experienced in explaining the failure of female influence, as well as the specifics of the explanation, point to linkages between gender and other areas of middle-class ideological engagement. Most notably, the temperance movement's gender troubles reflected the need to develop a political economy suited to middle-class formation during a period of rapid market expansion. Fears that strong drink and the liquor trade were defiling American homes and disrupting proper gender relations dovetailed with middle-class ambivalence and anxiety about the market revolution that was transforming the United States during the early decades of the nineteenth century. Ian Tyrrell identified correctly the majority of temperance supporters as "improvers," people eager to embrace market expansion, economic growth, and their accompanying social changes. Temperance reformers, Tyrrell explained, "hoped to create the conditions for permanent moral and material progress in America . . . [through] the removal of obstacles to the development of an acquisitive, industrial-commercial society."[10] Most of the middle-class temperance advocates who formed the core of the movement viewed the new financial and business opportunities engendered by regional, national, and interna-

tional market ties with great optimism. Still, they worried that the unbridled pursuit of economic gain made possible by the expanding market
threatened cherished notions of gender, community, and ethical behavior.

Discussions of the liquor trade provided an ideal venue to air these anxieties. In excoriating the traffic in ardent spirits, temperance advocates'
very language betrayed some trepidation about the omnipresence and in-
escapability of the burgeoning market, of which rumselling represented
only one component. Like the expanding market, liquor insinuated itself
into every corner of American life. Cheap and abundant spirits turned out
by factory-like distilleries covered the "surface of these United States, almost as universally and copiously as the dews and rains of heaven . . .
[they] have pervaded and polluted the city, and the village." Similar to the
ways in which the market enmeshed the unwary in its toils through the
seductive goods and services it offered, the liquor trade also lured in its
victims. Rumselling, urban reformer Robert M. Hartley fretted, "spreads
over the community in one vast network of temptation; and as the heed-
less multitudes perceive not their danger, it is more strange that some escape, than that many are ensnared to their destruction." John Marsh's account of the dimensions of the liquor problem bespoke concerns similar
to those who feared that factories, railroads, and the changes they motivated threatened the integrity of American society. Thirty thousand distilleries, Marsh stormed, poured out "annually forty-four millions of gallons,
to be consumed by less than twelve millions of people. These were grim
fortresses planted all over the land, and surrounded by the skulls and
bones of human victims. They needed only the terrific locomotive of our
day, with its cars of whiskey flying everywhere on the iron track, to complete a picture of hell's domination."[11]

As they lamented the effects of drink on women and American homes,
temperance reformers echoed larger concerns about the excesses of market
capitalism in their bitter denunciation of the liquor business's selfishness
and lack of regard for those it injured. Clearly rumsellers provided the
liquor that caused the domestic violence, crime, and pauperism that concerned so many Americans. They justified their pursuit of gain by arguing
that it was a legal business and that temperance violated their liberty to
make a living. To the brokenhearted wives who pleaded with them to forbear selling to their degraded husbands, the rumseller merely replied that
he was a "licensed poison-seller, reason-extinguisher, beggar-maker, body-
ruiner, and soul-destroyer, and that all trades must live." Or, as a satiric
ditty set to the tune of "Auld Lang Syne" had it, "What if the drunkard's
children cried,/ and wife for lack of food;/ Our trade with greater zest we
plied,/ All for the 'public good.'"[12]

Outraged temperance advocates contemptuously brushed aside this
sophistry. "Shall we be told that in *trading* or *commercial dealings*, everyone
must take care of himself, and judge his own interests," demanded one

critic. "Who tells us this? Is it Christ, or any authenticated source of divine truth? Plainly not, but it comes from the *self-interest* of the *dealer*." Americans must remember, argued another, that there are "obligations among men, which grow out of the relations of man to man, and of man to his Maker, from which all earthly power, and all human laws, cannot set them free." Regrettably many forgot these obligations in the scramble for gain. In the present "depraved" state of the country, lamented a clergyman, "selfishness controls the affections and conduct of the generality of mankind. Each individual aims supremely at his own private, separate good, and subordinates to this object the good of all others. . . . Provided my own interest is promoted, what need I care whether others are benefited or injured?"[13]

For many concerned observers, the liquor trade exemplified these disturbing tendencies. Yet temperance advocates had to tread with caution here, for though the traffic in ardent spirits put the selfish pursuit of gain in high relief, its practices were quite similar to those of other business enterprises. The liquor trade promoted a thriving business that employed farmers, distillers, and vendors, thereby advancing national prosperity. Worse, the financial success of a tavern owner lent an "aura of middle-class respectability to the sale of alcohol" and suggested that a vendor in spirits was "guilty of nothing more than being a hardworking businessman."[14] If their trade led to the impoverishment and injury of some, what business did not? How then could temperance forces criticize what amounted to liberal individualism, social mobility, and free markets in one context without questioning their moral status more generally? This conundrum proved particularly vexing for Whigs, who tended to support both temperance reform and market capitalism more than did their Democratic counterparts. Pro-market, pro-economic development temperance advocates needed to find a way to condemn and rein in the liquor trade without implying that the entire marketplace should be regulated or that economic individualism might be morally suspect.[15]

Middle-class temperance reformers also found, much to their dismay, that their opponents could turn against them the very discursive weapons they themselves had helped forge. The respectable middle class claimed to be the promoters and guardians of home, family, civic virtue, and economic prosperity. The liquor interests flatly contradicted them, arguing that pious middle-class outrage at intemperance cloaked the blatant pursuit of economic self-interest and political power, threatening the values they purported to cherish in the process. Some such attacks rested mainly on economics. Pennsylvania grain growers indignantly objected to the "Farmers' prosperity . . . [being] sacrificed" to the "hyper moral and utopian notions" of temperance advocates. When the "FARMERS, whom Jefferson has called the chosen people of God," who, like "good patriarchs support the whole human family, are denounced as criminals," they fulminated, only "ruin and universal bankruptcy" could result. Others read more sinister motives into reformers' sallies against their livelihoods. New Haven grocers, for instance, weary of attacks on their trade, lashed back at temperance reformers in 1838, insisting that the "real object of their conspiracy" was the acquisition of

> political power, to be wielded under the guidance of that fanaticism, which in all ages and all countries has been the mother of hypocrisy, the precursor of tyranny, and the handmaid of oppression, —whose conscience is her purse, whose piety the desire for universal dominion, and whose benevolence is the destruction of all who resist her mandates.

Another critic of the "Abstinence Enterprise" also dismissed professions of disinterested benevolence: viewing the movement's "*principles,* and the manner you manage your enterprize [*sic*], I cannot think you are sincere in your profession." The main "*object*," he charged, was "to obtain wealth, and form a political party for the purpose of obtaining the civil government."[16]

Other opponents of temperance took a different tack, ridiculing the middle-class movement's pretensions to superior virtue and religiosity. One celebrated anti-temperance pamphlet couched the campaign for total abstinence as intolerant and anti-Biblical, casting doubt on the religious propriety of such extremist views. Leonard Withington, a Massachusetts clergyman, lamented that the proliferation of temperance and other reform societies bespoke an "improper distrust of the wisdom of God," which could be found only in scripture. Pledges of abstinence amounted to pharisaical pretense; the "*thrilling facts*" presented by temperance literature confounded "pathos with argument and means with ends," operating on weak-minded "women and men like women." Let all Christians, Withington implored, "instantly disjoin themselves from these moral associations, these bands of faction, which attempt to promote moral purposes for political means. Fly, O fly, from this unhallowed ground!" Like Withington, Connecticut minister William Watson rejected membership in the staunchly bourgeois Sons of Temperance on the grounds that the church is the source of all virtue. "I consequently hold," Watson icily declared, "the use of all other instrumentalities as a slighting of God's plan, and involving a species of covert infidelity."[17]

Perhaps the most serious threat to middle-class pretensions, however, came from the suggestion that temperance undermined rather than protected the domestic sphere as an inviolable sanctuary beyond the reach of the outside world. By imposing total abstinence on American society, critics argued, temperance societies imperiled the prerogatives of family government and personal conscience. "What right has a set of men," demanded a Richmond clergyman, "to unite for the purpose of thus interfering with the right of private judgment? Is this not intolerance of the worst kind?" Harrison Gray Otis, the venerable Massachusetts lawyer and politician, agreed. Prohibitory legislation, Otis averred, constituted a "prelude to [a] system of sumptuary laws, which, if not resisted, will become a substitute for family government." Criticisms such as these drew upon persistent older visions of family and gender, which painted the household as a male bastion of patriarchal authority, rather than a female domain dedicated to the exercise of moral and religious influence. Middle-class temperance forces acknowledged the seriousness of these charges, admitting that only the ravages of alcohol justified the "all but social sacrilege" involved in lifting the "veil, and enquir[ing] after the purity and peace of the domestic circle." Still, they could not deny or ignore the "apprehension abroad" that the "friends of Temperance" themselves desired to "invade the sanctity of domestic society" through prohibitory legislation. The "habits and wishes of each family, within its own private circle, are to be held sacred," a Pennsylvania temperance convention insisted, "and not to be forcibly entered, even under the cover of law."[18] Later in the century, charges of hypocrisy, self-interest, and arrogance might have been dismissed out of hand, but in the antebellum period of class formation, before middle-class Americans could take their status, success, and self-confidence for granted, they stung. How then could middle-class temperance advocates disprove these accusations and also resolve the contradictions between their condemnation of the liquor trade and their support of the capitalist market that spawned it?

Demonizing Rum

To resolve this dilemma, temperance advocates defined "liquor" as a special commodity that produced social harm without any redeeming value. Middle-class temperance advocates hit upon a similar tactic to explain how women could become drunkards, despite domestic ideology's apparent inability to square the existence of female intemperance with its account of gender roles and characteristics. By the 1830s at least, middle-class apologists recognized the usefulness of denouncing alcohol as a uniquely evil commodity for resolving other ideological conflicts. Reflecting the centrality of respectable middle-class families to their vision of the good society, their efforts focused on the social damage inflicted by liquor through its invasion of American homes. Alcohol, a "liquid poison," reformers urged, attacked the "very elements of society, at the domestic altar." Temperance literature routinely depicted alcohol and the liquor trade in the process of making a travesty of the American family. George Burleigh, for instance, produced a humorous memoir of alcohol, portraying a being who denied that the "devil *is* my father. . . . I am the offspring and invention of *man*," but the "*devil instigated him to it.*" In the course of his memoirs, Alcohol related how he with his sons Brandy, Rum, and Whiskey and his daughter, Gin, entered families and "poisoned the cup of domestic joy." Similarly, a temperance newspaper printed a mock trial of Alcohol for murder, robbery, and other crimes. The defendant, it noted, had insinuated himself into so many families, causing "divisions and strifes," that many people "no longer called him Alcohol, but by a name they conceived more appropriate, viz. 'FAMILY DISTURBER.'" Other common images quite literally demonized liquor, likening it to a "demon of intemperance" that made the "mission of the demon of war to the domestic circle" appear as an "angel's visit," or a "MONSTER" made and sold by "beings in the shape of men." One writer painted it as a serpent that must be destroyed: "The viper! It comes with a track of shiney [*sic*] pollution across the cottage door of humble peace; it stretches its vipery length along the cheerful hearth, and hisses till fireside joys are driven away." In another monstrous form, alcohol appeared as a "most cruel hydra that is permitted to enter our dwellings," eventually "infusing its venom into all the sinuosities of the heart."[19]

As its ability to confound female influence and overturn proper gender relations demonstrated, liquor was intrinsically evil and thus could not be compared to other commodities. According to its detractors, liquor was "not only worthless, but mischievous. . . . [I]t is a pernicious, ruinous article, which endangers, in the case of your neighbor, all that is dear in life, or in eternity." In this light, any potential threat to private conscience from the promulgation of middle-class values through temperance reform melted away like April snow. Shall we "be told that private liberty is invaded," demanded a temperance address, "if we associate ourselves, and form, if we can, a bulwark against the farther encroachments of an invading enemy, which desolates everything fair and lovely, that comes beneath its tread? If I give up my liberty, when I do this, then let me be a slave, that I may be free."[20]

Having translated their gender-based condemnation of the hated commodity into the realm of political economy, middle-class reformers extended their invective to those who produced and trafficked in drink. Vending the poison that ruined so many lives constituted an "employment which violates the rules of morals which ought to regulate a man's business and conduct," insisted Albert Barnes in 1834. The liquor traffic, agreed another minister, carried "only poverty, wretchedness, and death into the homes of its victims," leaving no "spot on earth to which a man can go, and feel that he is safe from the rude assaults of drunkenness." The "rum-seller (a fiend in human shape)" appeared to those victimized by alcohol as a "curse and pest on the neighborhood . . . a sort of walking rum-barrel, impregnating the very atmosphere with a moral pestilence." Liquor dealers compared unfavorably with spiders sitting in their webs, preying on other insects. The spider, at least, preyed "not upon his own species. He sucks the blood of a different race. But to whom does the spirit dealer sell his baneful draught? To men—to husbands—to parents." Nor would the liquor trade's enemies countenance the argument that men who misused alcohol bore the responsibility for their own degradation. Rumsellers and the moderate drinkers who supported them could not "point us to the drunkard. The poor wretch, whose alcohol-sodden brain and physical fibre pronounce him a drunkard, is their abject creation—the drunkard springs from them *and only them.*"[21]

To counter arguments that the liquor trade, like any other legal business pursued for profit, benefited the national economy, temperance forces deployed a self-serving, specious political economy. Because liquor had no redeeming value, they argued, the traffic in it did not conform to the ordinary laws of economics. According to classical economic theory, demand for an item motivated producers to manufacture it. The liquor trade inverted this relationship. Liquor dealers employed every artifice to ensnare potential customers, such as the use of beautiful women to sell drinks, but this was not the only stratagem that aroused middle-class ire. The liquor trade's methods were "very numerous, and usually as disgusting as they are multiform." Vendors tinted the "poisonous fluid" to "all the colors of the rainbow," arranging it "tastefully . . . in bottles of finely ornamented cut glass, dazzling the eye with their brilliancy, and alluring the unwary to the gratification of appetite." In 1819 political economist Thomas Herttell argued that intemperance created grogshops, rather than the other way around. By the 1830s reformers rejected this earlier construction. Using its manifold seductive techniques to traffic in a habit-forming beverage, they charged, the "drinking-house" created the "love of strong drink," alluring "myriads of young men and boys to drink for the first time, and to continue drinking, who otherwise would never have touched a drop." Or, as prominent reformer John Marsh baldly put it, the "supply creates the demand. While in things essential the demand creates the supply, it is here all the reverse."[22]

Instead of producing economic growth, temperance partisans insisted that this perversion of natural economic law occasioned a "destruction of capital" so thorough that the funds might as "well have been buried in the earth, or cast into the caverns of the ocean." One ideologue likened buying liquor to paying a company of "jugglers" for entertainment. The capital is transferred to "those who are not productive consumers"; once they consume the money, "it is destroyed—it is a dead loss to the nation." Distillers who supposedly profited from their business, he continued, merely replaced the capital they expended in producing liquor without generating new profits. Nor did vendors fare better. "Where has a man lived," demanded Samuel Chipman, "who has amassed a fortune by the sale of liquor—has died sober, and left a fortune to sober children?" Because these reformers regarded capital as the "main-spring of the machinery of the nation," its supposed destruction had political as well as economic implications. The "sixty million gallons of liquid fire" purchased every year cost consumers $30 million and the country more than "three fourths of all the pauperism, taxation, crimes and wretchedness" it endured. Consequently, critics charged, the traffic in liquor was "therefore *anti-republican,* and hostile to the dearest interests of the nation."[23]

What motivated liquor dealers to pursue so heinous an occupation? Avarice, plain and simple, temperance advocates answered. Here middle-class reformers took the opportunity to stake their claim to moral respectability and allay qualms about their own embrace of market values by differentiating themselves from those who pursued wealth at any cost. The "pernicious practice" of intemperance, noted one reformer in 1821, "owes its origin as well as increase to the lovers of filthy lucre." Others agreed, and the vehemence of their denunciations increased as the years passed. "No motive but gain," averred the *Temperance Recorder,* "can influence any man, in any place, or under any circumstances, to traffic in, make, or sell ardent spirits as a beverage. And no passion of the human mind will steel the human soul and dry up the fountains of its kindness, so soon and so effectually as avarice."

Whatever the liquor trade's protestations to the contrary, prominent temperance figure Lucius M. Sargent warned a year later, "the all-absorbing object of the party [is] *how much money can we make by the traffic in* RUM!" The combination of avarice and, often, addiction to strong drink— "*interest* as well as appetite" that induced men to pursue a business "productive of naught but sorrow and tears"—hardened their hearts to the enormity of their offenses against their fellows. Justin Edwards, clergyman and temperance advocate, juxtaposed two kinds of murderers, inquiring which was the guiltier. On the one hand, he described the midnight assassin who kills an entire family to obtain their money. On the other, he depicted the rumseller who sells the father a "poisonous drink" that produces an "intemperate appetite" that the seller continues to feed until the man and his whole family become drunkards. The liquor dealer furnishes the "known cause" of their drunkenness, fuels their vice until the "father, the mother, and the children, one after another are all dead, and, as has actually been the case, laid side by side in the drunkard's grave. . . . Money was the object in both cases. One permitted the whole family to go down, each innocent; the other knowingly assisted to render all guilty, each of his own death."[24]

Middle-class temperance advocates thus portrayed alcohol and the liquor trade that promoted and distributed it as *sui generis,* unlike the morally respectable business pursuits and free markets that they championed. The uniqueness of this evil commodity, which originated in the public sphere of the market but was capable of invading the private sphere of the home, also provided a plausible explanation for why women could not eliminate intemperance. Female influence, a species of moral suasion, could not grapple with an evil that moved freely between public and private. Because the liquor trade's tentacles extended to the very domestic hearth, women could not defeat alcoholic depravity in their homes. Nor, given the inefficacy of women beyond their natural sphere, could they extend their influence into the marketplace to effect change. Numerous tales attested to unfeeling rumsellers' propensity for derisively dismissing women's most pathetic appeals. Liquor dealers, fulminated the American Temperance Society, would for 25 cents

> hear the scream of the children, and see them run away and hide, and hear the groans of her who cannot get away; and though she comes, when the storm is over, and beseeches him, with tears, not to sell her husband the madman's poison, for she and her children—and her tongue falters as she says *children*— cannot endure it; yet for 25 cents, he will sell it again and again.

One fictional wife resolved to "go to all the rumsellers, to implore them to save her husband. . . . It was of no use—she might as well have appealed to the stones." Female influence could not move men enmeshed in the excesses of the market, men "utterly dead to all other appeals, whose consciences are seared with a hot iron, on whom 'moral suasion' has no more effect than on stone walls." In the pursuit of gain, such men could "inhumanly push a woman out of their own doors, where she has come to beseech them with tears and on her knees" to cease feeding her husband's depraved appetite for liquor. "Talk of moral suasion with a man whom tears cannot move," scoffed a Pennsylvania clergyman in 1846. "You might as well attempt to set on fire the ice-bergs of Greenland, as to set on fire a dram-seller's heart. . . . Wives have entreated for their husbands and children for their fathers, and yet they sell to them. . . . God is disregarded; his warnings are sold for a six-pence!!"[25]

Ten Nights in a Bar-Room

All of these elements—the demonization of drink, the inefficacy of female influence, the destruction of families by the liquor trade, the contradictions of regulating or prohibiting liquor sales while championing free markets—crystallized in the most popular and influential statement of nineteenth-century middle-class temperance principles, T. S. Arthur's *Ten Nights in a Bar-Room, and What I Saw There* (1854).[26] Arthur, by the 1850s an established author of sentimental and reform literature, created a quintessentially American town, Cedarville, to limn the disastrous effects of liquor on families and communities. At the beginning of the novel, Cedarville, a town steeped in the agrarian past but experiencing the impact of market forces, had just acquired a new public house, the Sickle and Sheaf. An unnamed traveler who passes through Cedarville several times over the ensuing years narrates the tavern's harrowing career as a blight on Cedarville's moral and economic life. Throughout the book Arthur addresses all of the themes that bedeviled middle-class ideologues in general and Whigs in particular. A blatantly partisan work, *Ten Nights* discloses its loyalties early on. The first chapter introduces Judge Lyman, "who had a few weeks before received the Democratic nomination for member of Congress." Lyman speaks warmly of the "advantage of a good tavern in Cedarville" for promoting the town's prosperity, but his subsequent actions reveal him to be an unscrupulous, not to mention bibulous, tool of the liquor trade. By the middle of the novel, this Democratic congressman becomes the "rum candidate," aided by "easily swayed 'indifferents'" in sweeping "aside the claims of law, order, temperance, and good morals."[27]

Arthur uses Lyman and other characters as straw men who make the case for viewing liquor and the economic activity it generates as a benefit to American communities, only to refute them with the events of the story. Simon Slade, who owns the Sickle and Sheaf, for instance, praises tavern-keeping as an economic boon and a means of achieving middle-class respectability. Once he gave up being a miller and began "keeping a good tavern, and thus materially advancing the interests of Cedarville," he maintains, the town's "best people" began treating him with deference. The "very people who used to call me 'Simon,' or 'Neighbor Dustycoat,' now say 'Landlord,' or Mr. Slade, and treat me in every way more as if I were an equal than ever before." Initially Cedarville agrees about the benefits of the liquor trade, for its citizens celebrate Slade and his Sickle and Sheaf, enthusing further when Judge Hammond, another local worthy, announces his establishment of a distillery in the town. A distillery, Simon Slade notes, would raise grain prices and help area farmers: what he did for Cedarville, Slade modestly averres, is "a mere song compared to the advantage of an extensive distillery."[28]

Events undercut this rosy picture, however. Slade proves to be motivated more by sloth and greed than the desire to advance Cedarville's fortunes. When questioned by the narrator why he had abandoned a mill that cleared $1,000, which ought to have been a profit large enough for any man, Slade disagrees. "Every man desires to make as much money as possible," he observes, "and with the least labor." The innkeeper's devotion to lucre rather than hard work and community service led to a decline in the Sickle and Sheaf. By the middle of the novel, the narrator notes the decay of a once handsome establishment: "Now all was dusty and dingy, the air foul, and the bed-linen scarcely whiter than tow." Moreover, even his claims that the tavern benefited the town economically proved false. Twice drunkards themselves give the lie to the rum interest's deceptive artifice. "'If he gets richer, somebody will be poorer!'" chimes a garrulous drunkard at an opportune moment early in the text. Later, another "good customer at somebody's bar" expands on this theme, regaling the narrator with a temperance critique of Slade's political economy: "He does not add to the general wealth. He produces nothing. He takes money from his customers, but gives them no article of value in return—nothing that can be called property, personal or real. He is just so much richer and they just so much poorer for the exchange. Is it not so?"[29] Even brains befuddled by drink, Arthur seems to say, could penetrate the liquor trade's sophistries.

For all its partisanship and economic theorizing, however, *Ten Nights'* discursive power derives from its deployment of middle-class gender ideology to drive home the evils of the liquor trade.[30] Clearly Arthur conceived and depicted the traffic in strong drink in gendered terms, presenting it as a masculine activity that is wholly incompatible with feminine traits and characteristics. This emerges early on when Simon Slade throws his former business partner, Joe Morgan, now an impoverished drunkard, out of the Sickle and Sheaf after taking Morgan's last sixpence for liquor. Though Morgan accuses Slade of hard-heartedness, the innkeeper justifies his actions as merely good business. "Maybe my heart is growing harder," Slade retorts, "and it is time perhaps. One of my weaknesses, I have heard even you say, was being too woman-hearted." The marketplace, it would seem, was no place to indulge a woman's heart. Arthur enlarges on this point in a later discussion of the reluctance with which wives greet the news that their husbands have entered the liquor trade. Wives, he remarks, rarely "consent freely to the opening of taverns by their husbands." The decision often occasions a "breach of confidence and good feeling never afterward fully healed." In twelve words that encapsulate middle-class gender ideology, Arthur reveals the reason: "Men look close to the money result; women to the moral consequences."[31]

Throughout the novel Arthur accentuates the damage done by liquor to families, playing on middle-class notions of gender to make his point. The most pathetic and affecting passages of *Ten Nights* revolves around the injury done to innocent and helpless females by drunken men. Moral suasion as embodied in female influence, Arthur demonstrates, could not prevent a rapacious liquor trade from using demon rum to destroy individuals, families, and communities. In the three families that comprise the bulk of the novel's major characters, women strive and fail to protect or redeem their families from the ravages of liquor. Innkeeper Simon Slade ignored the warnings of his wife, a woman of "flushed and excited countenance, as if she had been over a hot fire." Mrs. Slade, who had ceased showing a "true smile on her face" since her husband became a vendor of spirits, worried about the immoral influence of the barroom on her children, twelve-year-old Frank, a boy with "deep blue eyes, from which innocence beamed," and sixteen-year-old Flora, a "neatly dressed" girl with "rather an attractive countenance." Abandoning the honest business of his grist mill to open a tavern, Mrs. Slade warned, could only result in Slade's breaking "hearts as well as commandments, if you keep on for a few years as you have begun—and ruin souls as well as fortunes." Slade "answered with an oath" and continued on his ruinous path. Several years later, Mrs. Slade's presentiment came true: Slade died at the hand of his son, Frank, in a drunken fight. Botching a suicide attempt, Frank wound up a "lonely prisoner in the county jail." The two Slade women fared little better: Flora devoted herself to caring for her mother, now the inmate of an "insane asylum, about five miles from Cedarville." Despite Flora's and her mother's best efforts, liquor doomed their family:

> Long before this, all her own and her mother's influence over her brother had come to an end. It mattered not how she sought to stay his feet, so swiftly moving along the downward way, whether, by gentle entreaty, earnest remonstrance, or tears; in either case, wounds for her own heart were the sure consequences, while his steps never lingered a moment.[32]

Nor was female influence more efficacious in the Morgan family. Joe Morgan's wife, Fanny, "one of the sweetest girls" in Cedarville, knew that Joe drank when she married him. She did not fear the future, however, believing that "her love was strong enough to win him from all evil allurements." Such was not the case, and though Fanny remained a "loving, forbearing, self-denying wife," she could not wean him from the poisoned cup. Joe's drunkenness took its toll: by the beginning of the story, after several years of living as a drunkard's wife, Fanny was becoming a nonentity. Her "person was very slender, and her face so attenuated that it might almost be called shadowy." Consonant with the view that women's endurance of male-induced suffering constituted a hallmark of femininity, *Ten Nights* found cause to admire the unhappy Mrs. Morgan. "She could not now be called beautiful; yet in her marred features—marred by suffering and grief—were many lineaments of beauty; and much that told of a pure, true woman's heart beating in her bosom."[33]

Joe Morgan did reform by the end of the novel, largely through the intervention of his daughter, but this plot contrivance, which mirrored a similar expedient in *Uncle Tom's Cabin,* hardly represented an endorsement of female influence. Little Mary Morgan often went to the Sickle and Sheaf at night looking for Joe in a pathetic attempt to coax the inebriate to return home with her. One night Simon Slade vented his anger at Morgan's continuing criticisms by throwing a heavy whiskey glass at him. Morgan ducked, but the glass struck Mary in the head just as she entered the bar in search of her father. Predictably Mary died of her wound but not before extracting on her deathbed a promise from Joe never to drink again. Though one might regard this as female influence, it is a partial and pyrrhic victory at best. A bout with delirium tremens stiffened Joe's resolve, and Mary, a child rather than a woman, only gained influence over Joe because of her impending demise. Recall that Mary's many visits to the Sickle and Sheaf to extract her father did not keep him from returning to drink the next day.

Perhaps the most spectacular and maudlin failure of female influence, however, involved the Hammond family. Willy Hammond, the promising young son of Judge Hammond, fell in with a gambler as the result of frequenting the Sickle and Sheaf. Willy spent his childhood at his mother's side, Arthur revealed, but forgot her moral teachings as soon as he left home to study law. Despite his mother's earnest warnings and entreaties, Willy continued drinking and gambling. When Mrs. Hammond, a woman "far past the meridian of life," with "lines of suffering and sorrow on her fine countenance" took to haunting the street outside the Sickle and Sheaf in a vain effort to find her son, Willy escorted her home but returned straightaway to the gaming table. Even financial embarrassment and his mother's illness, both brought on by his drinking, did little to reform Willy.

> He loved his mother, and was deeply afflicted by the calamity; but it seemed as if he could not stop. Some terrible necessity appeared to be impelling him onward. If he formed good resolutions—and I doubt not that he did—they were blown away like threads of gossamer, the moment he came within the sphere of old associations.[34]

Unsurprisingly Willy met a bad end. In a drunken brawl, the gambler Harvey Green inflicted a fatal knife wound on Willy. The boy lived long enough for his mother to be summoned and to cry out "save me! save me!" as she rushed to his side. Despite her assurance that she would save and protect him, Willy died a moment later. Initially unbelieving that Willy had died, Mrs. Hammond "looked wildly upon his face. One long scream of horror told of her convictions, and she fell, lifeless, across the body of her dead son!"[35]

At the end of the novel, the tally sheet of female characters stands thus: one woman and one girl dead, a woman driven insane, and another resigned to the self-abnegating role of her caretaker. Fanny Morgan disappears from the story completely. Despite Joe Morgan's reformation and the closure of the Sickle and Sheaf after Simon Slade's death, *Ten Nights* leaves the reader convinced that moral suasion, and especially female influence, is helpless against demon rum and the insidious liquor trade that promotes it. As the now-sober Joe Morgan, "or rather, Mr. Morgan" put it:

> [T]here is but one remedy. . . . The accursed traffic must cease among us. You must cut off the fountain, if you would dry up the stream. If you would save the young, the weak, the innocent . . . you must cover them from the tempter. . . . [They] can no more resist its assaults, than the lamb can resist the wolf. They are helpless, if you abandon them to the powers of evil.[36]

The demonization of liquor and the liquor trade, to which *Ten Nights* and other temperance literature contributed mightily, solved many of the ideological problems raised for the middle class by the failure of female influence and anxieties about the morality of market capitalism. Liquor was no ordinary commodity and the liquor trade no ordinary business. Both embodied an unmitigated evil that confounded and negated normal moral and economic laws. As in Cedarville, the economic activity produced by liquor impoverished rather than enriched communities. And, as was the case with the Slades, Hammonds, and Morgans, the moral evil generated by drinking proved impervious to female influence. Having outlined the demon's boundless evil and striking singularity, middle-class Americans could rest easy in the conviction that this horrific exception to the rule did not contradict or invalidate their faith in female domesticity and market capitalism.

Still if the demonization of liquor resolved some ideological difficulties for the middle class, it created others. If moral suasion and female influence could not eliminate intemperance, what course should the temperance movement follow? For many in the antiliquor ranks, the answer was legal and political action. Moral suasion had its place, they assured doubters, but so did legislation to limit severely or prohibit entirely rumsellers' ability to prey on their fellow citizens. "If moral means are no more sufficient to move and control the avarice of the dram-seller . . . then severer means become absolutely necessary and proper," declared one early supporter of the legislative approach in 1846.[37] This growing sensibility, which culminated in support for the Maine Law and other prohibitive legislation in the early 1850s, took seriously the social ills produced by intemperance and women's inability to protect themselves and their families against an aggressive liquor trade. It also, however, problematized women's continued public participation in temperance reform at a time when middle-class women began showing increasing interest in public activism. If female influence operated best in the home and men provided protection for the domestic sphere against incursions by the market, should women withdraw from public temperance work? The next chapter examines the differing responses of men and women to this question, as well as the implications for gender ideology.

6

Protecting the Home

The Maine Law and the Limits

of Women's Activism

By the late 1840s, the pendulum of temperance reform had begun to swing decidedly away from moral suasion and toward legal coercion. A number of factors produced this change in tactics. As outlined in the previous chapter, middle-class temperance reformers strove both to combat intemperance and insulate free-market ideology from scrutiny. Their campaign to demonize alcohol and the liquor traffic convinced much of the general public that no possible good could come from continued community toleration of the liquor trade. "Reliable statistics demonstrate," insisted Ohio temperance advocates, "beyond the possibility of a doubt, without appealing to your own experience, that this traffic has resulted *in evil, only evil, and that continually,* in Christian and heathen lands." Many Americans accepted assertions like this as the conventional wisdom, agreeing that in dispensing alcohol, the "destroyer of every sense of guilt," the liquor trade perpetuated vice by allowing the depraved to deaden the "stinging of an inward sense of shame" that might otherwise impel them to reform. As the 1840s drew to a close, a growing number of Americans had concluded that only legal coercion could stamp out such a monstrous vice.[1]

Toward the Maine Law

By 1850 most temperance supporters, male and female, had reconciled themselves to the failure of moral suasion and female influence to effect meaningful reform. Time and bitter experience had shown reformers that expecting female "angels" to follow drunkards to the "depths of iniquity" and lead them "back to virtue if [they] would but heed her voice" inevitably came to naught. The "unrelieved hideousness" and intractability of intemperance became apparent when "we remember how often it seizes even this angel herself, and drags her through all the gradations of drunkenness down to its loathsome death." The problem, the liquor trade's detractors came to believe, was that the unique evil of the commodity made its traffickers impervious to virtue, moral argument, and even the pathetic appeals of suffering women. Women's exercise of moral suasion through female influence simply lacked the potency of masculine legislation. Liquor traffickers constituted a "class of men," Presbyterian minister Albert Barnes thundered in an oft-reprinted tract, whom one "can never influence by moral suasion." He fumed: "They are men who enter no sanctuary; who place themselves aloof from argument; whose hearts are hard; whose consciences are seared; whose sole motive is gain; and who, if the moral part of the community abandons a business, will only drive it on themselves the faster."[2]

Such men could never be swayed by moral exhortation, for the lure of wealth generated by selling drink corrupted them beyond redemption. As one clergyman explained, moral power influences "accessible moral natures. But, among those who are doing so much to desolate our earth with the besom of intemperance are not a few, who, for all hopeful purposes, have no moral natures, —to *them*, justice and mercy cry out—apply the *law*." Other things being equal, moral suasion would be "greatly preferable" to harsher measures. But in the face of an obstinate and brazen liquor traffic, suasion was of no "more efficacy in destroying the rum trade than it would be in destroying counterfeiting or gambling." With those "governed merely by appetite or love of gain," asserted a Connecticut advocate of prohibition, "legal suasion saves breath and labor, and accomplishes the object in the simplest manner possible."[3] Only "restriction by legislative enactments," not pathetic appeals, would answer the pressing need for reform. Or, as a Pennsylvania lawyer argued of his state's failed system of regulation through licensing liquor vendors, nothing "but an act of Assembly now sanctions and supports this traffic; and nothing but an act of Assembly is required to undo the mighty evil already done, and redeem the State from the incubus which rests upon her."[4]

For some women, frustration with the glacial pace at which men moved to dislodge this demon proved too great to bear. Beginning in the mid-1840s and continuing through the 1850s, women in many parts of the country resorted to direct action, descending upon liquor vendors, attacking their establishments, and destroying their wares. From Baraboo, Wisconsin, to Kewanee, Illinois, to Syracuse, New York, women in small northern towns and cities physically blockaded liquor dealers' shops, excoriated rumsellers and demanded that they quit their business, or took axes and hatchets to casks of liquor. In 1854, for instance, two drunkards' wives secured "protection from personal harm" from "respectable and influential men" in Otsego, Michigan. They proceeded to "one of the rumholes with axes in hand" and destroyed liquor barrels. The "fire-poker was then called into battle, which caused a collision with the bottles in the bar, and resulted in a perfect smash up."[5]

Many temperance men supported this sort of action, accompanying female vigilantes to see that no harm befell them or paying their fines if they were arrested. These men viewed women's vigilantism as "righteous anger against a deeply entrenched evil [and] a legitimate extension of women's role as preserver of the home" as "essentially domestic in nature." Some women may have understood it differently. Amelia Bloomer insisted that if the "law lets loose a tiger upon her," woman "may destroy it." Her newspaper, *The Lily*, reflected this sentiment:

> If the rulers of our land will do nothing to stay, the ruin caused by intoxicating drinks—if they will do nothing to protect the innocent wife and children from being crushed and trodden to the earth by the tyrant rum-seller, then it is time that woman bids defiance to our unjust laws, and shows a spirit of determination to protect herself. We only wonder that she has so long tamely submitted to them.[6]

The same frustration and sense of urgency that made female vigilantism acceptable also produced a newfound willingness to switch tactics and support coercive legislation. Enthusiasm for legal remedies to the drink problem culminated during the early 1850s in the passage of prohibitory legislation by thirteen states and territories, mostly in the Northeast and Midwest, beginning with Maine in 1851. In many cases, this embrace of prohibition built on earlier town and county campaigns to restrict liquor sales by limiting or forbidding the granting of licenses to sell. Under the leadership of Portland mayor Neal Dow, Maine legislators approved a prohibitory act that in scope and severity surpassed any previous liquor regulations. The Maine Law, as it came to be called, attempted to close loopholes in earlier liquor laws by eliminating prosecutors' reliance on testimony to prove that an illegal sale had taken place. While the Maine Law prohibited the manufacture or sale of liquor, it also bestowed broad search and seizure powers on local officials, empowering them to destroy seized liquor and levy stiff penalties on violators. Dow's Maine Law appealed to frustrated liquor adversaries in other parts of the country: in the four years following its passage, ten states (Massachusetts, Rhode Island, Vermont, Michigan, Connecticut, New York, Indiana, Delaware, Iowa, New Hampshire) and two territories (Minnesota and Nebraska) enacted similar legislation. In Ohio and Pennsylvania outright prohibition failed narrowly, but both states did pass more restrictive regulatory laws than had been on the books previously. This sea change in antiliquor tactics even ramified into the South. Both Texas and Mississippi passed new, more stringent license and sales laws in the wake of the Maine Law.[7]

On the face of things, the success of the Maine Law represented a victory for temperance advocates, women among them, who had for years called for legal protection from the liquor trade. Radical women in particular had long decried the legal imprimatur given to rumsellers by state licensing, insisting that what "is in itself wrong, law can never make right, and legalizing the cruel and deadly business of vending alcoholic poison, has too long stood a foul blot on the statute books." In this Amelia Bloomer's newspaper, *The Lily,* took the lead, seeking to deny rumsellers the cloak of respectability provided by the license system to redefine liquor selling as a moral *and* legal transgression. "Rumselling is a crime," *The Lily* stated baldly, adding that measures short of legal prohibition would "no more work out the shutting up of the grog shop, than they will protect society from the depredations of the thief and the highwayman." Articles in *The Lily* routinely condemned selling rum as administering poison to an unwitting victim or applauded legislation that restricted the sale of liquor or protected the rights of drunkards' wives.[8]

In Maine, where prohibition began, women figured prominently in the move toward coercive legislation. An 1846 prohibitory statute, a precursor of the more rigorous 1851 law, emerged in part from the petitioning of a husband and wife, Lydia and James Merrill. The Merrills' 1846 petition to the state legislature conjured for lawmakers images of women with "no hope but in the reformation of their deluded husbands . . . poor mothers . . . cast down too low to petition, or even hope for relief." The Merrills promised the legislature that the "blessings of millions of maids and mothers will pour upon you like a golden shower," if they answered women's prayers and "abolish[ed] the sale and use of ardent spirits in this State by your votes!" Reminiscing some years later, Neal Dow attested further to women's desire for prohibition, attributing his idea for the Maine Law to an interview with a heartbroken drunkard's wife in 1844. The woman had pleaded with a "publican" to stop whiskey to her husband. He replied that he was "licensed to sell," the woman reported tearfully, beseeching Dow's aid. "By the help of God, I'll change that law," Dow replied. Dow's remembrances, as well as other contemporary accounts, suggest that women enthusiastically supported what many considered the most controversial provision of the Maine Law: its authorization of the destruction of liquor. A delegate to an 1851 temperance convention reported, for instance, that when a liquor establishment burned, a woman said she had "prayed for that, and there are thousands of wives praying for just such fires. . . . Here is the spirit over this nation. There are 30,000 wives in Ohio, praying for the destruction of liquor. . . . This is the last step; destroy the liquor."[9]

Female Skepticism about Male Legislation

To some women, the Maine Law's passage seemed like a prayer answered. Even as support for the prohibition continued to spread throughout the North, however, female temperance advocates expressed skepticism at the law's effectiveness, doubts about men's motives for passing it, and exasperation at the patronizing attitudes of male-dominated temperance societies that marginalized female voices and concerns. Some women feared that because they lacked a public voice, their interests would not be represented in the political conflicts surrounding prohibition. Temperance proved a thorny issue during the Second Party System, and in the rush to win votes, political expediency often trumped moral principles for both Whigs and Democrats. In this, life imitated art. Edwin Tompkins, a senator in a temperance novel, politely refused to honor his wife's entreaty that he "advocate and defend the 'Maine Law' with all the power you possess" and take "a bold and fearless stand for virtue and temperance." Tompkins, the practical politician, demurred, objecting that such a stance "would destroy my political prospects for all time to come. . . . I am unwilling, at this time, to espouse the Maine Law."[10] Tompkins may have been a fictional character, but he expressed sentiments shared by many real politicians.

This proclivity to sacrifice temperance interests to gain advantage at the polls incensed female temperance workers. Women recalled that the "high license" and "no license" campaigns would have effectively prohibited the liquor traffic but foundered because men failed to enforce them vigorously due to political and pecuniary concerns. Too often, women pointed out, temperance men wavered when adherence to cold-water principles would cost them votes. "Why do they cringe to an inferior force," demanded *The Lily* in 1850. "Why yield up their cherished principles and join hands with a drunken, dissolute class, and aid in strengthening its power? All this seems to us strange and inexplicable, and we strive in vain to solve it." Temperance women, along with many male counterparts, feared that the Maine Law, like previous attempts at coercive legislation, would come to nothing because men would not enforce it. Men's attempts to reassure women on this score often sounded hollow. "More than one half of the legal voters of the State," a Massachusetts minister argued in 1852, to say nothing of the tens of thousands who are not legal voters, have voluntarily petitioned the legislature for its existence. It is believed that three fourths of all our population are in favor of the law, and would rejoice to see it universally executed. With all this numerical and moral strength, and, I may add, enthusiasm in its support, why should the law fail?[11]

Yet the laws did fail, either through non-enforcement, political skullduggery, or constitutional disqualification. Prohibition could not extinguish the liquor trade if local officials declined to prosecute offenders vigorously because they feared losing political support. Thus despite the passage of laws for which women had pleaded, they could still, as Ian Tyrrell noted, regard "male legislators and even some male temperance reformers as unresponsive to the demands of women for protection of the home against the impact of intemperance." Men's commitment to politics, it became apparent, undermined their attachment to temperance principles. The blame for the non-enforcement of Rhode Island's prohibitory law, fulminated one reformer, was "justly chargeable to a great extent to PARTY; not to any one party exclusively . . . but to both—to PARTY . . . and an habitual servile truckling to partizan [*sic*] feelings and party interests."[12]

Making matters worse, by mid-decade, the Massachusetts, Rhode Island, Michigan, and Indiana state supreme courts had each declared their state's version of the Maine Law unconstitutional. It is not surprising then that female temperance activists expressed frustration and contempt for male efforts to represent women's interests or legislate for their protection. In 1852, for instance, an astonished writer for *The Lily* reported on a New York election in which temperance men "subjected themselves to much odium and ridicule by getting up a *temperance* ticket with a *vender of intoxicating drinks at the head of it*." The reasons behind this stunning turn of events, she continued, may be clear to "*voters,* but we who are denied our right to vote, are quite in the dark on this subject." This incident may have motivated Elizabeth Cady Stanton to remark in her presidential address to the Women's New York State Temperance Society three months later that man "has so much intrigue and worldly wisdom, and the best of them do so continually sacrifice principle to expediency, that we had great fears in taking him as a counsellor on any moral question." In short, women "stood helpless and watched as male voters and male-dominated political parties brought about the collapse of political temperance reform."[13]

At the same time that women became restive and dissatisfied with political horse trading on liquor reform, men grew increasingly impatient with women's continued demands for a public role in the temperance movement. As shown in earlier chapters, women's temperance activism changed over time, becoming more organized, assertive, and public by the

1840s. Women organized female temperance societies, mounted petition drives for antiliquor causes, importuned businessmen to desist from selling ardent spirits, published temperance newspapers, and, increasingly, spoke in public against the liquor trade. All these activities could be depicted as moral suasion and justified as legitimate female exertions against a threat to hearth and home. With the shift from suasion to coercion, however, the temperance crusade became, "almost overnight," a movement for prohibition "and therefore, inevitably, a political movement." While middle-class temperance supporters could approbate women's public, even at times vociferous, advocacy of a domestic cause, they could not countenance female interference with a political issue. As Jed Dannenbaum noted, when "temperance tactics shifted from the advocacy of moral suasion to that of prohibition, women were left without a meaningful function to perform in the movement."[14]

Male Backlash

Having given women the legal protection against the liquor traffic they had long sought, men reasoned that their wives, sisters, and mothers should abandon public reform and return gratefully to their firesides. Instead women criticized men's failures to make the Maine Law work and insisted on retaining public prominence in the temperance movement. Even worse, some radicals began to militate for expanded political and property rights so that women could protect themselves against the impact of intemperance when, as they predicted, legislation failed. This seeming ingratitude and recalcitrance occasioned a savage backlash among many middle-class male temperance proponents, who heaped contumely on female reformers and moved to limit their participation in the movement. Now that the battle against liquor had left the realm of morality and entered the arena of law and politics, men deemed that women no longer had a public role to play. Any further female agitation within the temperance movement seemed not genuine efforts to eradicate a moral blight but devious attempts to disturb the movement with "their stuff and nonsense about 'Women's Rights.'"[15]

The major temperance societies took the lead in writing women out of the movement. The Sons of Temperance, the largest fraternal temperance organization of the 1840s and 1850s, consistently denied women the opportunity to speak at its meetings. The Sons did admit women to the order as "visitors" in 1854 but circumscribed their rights to participate in meetings. At mass meetings, too, women received a cold reception in the wake of the Maine Law's passage. In January 1852, for instance, at a gathering in Albany of all the New York "divisions" of the Sons of Temperance, the male leadership received a delegation of the Daughters of Temperance, which included Susan B. Anthony, Mary C. Vaughn, and Lydia Fowler as members of the convention. When Anthony attempted to speak, however, the Sons prevented her, informing the Daughters "that the ladies were invited to listen, and not to take part in the proceedings."[16]

A year later, at the Whole World's Temperance Convention in New York City, the backlash against women reached its apex. The meeting convened, accepting the credentials of male delegates, then admitting women representing the Woman's (New York) State Temperance Society as an afterthought. Thomas Wentworth Higginson's motion to add Susan B. Anthony, the secretary of the Women's State Temperance Society, to the convention's business committee produced an immediate uproar. "D.D.'s, M.D.'s, and Honorables were horrified," one observer noted. "Speech followed speech in rapid succession, with angry vehemence." Abby Kelly Foster attempted to explain the women's position but was shouted down. A male delegate moved that a credentials committee be appointed to determine who were members of the convention. The three-man committee deliberated only fifteen minutes before reporting that the meeting "was not intended to include female delegates, and [as] custom had not sanctioned the public action of women in similar situations, the credentials of the ladies should be rejected." The motion passed by a narrow margin, all the women present voting in the negative. After "another disgraceful scene" when the convention refused to pay the expenses of the women who had come as delegates and been dismissed, the female delegates left, along with some male supporters. The men's vituperation did not cease with their exit, however. Rev. John Chambers of Philadelphia excoriated Abby Kelly Foster, "charging her with outraging the proprieties of her sex, trampling the very Son of God under her blasphemous feet." Chambers exulted in the women's absence, adding that "they had thus gotten rid of the scum of the Convention." Others concurred. S. C. Barstow, the mayor of Providence, Rhode Island, and president of the convention, "referred to '*women in breeches*' as a disgrace to their sex. . . . He did not know what such women were good for. He believed they were never *productive* in anything but mischief. (Laughter and cheers.)"[17]

Why did men act with such ferocity against women at precisely the time when common support for prohibition should have united the sexes? How do we reconcile women's dissatisfaction and the male backlash against them with what should have been a resounding victory for both? Men had long lauded women's efforts in the battle against liquor, and women had labored tirelessly in petition campaigns to support male-sponsored prohibitory legislation. Even if women did feel somewhat marginalized by the temperance movement's entry into the male realm of politics, they had, after all, finally been given the legal protection against liquor for which they had long clamored. What caused such hard feelings on both sides? Ian Tyrrell, the closest student of antebellum temperance, attributed the impetus for the Maine Law to middle-class social and economic anxieties during the late 1840s. Increasing Irish and German immigration, persistent patterns of working-class drinking, and structural economic changes that produced a higher incidence of transient labor, the "prosperous and respectable classes" feared, would increase crime, pauperism, and, worst of all, property taxes to pay for the amelioration of these social ills. In Tyrrell's trenchant analysis, the Maine Law served the interests of middle-class social ideology and political economy. While this explanation accounts for the class dimension of reactions to the Maine Law, it does not elucidate women's frustration or men's resentment after the passage of state prohibition. Nor does Jed Dannenbaum's insight that the shift to prohibition from suasion left women with no meaningful role in the temperance movement explain completely the bitterness and obloquy on both sides. To resolve this problem satisfactorily, both the socioeconomic aspects of prohibition and also the gender implications of the Maine Law for middle-class ideology must be considered.

Viewed from the vantage point of gender politics, men's support for the Maine Law represented an attempt at ideological as well as legal closure. In prohibition, middle-class men saw not just a means to resolve troubling questions about the morality of market capitalism posed by the liquor trade but also a way to settle disturbing contradictions in female gender roles occasioned by women's temperance activism. Unlike female antislavery activism, which could be dismissed or discredited more easily because of the controversial and often unpopular nature of the cause, women's public support for temperance could be portrayed easily as a natural extension of the moral duties attendant upon womanhood. Clearly women had a justifiable interest in preventing the violence and disorder caused by liquor from destroying the domestic sphere, and it made sense that their efforts might have to be directed beyond the home at the source of this evil. But, just as liquor dealers' invocation of free trade created quandaries for bourgeois political economy, women's appeal that their innate moral power had to extend beyond the home posed problems for middle-class gender ideology. Prohibition allowed middle-class ideologues to contain the former difficulty by demonizing liquor and its traffickers, thereby differentiating it from other items of legitimate trade in a free market. But banning liquor moved temperance reform into the legal and political realm, thereby also effectively placing women's public activism on this issue beyond the pale of respectability. Considered in gendered terms, the Maine Law's denial of a meaningful public role for women in the temperance movement was not coincidental or unintended but a central objective of the legislation. Allowing women to use temperance as a platform for extremism risked both undermining the battle against liquor and legitimizing in the larger community opinions and behavior antithetical to middle-class gender ideology. The gender politics of the Maine Law, then, represented middle-class men's efforts to reseal women in the domestic sphere, both for their own safety and to prevent them from infecting the public sphere with the perverted womanhood of the manipulative belle and undutiful wife. Understanding fully the backlash against women during the Maine Law period, then, requires attention to the context of the gender politics in which the move toward prohibition was imbedded.

Roots of the Backlash against Female Activism

Neither the tactical shift from suasion to coercion nor the backlash against women's temperance activism took shape overnight. Long-term, subtle changes in the gendered discourse of alcohol reform accompanied by growing male discomfort with the tenor and trajectory of women's public role paved the way for the recriminations of the early 1850s. At the dawn of the temperance movement in the opening years of the nineteenth century, citizens concerned about the prevalence of drunkenness expressed their anxieties in class terms. Elite reformers believed that social influence and example flowed downward, from the better classes to the lower ranks of society. Though the gentry might be able to drink temperately, they had to be chary of the precedent that their habits set for their less elevated neighbors. In this view elites could stem the tide of intemperance by setting a good example for their social inferiors. The "sentiments and example of persons of substantial characters and temperate habits," noted a Pennsylvania reformer in 1810, "has had a more extensive and impressive effect to promote intoxication, than all the unguardedness of the vulgar, and the sensuality of the sot united together." An anonymous commentator made a similar point to the religious community in Connecticut three years later, condemning "the countenance which has been extensively and incautiously given, in worthy and serious families," to social drinking. The "example thus set in high places," he continued, "has had a baleful influence in the humbler walks of life. If the rich drink at their social visits, the poor will drink at theirs." The upper-crust members of the Massachusetts Society for the Suppression of Intemperance, which in 1813 emerged as the nation's first statewide temperance organization, took a similar tack. A circular to its members expressed concern about drinking among some "gentlemen of talents" as well as the "labouring classes." The MSSI urged members to "exert a prudent influence" to check intemperance by changing the "fashion of entertaining guests and visitors" through the presentation of "mild and safe substitutes" to ardent spirits.[18]

As the MSSI circular reveals, early nineteenth-century American elites often conceived of themselves as arbiters of fashion, trendsetters who influenced the rest of society. Thus social critic Thomas Herttell insisted in 1819 that the "*intemperate use of ardent liquor, originates in the fashions, habits, customs and examples, of what are called the upper or wealthy classes of the community"* and then spreads downward to the lower classes. Breeding, social position, and prosperity shielded the upper classes from the pernicious effects of intemperance, but their social inferiors fared less well. In Herttell's view, elites bore responsibility for the spread of immorality:

> The examples of the rich give a currency to vice, which, under the imposing influence of fashion, passes thro' every grade of society, uncensored and unrestrained, till stripped naked of the influence of *wealth* and *education*, it exhibits itself in the lower class; where recognized by its native deformity, it takes its true name and character, and receives that merited animadversion, which, unfortunately, for the cause of morality, it escapes in the higher walks of life.

Boston physician John Ware struck a similar chord in an address before the MSSI in 1825. How could the better sorts "censure so deeply the excesses of the less informed and enlightened classes," Ware chided, when the "higher set them an example, by indulgences which only their better education or their regard of character, prevent from leading them into habits equally pernicious!" However "insensibly it may be exercised," Ware insisted, elite influence on the lower ranks of society "is immense." Upper-class "habits of living and thinking, as well as their fashions, always descend in some form, and have their counterpart, among their inferiors."[19]

Fashion, then, understood in class terms, exerted an enormous influence on the extent of alcohol use and abuse. Temperance activists continued to speak and write in these terms throughout the antebellum era, identifying the upper and, increasingly, middle class as the arbiters of manners and fashions. An 1837 tract, for example, lamented the "fashionable drinking" of its young, middle-class protagonist, who sought social recognition and influence by entertaining the "gay votaries of fashion" with drinking parties. The *Temperance Text Book*, a popular compilation of stories and statistics, regretted the influence of genteel manners and hospitality on drinking in the same year: if gentlemen offer ladies wine at dinner, and it is thought uncivil to refuse, wine will be freely used "among both fashionable people, and those who desire to be thought such." A Pennsylvania temperance advocate reported ruefully in 1840 that "wine drinking is tolerated, and even regarded as fashionable, and a mark of social pre-eminence by a certain class of the community." Despite the progress of the antiliquor cause, a concerned physician observed in 1847 that the "habits, fashions, customs and examples, of what are called the upper classes," continued to present the "greatest obstacle to the temperance reformation."[20]

The Gendering of Fashion

The linkage of fashion with class remained fairly constant throughout the antebellum era, but two important changes in discourse did occur. First, as Karen Halttunen has argued, in the wake of the French Revolution, the "middle classes seized upon fashion as a means to segregate themselves from the less deserving lower classes." Nowhere, Halttunen added, "was this phenomenon more pronounced than among the American middle classes in the Age of Jackson." As this occurred, fashion acquired a somewhat morally questionable connotation, bespeaking pretension and hypocrisy rather than the sincerity and honesty upon which the emerging middle class prided itself. Second, fashion became gendered as female. Early in the century, the "gentleman of fashion" had been a common figure in literary and social commentary, but by the 1830s at least, women had become the dominant cultural referent for fashion. Fashion became both a preoccupation and a problem for middle-class women during the middle decades of the century. Charged by middle-class ideology with upholding morality, American women, "whose highest moral responsibility was to preserve sincerity in the parlor, threatened to poison parlor society with the hypocrisy of fashion." The changing and problematic status of fashion may explain why it was referred to in terms both feminine and ambivalent, if not derogatory. "Fashion rules the world," a women's temperance newspaper sighed in 1846, and "a most tyrannical mistress she is, compelling people to submit to the most inconvenient things imaginable for her sake."[21]

Woman's role as hostess and supervisor of domestic entertainment grew increasingly important during the antebellum era as middle-class temperance crusaders fretted that enforcement of public sobriety might only drive intemperance into the private realm. Only by reforming private habit and custom, they urged, could intemperance be totally eliminated. Here women's support would prove invaluable. As the "arbitress of manners," observed another opponent of liquor, no "license can exist in society but by her assent. . . . As the censor of morals, her countenance reassures virtue, and her frown checks the serpent like advances of vice in the walks of private life." The temperance movement had chased intemperance from the public eye, asserted another reformer in 1842, but it had retreated to the "sacred retreats of the social and domestic circle," and here women must combat it among the "fashionable" set.[22]

The identification of women with fashion can be seen clearly in the larger sweep of antebellum popular culture, as well as in temperance literature. In the popular press, *Godey's Lady's Book* and similar publications offered women commentary, illustrations, and patterns for fashionable clothing and furnishings. Anna Cora Mowatt's 1845 play *Fashion* revolved around the threat to her husband's legal and financial standing posed by

Mrs. Tiffany's addiction to fashionable attire and entertainment. Popular fiction, too, linked women to fashion. Novels and stories held the tavern keeper's wife up to scorn for her willingness to tolerate her husband's infernal business because of the luxuries it afforded her. One resentful drunkard's wife regarded the liquor dealer's wife as a "mere butterfly of fashion" who reaped the rewards of destroying families with liquor. In another tale, a rumseller's wife throws a "fashionable party" to ensnare the protagonist, Dick Wilson. But ordinary women, as well as those allied with the liquor trade, came in for criticism as well. The aforementioned Dick Wilson, for instance, lacked the fortitude to resist temptation owing to a deficient upbringing. Dick's mother, an otherwise "excellent woman," was "so pressed by the continued calls of fashion" that she lacked sufficient time to spend with her children. The "tyranny of a morbid fashion, which has mingled itself with the rumseller's doings" explained a relative, "robbed" Dick of the maternal solicitude necessary to his proper moral development. Similarly another woman "allowed the power of fashion . . . to triumph over the still small voice of conscience," and failed to oppose the liquor traffic. Even women inclined toward temperance might succumb to the lure of fashion. In popular novelist Metta V. Fuller Victor's *Fashionable Dissipation,* the Lee sisters, Margaret, Lily, and Rosa, express support for temperance but resist a proposal to attend a temperance lecture, considering it boring compared to more elegant amusements. Soon thereafter the sisters arrange a bucolic picnic for their brother and some guests. "When the ladies had arranged their rural repast upon the grass, contrary to all customs of the shepherds and shepherdesses they should have imitated, a basket of wine made its appearance." Predictably their adherence to the fashion of serving wine ended disastrously, with one of their guests getting drunk, ruining the party, and embarking on a lengthy alcoholic debauch.[23]

By general acclamation the upper and prosperous middle classes still set the styles, but commentators increasingly identified their female members as the arbiters of manners and fashions. This control over fashion, one moralist noted, extended woman's power beyond the domestic sphere. "*Society* is her empire, and she governs almost at will. . . . She is the arbitress of taste and manners. It is her province to *adorn* social life . . . by making it lovely and attractive, pure and improving." The gendering of fashion fed into discussions of female influence, for it attributed enormous social authority to women. Thus female control of fashion implied an important role for women in the battle against intemperance. In "regulating the habits and customs of society . . . females may exert the most powerful and permanent influence. In all matters of taste and fashion, they are the acknowledged arbiters." Women had power, a temperance journal asserted, "over those fashions which govern, and we may say ruin the community." Ladies must join temperance societies, urged reformers, because they "control the fashions of the day, and especially as it [*sic*] relates to the entertainment of company."[24] By the 1840s, then, the class-based temperance discourse of elite influence that had emerged earlier in the century took on a gendered dimension. The fashionable classes still had to set an example for their social inferiors if temperance were to prosper, but reformers increasingly held women responsible for the success of that enterprise because of their identification as the arbiters of fashion.

This identification proved problematic when, on the one hand, women gravitated toward some of the less salutary manifestations of fashion and, on the other, female influence did not eradicate intemperance. Observers complained that some middle-class women embraced not the uplifting aspects of fashion but the vapid, superficial, and destructive ones. Temperance newspapers lamented that ladies patronized fashionable ice cream establishments that served liquor or visited pleasure gardens and salons that were little more than liquor shops, where four-fifths of "'fashionable amusements' and 'fashionable attentions' mean the destruction of female morals." Women, it seemed, succumbed to the tawdry side of fashion, acquiescing in questionable practices to enjoy the elegance and opulence made possible by middle-class prosperity. The *New York Organ* reacted indignantly to women's patronage of Broadway's "magnificent drinking saloons," which were "furnished with every dazzling attraction that can lure the sensual." Reflecting on how many men met with ruin in these gilded dens of vice, the paper marveled that "fashionable, genteel and beautiful ladies can be found to add their charms to the fascinations of liquor and cigars, in alluring men to dissipation." Even the friends of female temperance activism held women responsible for the "evils and calamities growing out of the fashionable custom of using intoxicating drink, which [they] had taken so active a part in sanctioning, if not introducing far and wide through the community."[25]

Critics continued to sound this tocsin throughout the antebellum years. Writing on the eve of the Civil War, Alonzo Potter summed up sentiments that had coalesced over the past two decades. Asking where drunkenness came from, Potter averred that it did not result from "*appetite, but from deference to custom and fashion.*" Drinking usages, he continued, constituted the "chief cause" of intemperance and derived "their force and authority, in the first instance, wholly from those who give law to fashion." At first, Potter emphasized the class position of these law-givers, alluding to the "abodes of the rich and admired." In the homes of the prosperous, he went on, where "friend pledges friend" with wine to "lend animation to gaiety," intemperance originates. But then the discussion turned away from the socioeconomic roots of drunkenness, for Potter revealed that the "most dangerous decoy" is the "sparkling glass" that is raised by the "hand of [a] beautiful and lovely woman." Must not the less elevated emulate this example and consider that "proper, and even obligatory," which boasts the "deliberate and time-honored sanction of those who stand before the world as the 'glass of fashion,' and 'rose of the fair state'?"[26] Here class and gender ideology intertwined to indict women for the perceived failure of middle-class reform. In essence Potter and others like him retained the class-based model of social influence from earlier decades but refracted it through the lens of a misogynistic middle-class gender ideology.

Washingtonianism and the Gendering of Suasion

The discursive changes surrounding understandings of fashion and class put middle-class women in a particularly difficult situation, for a similar process of gendering was undermining the one weapon at their disposal in the battle against liquor—moral suasion. Ironically the devaluation of women's contribution to the antiliquor crusade proceeded from a development that at first glance might have been expected to raise the stock of female influence and persuasion as reform tactics. The rise of the Washingtonians, a self-help group established in 1840 by working-class drunkards in Baltimore, reinvigorated interest in using persuasive rather than punitive measures to ameliorate intemperance. Washingtonian societies, usually led by reformed inebriates rather than respectable citizens, encouraged members to give public testimony about their own horrific experiences with alcohol to convince drinkers to sign the total abstinence pledge. Washingtonian "experience speeches," which detailed the male speaker's alcoholic degradation and path to regeneration, relied on overtly emotional and pathetic appeals to reach their audiences. The tears, lamentations, and admissions of failure and helplessness distinguished the largely working-class Washingtonians from their middle-class counterparts in the mainline temperance movement. Though middle-class temperance literature and oratory also appealed to their audience's sympathy for the victims of intemperance, they utilized rhetorical strategies gendered as male, such as rationality, logic, and righteous anger, to make their case against the liquor trade. Washingtonian experience speeches, by contrast, tugged at the hearts and played on the emotions of listeners, employing sympathetic and sentimental appeals more commonly associated with women. Washingtonian lecturers pleaded with audiences to avoid the alcoholic lures that ensnared them, vividly describing the horrors of intemperance while soliciting compassion and support for the degraded and miserable drunkard, rather than fomenting anger and enmity against liquor dealers. In his study of public sentimentality in nineteenth-century American literature, Glenn Hendler suggested that Washingtonian experience speeches had their "nearest relative as a narrative form" in the "nascent genre of sentimental women's fiction, which was similarly centered on the enactment or performance of sympathetic identification [and] an exchange of affective experience." Though Hendler argued that the boundary between masculine and feminine narrative forms was "more porous than we usually assume," it is undeniable that Washingtonian sentimentality partook of practices and qualities coded as feminine in mid-nineteenth-century America.[27]

Certainly women embraced the Washingtonian movement, praising it extravagantly in middle-class female temperance papers and forming cross-class Martha Washington societies to support the efforts of men. As part of this process, women invested moral capital in the Washingtonian approach to reform, tying their fortunes within the temperance movement to suasion rather than coercion. Along with their affective displays, impassioned appeals, and sympathy for drunken men, Washingtonians opposed punitive laws, preferring to persuade rather than compel. This approach, which they claimed would be the most effective in reclaiming drunkards and, ultimately, eliminating the demand for liquor, resembled more closely female emotionalism than male rationality. Hence women gravitated toward Washingtonianism, for it validated existing female contributions to the battle against liquor as important and efficacious. Endorsing Washingtonian suasionist tactics also promoted women's claims to a prominent place in the reform, for who could deploy sympathy and sentimentalism as well as women? As *The Olive Plant,* a woman's temperance newspaper, put it, "Moral suasion is the basis of the Washingtonian movement. Who can wield that weapon so effectually as woman? Indeed she has no other means at her disposal." Thus the Washingtonian movement's emphasis on sentimental persuasion attracted woman to its vanguard, while identifying, more closely than ever before, female participation in the temperance movement with moral suasion.[28]

Less than ten years after its founding, however, the Washingtonian movement began to unravel as ostensibly reformed drunkards fell off the wagon and the liquor trade continued its depredations unabated. Its demise undermined women's position within the temperance movement by casting serious doubt on the viability of moral suasion as an effective weapon against the liquor traffic. Male liquor reformers suspected that rumsellers seized upon Washingtonianism as a way of preventing any meaningful action against them. Professing "great interest in the Washingtonian reform," calculating liquor dealers duped the reformed drunkards and their allies, persuading them that "as they were operated upon and induced to abandon their cups, by example, and kind and earnest appeals to heart and conscience, so no coercive measures against the rum traffic should be countenanced" by the Washingtonians. "Why all that the dealers in strong drink could desire at the hands of the temperance movement," another advocate of coercion fulminated, "is that its apostles would just stick to this old policy of moral suasion." By the early 1850s, the conclusion that moral suasion, a tactic gendered as feminine, remained powerless over those "who ply the liquor traffic" became the conventional wisdom. Failure to abandon suasion for coercion promised not only defeat but a degrading feminization. "Are we so lost to honor," demanded one reformer, "are we so effeminate, so pusillanimous as to succumb to the rum tyrants of the nineteenth century? It cannot be!"[29]

Gendering suasion as feminine and dismissing it as ineffective opened female temperance advocates to misogynist attacks. During the late 1840s, some male temperance activists disparaged women's support for suasionist tactics as unwitting or malicious aid to the enemy. An exchange between the *New York Organ*, the official publication of the Sons of Temperance, and New York's *The Pearl*, a women's temperance paper, illustrates this tension. In early 1847, the *Organ* accused *The Pearl* of being the dupe of the liquor trade. Mrs. Virginia Allen, editor of *The Pearl*, took umbrage at this charge, upbraiding the *Organ* for criticizing *The Pearl*'s support for suasion as "'advocating rumselling.'" The *Organ*'s attack backfired, as Allen and others concluded that the paper's editor was "'no gentleman.'" After a bit more sniping, the *Organ* admitted to "ungenerous" remarks, but its position carried the day.[30] No longer would moral suasion be taken seriously as a weapon in the war against intemperance.

Instead temperance men advocated more stringent, coercive measures in conjunction with suasion or alone. A Massachusetts temperance paper, for example, in 1844 approved the motto "Moral suasion alone for the drunkard, moral suasion and legal action combined, for the drunkard maker." Women, especially radical ones, also recognized the limitations of persuasion. "Gentle means—moral suasion alone," noted Amelia Bloomer's *Lily*, "will no more work out the shutting up of the grog shop, than they will protect society from the depredations of the thief and the highwayman." John Marsh put it more forcefully in 1851: "'But dissuade the drinker from drink, and then the traffic will cease.' The assumption is false in its basis, for men will never cease drinking while the traffic continues." Moral suasion might accomplish much, but it had failed to put down the drink trade, for the "appetites of men stimulated by the unscrupulous avarice of manufacturers and sellers, being as usual too powerful to be overcome by any motive however strong which it is able to present, what next? . . . MANIFESTLY COERCION OR NOTHING." Suasion might help, but it could not replace legal measures in the struggle to destroy the liquor trade. "It need scarcely be necessary to answer the antique objection," snorted a Philadelphia lawyer in 1852,

> against [prohibitory legislation], that *moral suasion* alone ought to be used in such a case as this. The most powerfully concentrated moral suasion has been brought to bear in favor of this reform, with all its thousand batteries during the last forty years, yet the vice has increased, and its supporters have laughed to scorn the inept struggles of their foes. Surely it is time to try another measure.[31]

The implication, of course, was that the reform tactic identified with women had been tried and found wanting. Persuasion, whether plied by middle-class women or feminized working-class Washingtonians, proved powerless against the liquor trade. Only legal measures enacted by men in the political sphere could save the day. "So long as we have those among us," insisted a clergyman in the 1850s, "who will drink ardent spirits if they can get it, so long as we have those among us, who will sell it if they can find purchasers, so long we need the application of rigorous law." This message emerged not just in formal pronouncements by temperance societies but in popular culture as well. An ephemeral genre, the Maine Law novel, appeared during the 1850s to support prohibitory legislation with portraits of debilitated men and powerless women, all victimized by intractable and voracious rumsellers. First and foremost, these literary interventions in temperance politics insisted upon the total incapacity of moral suasion in general and female influence in particular to prevent the liquor trade from corrupting men. Under the influence of liquor, Erastus Baker, a character in an 1853 novel, "seemed to forget his wife, or at least the obligation he was under to love, protect, and support her . . . the tears and anguish of his broken-hearted wife had no power to reform or even restrain him." Baker lived only to "gratify his appetite," going so "far as to take, without the knowledge of his wife, her wedding dress, and sell it . . . for liquor." Nor could familial bliss protect against the depredations of liquor. New father Edward Lee, for example, kissed his wife, Alice, as they fondly contemplated their newborn in his crib. Alice noticed with concern that her husband had been drinking brandy, though he swore that he would "never, never, take anything stronger than wine." As one male protagonist explained it to his wife, the appetite for liquor, once awakened, obliterated all other concerns. Not "a want of love for you and our little ones" accounted for his chronic drunkenness and disgrace, Charles Douglass assured his wife, Amelia.

> No; I love you as I do my own soul, —I could die for you. I do verily believe that if a loaded pistol were pointed at me, and I knew that the first drop I tasted would discharge its contents into my heart, it would be no restraint, in that state of mind, to my drinking. I should be so exclusively absorbed by my appetite, and the means of its gratification, as not to regard my own life more than I regard you and the children.[32]

Female characters in Maine Law novels recognized the uselessness of appeals to duty, obligation, or love against the allure of drink. In contrast to avowals of the power of female influence in earlier years, temperance novels of the 1850s depicted its impotence to reform drunkards. Though wives and mothers might mount a "mighty array of Christian domestic influence," the "irresistible incantation of wine" more than counterbalanced it. With "threads of silver and gold" virtuous wives endeavored to keep their husbands "within the sacred circle of the home, where the evil genii that surrounded him in the outer air could not intrude," but to no avail. Once the "worm of the still" fastened its eye "upon a victim," it "exercise[d] a fascination more alluring than the dreaded enchantment of the rattle-snake." A distraught sister, for instance, lamented that as her brother had already broken a vow of total abstinence "that he made to a dying mother, and in so short a time, there is nothing that can restrain him now. My love will come to naught; it will be powerless." Another beleaguered wife admitted that she had "hugged the delusive hope that I should, sooner or later, be able to reform him; but entreaties, tears, and prayers, are alike unavailing; and he seems to be letting himself down, lower and lower, and every succeeding day cutting himself more and more effectually loose from every restraint."[33]

If the Maine Law novels argued for the futility of female suasion, they contended just as fiercely for the efficacy of masculine law. Reformed drunkards and their wives affirmed the necessity of legal coercion to provide real protection against the liquor traffic. "Nothing but a physical impossibility, my dear," explained one inebriate to his wife, "can keep me from drinking." Other characters concurred. A long-suffering woman noted that her husband and sons had "lost all control over their wills, when exposed to temptation; and my only hope now, is to place them beyond the reach of temptation, through the enactment of the Maine Law." A male character, eager to reform, struck a similar chord, embracing the "necessity and importance" of the Maine Law's passage as the only means of "freeing himself from the temptation that would beset him" from all sides if liquor continued to be available. The Maine Law novels reflected and expressed a general dissatisfaction in the temperance movement's reliance on suasion "for the restraint of intemperance." Suasion had "spent its force, and it has done much . . . [but to] refuse to go further is to retrograde in this great moral enterprise."[34]

Suspicion about Temperance and Women's Rights

The changes in discursive practice surrounding fashion and moral suasion became pronounced during the mid- to late-1840s amid a climate of suspicion about women's true intentions and motives in supporting temperance reform. As noted earlier, women's temperance activism evoked concern and criticism among middle-class ideologues eager to bolster the ideology of separate spheres. By the end of the 1840s, this suspicion heightened what historian Nancy A. Hewitt has called the "ultraist" wing of female activism with a variety of reforms, temperance included. Temperance, formerly a respectable, middle-class cause, now threatened to undo the ideological work of the past two decades by encouraging women to move beyond the domestic sphere to militate for their rights. The growing linkage of temperance activism and women's rights militancy manifested itself clearly in the pages of *The Lily,* Amelia Bloomer's temperance newspaper. In early 1849, for instance, *The Lily* advocated the formation of female temperance societies but averred that they should "be conducted in a manner becoming the retiring modesty of our sex—without noise or parade, and in accordance with the strictest rules of propriety. The influence we exert in the community is not like the noisy bubbling but like the quiet course of a deeper stream." Later in the year, however, the paper adopted a more strident tone, calling for protection for married women's earnings against the profligacy of drunken husbands, engaging in political commentary and advocacy in relation to prohibitory laws and applauding the efforts of one woman who, finding that "moral suasion was worse than useless, and knowing the law had no protection for her," took matters into her own hands and destroyed a vendor's liquor to prevent him from selling to her husband. This trend continued during the next few years as activist Mary C. Vaughn reversed her opposition to women's political participation, arguing that man's inability to provide adequate representation of women's interests dictated that women must legislate for themselves.[35]

Not surprisingly, men reacted with outrage and alarm. Temperance, a Virginian complained in 1853, had

> engendered *woman's rights societies*—societies whose object is to invest the frail and modest part of the race with the political power of men—to appear on the hustings, in the dirty arena of politics, in the jury box, on the bench, and in our deliberative bodies—measuring arms with the lords of creation, and leaving the sustenance and moral training of their children to chance or accident at home.

In all parts of the United States, men reacted during the early 1850s with alarm to the increasing tendency of temperance women to espouse women's rights. *The New York Evangelist* declared it "morally wrong, and utterly inexpedient, to attempt to compel all those who love the cause of Temperance, to accept the notions of a few, on another and different subject, whatever the subject may be, or to abandon the cause." The not yet venerable *New York Times* reported that an 1853 temperance meeting at Metropolitan Hall convened "nominally to promote the cause of Temperance, but virtually to propagate all the wild extravagances of Woman's Rights." Commenting on the "Amazons and their male backers" who organized the event, the *Times* derided them as "awkward sailors, all" whose "Turkish trousers" could not hide their "lubberly movements" on the deck of the "ship of controversy which they are vainly endeavoring to navigate." Along similar lines, a Washington, D.C., periodical ridiculed a newspaper's laudatory story on Pennsylvania women who militated for a temperance candidate to the state legislature. "Look round upon these women," the writer spat: "we do not say *our* women, because there are some, many high-minded females in the country, sensible and accomplished, who have too much respect for themselves to usurp the prerogative of the other sex, who were designed by their Maker to be lords over women." On a lighter note, the *Spirit of the Times* reported on a "Miss Pellet" who lectured in California "throughout the mines on 'Woman's Rights' and Temperance." She charged admission to her lectures, the paper noted wryly, "no doubt [with] an eye to some of the big lumps being presented to her by the miners."[36]

Organizational changes in women's temperance societies during the late 1840s contributed to the impression that female support of liquor reform masked a campaign for women's rights and an expanded public role. The call for separate women's temperance societies alarmed many middle-class men, who considered it unnecessary, presumptuous, and dangerous. Most middle-class men, along with many women, agreed with the *New York Washingtonian*'s 1847 endorsement of "unobtrusiveness" in woman's temperance work as a preventative for a female "tossing about on the waves of dissension and discord, and struggling in the surf created by the conflicting seas of moral suasion and legal coercion . . . she has thus far been preserved from the curse of such a position." Yet infighting and discontent in the staunchly middle-class Daughters of Temperance, the female auxiliary of the Sons of Temperance, appeared to be leading in precisely this direction. Temperance women appeared to be contending for organizational influence, power, and pride of place, rather than solely for the cause of total abstinence. Dissatisfaction with their subordinate, secondary status moved the Daughters to establish separate Unions so they would have more control over their own affairs. Female sympathy, critics charged, had been withdrawn from the Sons of Temperance out of "sheer opposition" to women, and women's desire "that they might be doing something" for the temperance cause. In apparent criticism, the Daughters called their organizations Unions, as opposed to the Divisions of the Sons. The Sons reacted with condescension to this development, denying that they had lost female support ("Do not Bible and banner presentations all over the country, give it a significant contradiction?") or sneering that the only union women really wanted was to a man in matrimony ("Among the Sons, what great Divisions rise,/ But loud for Union every Daughter cries./ Shame on the sex that to divide began;/ The ladies are for union—to a man!").[37]

Male temperance forces responded with alarm to the spectacle of women engaging in the male activity of institution building and the infighting that accompanied it. By 1847 Daughters of Temperance chapters had proliferated to the point at which state organizations began to demand recognition and autonomy from the first DOT union established in New York in 1845. The New York union had granted charters to DOT groups in other states to organize unions but wished to retain control and authority over them. New York Union No. 1, the first DOT organization, styled itself the "Original Daughters of Temperance" and disparaged the new Grand Union that was coalescing in New York from local unions previously under its control. As a commentator explained a few years later, the Original Daughters consisted of "a comparatively small number of *unions,* as the several separate societies are denominated" run by a "board of directors, who are members of the New York Union, No. 1." The larger DOT group vested power in "representatives from the single unions, in a number of states, that are called Grand Unions." The separation process produced hard feelings among the Daughters of both varieties, and dissension and infighting ensued. In January 1847, Jersey City Union No. 1 abandoned the Originals for the new Grand Union. For its part, the Grand Union attempted to exert control of its own, expelling the Geneva (New York) Union for "insubordination." The Geneva Union promptly allied itself with the Originals, firing back a reply to the "slanderous imputations" of the Grand Union: Geneva complained of high-handed treatment, attributing its expulsion to its members having "refused to bow as menials" to the new organization. Responding to this rancor, the Grand Union regretted that these "difficulties, which arise in the 'best regulated families,' should be published to the world, and be a cause of scandal . . . the only rivalry among sisters should be which can do the most good."[38]

At this juncture male temperance supporters' discomfort with female activism grew. It was during the initial DOT schism in 1847 that the previously noted men's doubts about the efficacy and intentions of moral suasion, which the Daughters advocated, began to surface in the press and elsewhere. As the Grand Union expanded, men's worries about unsupervised women increased. The Grand Union had issued charters to women all over the country so that by 1848 every state had a Grand Union of its own. It became apparent that the movement's size necessitated the formation of a National Union, a prospect welcomed by the Daughters. Men were not so sure, seeing "serious difficulties in this. Some ask—Have ladies had sufficient experience in legislation to undertake the management of such an extensive organization, unaided by the action and counsel of gentlemen?" Men registered continuing worry as the Daughters met in New York in April 1848 to establish a national organization. The ladies' "deliberations . . . were singularly harmonious," except for a "misunderstanding" between representatives from other states and the Grand Union of New York, which appears to have wanted to use the convention to consolidate, rather than decentralize, power and authority. The whole matter should be submitted to a council of the Sons of Temperance scheduled to meet in June, a newspaper commentator prescribed, and there would be "no doubt but all grievances will be satisfactorily explained or removed." Apparently the Daughters did not heed this advice, for in July the "unhappy difference" persisted, with the "senior Grand Union of New York" still refusing to "acknowledge the power of the National Union." By September 1848 the competing factions of New York Daughters vied for public support and recognition with prominent advertisements in the press. The Grand Union, comprised apparently of the "Original" Daughters, decried the newer National Union, insisting that it had "not surrendered its power as head of the Order, nor does it recognize the National Union, the same not having been legally properly organized." The National Union rebuffed this claim, contending that the National Division of the Sons of Temperance recognized their organization and that concerned DOT chapters need not "entertain doubts of forfeiture of charter, moneys, or property by declaring for the National Union" and rejecting the Grand Union. The National Union appears to have prevailed in this struggle: by 1850 it boasted nearly 18,000 members in eight Grand and forty-four subordinate unions.[39]

But this success did not necessarily allay suspicion about the trajectory of female temperance activism. If men had concerns about the intentions and effects of women's temperance activism before the DOT imbroglio, their qualms could only have increased after it. In it they witnessed not the excess of the most radical female activists but respectable middle-class women engaging in the kind of public infighting and organizational politics usually associated with male, not female, spheres of action. A combination of factors—the changing discourse of class and fashion; the gendering (and discrediting) of suasion as female; and the unbecoming rivalry among temperance women—convinced many men of the need for a change in tactics and policy both to address the ravages of the liquor traffic and to contain women's efforts to expand their public role through the temperance movement.

These factors precipitated both the wide support for the prohibitory Maine Law and the backlash against women in the wake of its passage by thirteen states and territories. The Maine Law seemed an ideal solution to many of the difficulties faced by middle-class male temperance advocates. In supplanting moral suasion with legal coercion, it asserted the primacy of masculine over feminine approaches to remedying social ills. By enacting prohibition, it gave women the legal protection against the liquor trade for which they had long implored. As an expected permanent solution to the problem of intemperance, it also obviated the need for women's further work, at least publicly, in the temperance movement. For middle-class men the Maine Law served the dual purposes, or so they thought, of solving the liquor problem and policing the boundary of the domestic and public spheres. The conviction that the liquor problem had been settled helps to explain why middle-class temperance men reacted so ferociously when women continued to insist on a voice and a role in the movement, rather than receding back to their firesides. Once temperance became a political issue, as it clearly had in the debates surrounding the Maine Law, women could have no further role in the matter, unless they were using the antiliquor cause to push a women's rights agenda.

A New Role for Women in Temperance Reform

Still, men had to offer some role for women, and the one they provided reveals the extent to which they intended the Maine Law to reinscribe gender boundaries that had been comprised by decades of women's public temperance activism. Moral suasion, even when exerted as women's heartrending appeals to liquor dealers to cease vending their poison, availed nothing. This acknowldgment posed a problem for middle-class ideologues, especially since any overt or expanded political role for women remained unthinkable. If women's only legitimate weapon against the liquor trade proved useless, what became of the moral power that middle-class ideology claimed inhered in womanhood? How could claims of female agency, upon which the superstructure of middle-class gender ideology rested, be supported in the absence of any demonstrable efficacy of woman's moral power?

Middle-class men answered this conundrum by reformulating female influence to suit the needs of the changed political landscape and the re-quirements of bourgeois gender ideology. Though the Maine Law ensured triumph over those deaf to "reason and justice," the "curing of the Social Heart" remained to be done. Through their sway over men, women could "magnify the law and make it honorable, by creating a *sentiment* toward it that shall make it an honored and essential institution." How might women cure the Social Heart? Not, as it emerged, through civic activism, for thirty years of temperance reform had demonstrated that women's powers of persuasion proved useless in the public sphere. In any event, as one commentator observed well after the adoption of the Maine Law, woman's mission "is not, and has not been, to sway multitudes, or to mould political or ecclesiastical measures from the forum or pulpit. Propa-gandism is not her sphere; and every effort she makes to upheave public opinion, by addresses to mature minds, will be as temporary in effect as the stone cast upon the bosom of a placid lake." In other words, women were not cut out for public activism; their impact on "mature" (read: male) minds would always be limited. But this incapacity did not rule out all possibility of meaningful work. With the shift from suasion to coer-cion, women's "true work" was to "fashion the public taste; to sway the heart" toward greater acceptance of a sober society.[40]

Rather than boisterous advocacy of reform, women contributed most effectively through a "peculiar missionary effort by which the heart more than the reason, and hearts in detail and in private, rather than in masses and in public" could be reached and converted to temperance principles. Female influence might be enlisted in this missionary effort by making ("so far as you can effect it") the Maine Law "the law of your house." Proponents urged middle-class homemakers to emulate the "women of the Revolution . . . [who] considered tea the instrument of tyranny, and [made] its entire banishment" the law of the house. In their roles as hostesses and social arbiters, women could insist upon Maine Law principles at "social parties," as well as at "holidays and annual festivals." Moreover, even in the bosom of their families, women could make the Maine Law the "subject of thought, of reflection and conversation." Women might even implore legislatures for prohibition, provided they remembered their place: "If you cannot legislate, you can petition . . . you can demand protection from those who have power to bestow it." But women's influence for temperance "is not confined to the domestic circle," as these dicta might suggest. Women could "materially advance" this "enterprise of colossal moral grandeur," noted one clergyman without a hint of irony, by "ATTENTION TO ITS CLAIMS, IN THE MENTAL AND MORAL EDUCATION OF CHILDREN."[41]

In essence then, middle-class men entreated women to abandon aspirations for public authority and retreat to the safety of their firesides, where they might more effectively bring a redeemed and reconstituted female influence to bear upon men and children. This represented their desire to restrict women's participation in the increasingly political world of temperance reform, rehabilitate woman's sullied moral agency, and reaffirm the separation of public and private, marketplace and home. Prohibitory legislation as embodied in the Maine Law and similar enactments in other states and territories promised to solve a pressing social problem while shoring up a gender ideology buffeted by political controversy, economic change, and female restiveness. Though supporters of temperance were, as Ian Tyrrell has observed, "improvers" rather than reactionaries their program contained a significant amount of nostalgia for a less complicated past.[42] Their recommendations for women's moral role in the wake of the Maine Law in many respects harked back to earlier models of republican womanhood in which virtuous wives and mothers shaped society by steering husbands and children off the paths of vice. When some women balked at this proposed retreat from public life, male anger flared. As the backlash against female temperance activists in the early 1850s attests, the middle-class male architects of prohibition considered any continued female demands for representation—now that women's pleas for legal protection had been answered—as evidence of bad faith and a decidedly unfeminine desire for political power. In this sense, men attempted through the Maine Law to reseal women in the domestic sphere both for their own protection and for that of men: allowing women to use their feminine wiles beyond the home threatened to corrupt the already sordid world of male politics. The resulting male intransigence and resentment restricted middle-class women's opportunities for participation in temperance reform while driving the most radical women from the movement altogether.

In the end the impact of the gender politics of the Maine Law outlasted that of the legislation itself. Within ten years most state prohibition laws had been repealed, declared unconstitutional, or abandoned as unworkable. Nonetheless, middle-class male efforts to marginalize and silence female temperance activists produced far-reaching consequences. In 1851 the Sons of Temperance's suppression of the Daughters of Temperance resulted in the establishment of the Women's New York State Temperance Society, perhaps the most influential women's temperance organization prior to the Civil War. Headed by Elizabeth Cady Stanton, the Society excluded men from leadership positions and demanded, more stridently than before, that women's voices be heeded by temperance men. The 1853 debacle at the Whole World's Temperance Convention produced a rival convention organized by the dismissed female delegates and their male compatriots. Dubbed the "World's Temperance Convention," this meeting lambasted the pretensions of what its organizers called the "Half World's Temperance Convention" in depicting itself as something other than an "Orthodox White Male Adult Saints' Convention."[43] Women's expulsion from the male-dominated convention, like previous similar incidents, radicalized further many middle-class female temperance advocates. For women like Elizabeth Cady Stanton and Susan B. Anthony, the fierce backlash against female temperance activism after the Maine Law signaled the need to abandon temperance for the larger concerns of suffrage and women's rights. While heightened male hostility limited women's roles in alcohol reform well into the 1870s, ironically it also convinced female activists to create a separate women's rights movement, the influence of which persists into the twenty-first century.

CONCLUSION

The Legacy of Middle-class
Temperance Ideology

Following the expulsion of female activists from prominent roles in the temperance movement during the early 1850s, women's visibility and influence in alcohol reform waned. The post–Maine Law backlash against public female activism proved quite effective, particularly in the middle class, at suppressing women's attempts to extend their moral authority beyond the domestic sphere. In response to this successful rearguard action by middle-class men, the most radical female temperance activists, Susan B. Anthony and Elizabeth Cady Stanton foremost among them, abandoned the temperance movement altogether. Radical women concluded that their best hope for effecting positive changes lay in militating for women's rights rather than more conventional and limited reforms. As Stanton put it in a letter to Anthony, "I do beg of you to let the past be past, and to waste no powder on the Woman's State Temperance Society. We have other and bigger fish to fry."[1] Others remained with the movement, convinced that intemperance constituted such a moral evil and threat to women's interests that it had to be combated at all costs. If this meant satisfying themselves with a decidedly secondary and subordinate role, so be it. To be sure, male temperance advocates did throw a conciliatory bone to women now and then throughout the 1850s. The Carson League, a New York organization devoted to closing dramshops, endorsed female activism, but its influence did not extend far. A new temperance society, the Order of Good Templars, admitted women to membership on terms of nominal equality. In practice, female Templars remained second-ary members, their participation and activities circumscribed by gender roles quite congenial to middle-class ideology. In any event, the Templars exerted little influence until after the Civil War, when the race, rather than the gender, of prospective members became a significant issue for the society. Even the staunchly middle-class Sons of Temperance appeared to extend an olive branch to women during the late 1850s by amending its rituals to permit the admission of women into the order. Women over four-teen years old could join as "visitors, at such times as may be deemed appro-priate," if a membership committee judged the women acceptable and the rest of the members voted in favor. The changes, as reported in a published ritual, were not to be construed as "*forbidding* Divisions to invite visitors to speak and aid and counsel the members of the Order" [emphasis mine]. The 1860 ritual undercut this somewhat hopeful gesture, however, by making clear that Divisions *should* interpret the new rules as "only" debarring female visitors "of the privileges of voting, (except for Lady visitors), holding office, and participating in the special business matters of the Order." Here, as was the case earlier in the decade, temperance men strove to laud women's role in the movement while simultaneously reducing it to virtual insignificance.[2]

While the Civil War furthered the decline of women's public temper-ance activism, it did provide some opportunities for women, mostly in the North, to engage in limited temperance work. Women exerted themselves in the context of male direction of the war, however, and their efforts were nearly always subordinated to male goals, despite the appointment or ascendance of some women to positions of authority and influence. The prominence of women as nurses and nursing administrators is well known, but their experience extended to other activities more closely re-lated to temperance. Northern middle-class women, for instance, worked for the Sanitary Commission as fund-raisers, organizers, and advocates, with the goal of facilitating healthful and morally uplifting camp life for Union soldiers. Part of their duties involved the promotion and advocacy of temperance under circumstances that leant themselves to alcoholic ex-cess whenever troops, whose lives alternated between the boredom of camp life and the terror of combat, could obtain liquor. Upholding tem-perance, respectability, and morality in the army, though consistent with antebellum gender roles, proved to be of marginal utility in the desperate struggle that the war rapidly became. Men and women soon realized that the most meaningful female contributions to victory lay elsewhere: in car-ing for the sick and wounded, raising funds to provide for the welfare of the troops, and filling essential jobs for which no men could be spared.[3]

Moreover, due to its unique context, women's wartime work for tem-perance or other causes did not present the same opportunities for testing gender boundaries that antebellum reform had offered. With both the Union and Confederacy focused on national survival and military triumph,

women's entrance into areas previously considered unsuitable for females—nursing, office work, or manufacturing, for instance—could be understood as a patriotic sacrifice demanded by extraordinary circumstances
that should be lauded and abandoned as soon as hostilities ended. Some
radical women who had promoted women's rights during the antebellum
era seized the opportunity presented by the national crisis to promote
women's activism and participation in public affairs. Former temperance
advocates Elizabeth Cady Stanton and Susan B. Anthony, for instance, organized the Woman's National Loyal League, which mobilized tens of
thousands of Northern women in the Union cause. By and large, however,
women's temperance activism, already diminished by the backlash of the
1850s, receded still further during the war years.[4]

Not until the early 1870s did women resume public militancy against
intemperance and the liquor trade. In late December 1873, a number of
respectable, middle-class women in the Ohio towns of Hillsboro and
Washington Court House, inspired by the popular lecturer Diocletian
Lewis, organized to combat the liquor dealers in their communities. Gathering together groups of pious wives, mothers, and sisters, the women
marched to local drugstores, groceries, and taverns, praying with the own-
ers and exhorting them to sign a pledge to abandon selling liquor. This
new activism struck many, including some of the participating women
among them, as unprecedented and controversial. Praying in public, let
alone exhorting men and advocating a position on a provocative issue, violated gender norms that many in the middle class and beyond had come
to regard as natural. Still, buoyed by the conviction of their religious obligation to resist evil as well as a sense of aggrieved womanhood produced
by the depredations of the liquor trade, the women persisted, and their efforts bore fruit. Several liquor vendors agreed to forsake the trade, and
tales of this success circulated quickly to nearby towns, where other
women emulated the tactics and approach of their sister activists. The
Women's Crusade, as this movement came to be known, "swept the Midwest like a prairie fire and spread through the West and parts of the East
during the winter of 1873/74. Thousands of women in hundreds of communities took to the streets and invaded saloons and shops that sold alcoholic beverages, in an attempt to disrupt and close down the liquor trade."
Though the direct results of the Women's Crusade proved ephemeral, the
revivification of female temperance activism it produced contributed directly to the establishment of the Woman's Christian Temperance Union
in 1874. Ultimately, the WCTU grew into an international women's organization that engaged directly and independently in public activism,
advocated a variety of women's rights causes as well as temperance, and
figured prominently in the political campaigns and debates that would
culminate in the constitutional amendments that established prohibition
and woman's suffrage in the early twentieth century.[5]

It would be easy to conclude from the closer proximity of postbellum women's temperance activism to national prohibition and women's suffrage that the developments of the late nineteenth century, rather than those of the antebellum era, demand scholarly study and recognition. Certainly historians have devoted more attention to the WCTU and postwar temperance activism than to its precursors. A closer look reveals, however, that the more assertive, politically oriented, and expansive temperance campaigns that women pursued in the 1870s and beyond owed much to the gender ideology elaborated by middle-class reformers early in the century. In personnel, rhetoric, and tactics, antebellum middle-class temperance ideology influenced female participation in alcohol reform and the campaign for women's rights in ways that shaped later efforts. Furthermore, the gendered components of middle-class temperance ideology shaped American culture—particularly its depiction and treatment of women—in similarly lasting ways. We will conclude by considering in turn the impact of the antebellum temperance movement's ideology of gender in each of these areas.

Many of the women who assumed leadership roles in the Woman's Crusade of 1873/74, and later in the WCTU, had personal experience or family background in the antebellum temperance movement. Eliza J. Thompson, one of the early leaders of the Woman's Crusade in Hillsboro, Ohio, for example, had supported temperance for decades. A fifty-seven-year-old wife and mother in 1873, Thompson grew up in a prosperous, solidly middle-class home where she internalized ideas about gender that led her both to oppose alcohol and to hesitate to speak out against it in public. A sense of duty to employ woman's superior piety as a weapon against the liquor trade won out over her public reticence, as it had for many women during the antebellum years. "Mother" Eliza Stewart, another stalwart of the Women's Crusade, also grew up during the antebellum years. Born in 1816, she matured during the height of middle-class formation and temperance reform. Her opposition to the liquor trade grew during this critical period, and work for the Sanitary Commission during the Civil War gave her organizational experience she would later use in the postbellum temperance movement. Similarly, Frances Willard, perhaps the most influential female temperance reformer of the nineteenth century, acquired an antipathy to alcohol during her middle-class Methodist upbringing in the decades before the Civil War.[6]

In tactics and rhetoric, women's postwar temperance activism owed much to its antebellum roots in middle-class ideology. The tavern visitations and later vigilante actions pursued by militants like Carrie Nation replicated and extended tactics pursued by antebellum women. Women's postwar political action, which included petition drives, appeals to legisla-tors, and temperance publishing, had precedents in the activities of mid-century female activists. More importantly, the emphasis on liquor as a woman's issue that originated during the antebellum period of middle-class ideological formation persisted as a dominant focus for female activism and public discussion of alcohol abuse. The threat posed by drinking and drunkards to women and middle-class homes, and women's responsibility to use their superior moral authority to protect those homes, have proved to be key themes and effective rhetorical strategies in debates about gender, alcohol, woman suffrage, and a variety of other policy issues.

A few examples illustrate the continuing significance of gendered discourse within alcohol reform. During the height of the WCTU's influence in the late nineteenth century, leaders such as Annie Wittenmyer and Frances Willard confronted the same resistance to female participation in public affairs that their antebellum counterparts in the temperance movement encountered. Their strategy to legitimatize public advocacy of prohibition and other issues centered on presenting the WCTU program as activism in the service of "Home Protection." Women entered the public, even political, realm in the interests of preserving and protecting the home as a refuge from the corrupt outer world; here women could minister to work-weary men and nurture innocent children. Women's innate religious and moral sensibilities suited them to this role within the home, while the past fifty years of unsuccessful male attempts to protect home and family from the liquor trade demonstrated the necessity of women's intervention beyond the domestic circle. As should be apparent by now, both this strategy and the ideology of gender on which it is based emerged during the process of middle-class formation earlier in the century. The WCTU's appropriation of it proved wildly successful, particularly at drawing women who would otherwise eschew a public role into the battle against liquor. As historian Elaine Frantz Parsons noted, "it was precisely reformers' insistence that their ultimate goal was to return to the home that made the WCTU so successful in convincing moderate women to embrace their radical, invasive tactics."[7]

In the same way, American women's embrace of the gendered rhetoric of alcohol reform profoundly influenced the female entry into politics. Alcohol, argued Catherine G. Murdoch, "more than slavery or suffrage or any other single cause, effected American women's politicization." By making activism and political participation respectable, even admirable, the gendered rhetoric of reform that emerged from the antebellum middle class facilitated broad female participation in the campaigns for suffrage and legal equality. This proved particularly important as the dual struggles for suffrage and prohibition intensified during the early twentieth century. Ideas, concepts, and linguistic conventions that originated during the early nineteenth century "permeated the rhetoric of woman suffragists who blamed the 'liquor interests' for the defeat of both suffrage and Prohibition." Clearly the antebellum awakening of non-radical women's political consciousness as well as the recruitment of these women into political causes shaped the course of women's rights agitation in significant ways.[8]

The salience of woman's responsibility to protect the home from the depredations of drunkenness, even if she had to leave her fireside to fulfill it, continued into the twentieth century. Appeals by female activists who cited the importance of protecting men from the seductive lure of the saloon and their families from the penury and disgrace that proceeded from male patronage of these dens of vice figured prominently in the campaign for prohibition that ultimately resulted in the adoption of the Nineteenth Amendment. Even after the enactment of prohibition, the gendered ideology of reform that originated in the antebellum middle class's battle against alcohol retained its rhetorical purchase. During the political maneuverings that surrounded efforts to repeal the prohibition amendment, for instance, women on both sides of the issue deployed the imperative of home protection as justification for their position. Among the "drys," women argued for the continuing need to defend American families against the manifest evil of liquor and the crime that accompanied its smuggling and sale during Prohibition. Their "wet" counterparts, on the other hand, contended that the ill-considered and unenforceable ban on liquor threatened the moral fiber of American families by making disregard for the law acceptable and common. The federal government's inability to suppress bootlegging and related criminal activity, they urged, made lawlessness glamorous and profitable. Mothers concerned about promoting a home environment consistent with effective moral education and respect for law, in this view, could only support repeal.[9]

In popular culture, too, the middle-class ideology of gender that emerged from the early nineteenth-century temperance movement exerts an influence that has lasted into the twentieth-first century. In particular, temperance literature's frequent recourse to images of male violence against women and female fortitude in the face of male abuse both shaped and reflected popular representations of women. Depictions of innocent women imperiled by debauched men in temperance tracts, lectures, short stories, and plays represented one arc in a larger Anglo-American cultural trajectory that had its roots in the seduction tales of the early eighteenth century. In novels such as those by Samuel Richardson, as well as in other print genres, authors portrayed women beset by men's immoral advances, their virtue threatened by superior guile or physical force. Stories of virtuous maidens tempted, seduced, or ruined by lustful men valorized female resistance to male mistreatment, thereby buttressing emerging bourgeois notions about the moral attributes of the sexes. In the process, various forms of popular culture eroticized female endangerment and suffering, depicting as attractive and desirable the woman who could resist seduction and abuse, whatever travails she had to endure in so doing. This tendency found expression in the literature produced by a variety of middle-class reform movements during the early nineteenth century: moral reform, anti-prostitution, antislavery, and others, in addition to temperance. As we have seen, temperance literature's distinctive contribution to this cultural tendency lay in its positioning the loyal and long-suffering drunkard's wife as the ideal of womanhood, her femininity linked to, perhaps even made possible by, her experience of male violence. This ideological trajectory continued beyond the nineteenth century, adapting to new circumstances, as well as new media. The advent of film, for instance, in conjunction with more liberal attitudes toward sex, has sexualized, as well as eroticized, depictions and images of violence against women. The reach of film, and later television and video, moreover, has saturated popular culture with these images. One need only consider films ranging from the silent era's *Perils of Pauline* to slasher films of the late twentieth century to the genre of "extreme" pornography in the twenty-first to recognize the continuing resonance of representations of women and gender popularized and made respectable by antebellum temperance literature. Literary critic Glenn Hendler has argued for the significance of Washingtonian narratives as "unlikely but significant progenitor[s] of many popular cultural forms." The "reformed and transformed drunkard," Hendler contends, "stands near the beginning of a history of American mass culture." If Hendler is correct, it would be equally appropriate to note that the drunkard's wife stood by his side at this moment of cultural origin.[10]

Thus while temperance has lost currency as a political issue and prohibition has long been abandoned as a viable tactic in the war against drunkenness, the issues and ideologies created by middle-class Americans during the early years of the nineteenth century remain powerful and relevant. The denomination of women as the primary victims of drunkenness as well as the most obvious moral arbiters in the battle against destructive drinking ramified beyond the middle class to pervade American society. The organization is, after all, Mothers against Drunk Driving, not fathers. Other notions of gender and temperance have survived their middle-class antebellum origins as well, especially those associated with women's abuse of alcohol and other drugs. Over the last twenty years or so, increased attention has been directed to providing treatment options tailored to the specific needs of female alcoholics and addicts. These initiatives, though often well-intentioned, sometimes proceed from the assumption that modern women's departure from the domestic sphere for the workplace produces stresses that result in substance abuse and have done little to eliminate the "special stigma" attached to women, especially mothers, who abuse alcohol and drugs.[11] Thus while the conditions that led an anxious middle class to employ temperance reform in order to construct an ideology of gender that disadvantaged women have changed, that ideology's effects continue to be felt.

Notes

Introduction—Temperance Literature and Misogyny

1. Ian R. Tyrrell, *Sobering Up: From Temperance to Prohibition in Antebellum America, 1800–1860* (Westport: Greenwood Press, 1979); Jed Dannenbaum, *Drink and Disorder: Temperance Reform in Cincinnati from the Washingtonian Revival to the WCTU* (Urbana: University of Illinois Press, 1984); and Jack Blocker, Jr., *American Temperance Movements: Cycles of Reform* (Boston: Twayne Publishers, 1989). For women's participation in temperance, consult Ian R. Tyrrell, "Women and Temperance in Antebellum America, 1830–1860," *Civil War History* 28, no. 2 (1982): 128–52; and Ruth M. Alexander, "'We are Engaged as a Band of Sisters': Class and Domesticity in the Washingtonian Temperance Movement, 1840–1850," *Journal of American History* 75, no. 3 (1988): 763–85. William J. Rorabaugh's classic *The Alcoholic Republic: An American Tradition* (New York: Oxford University Press, 1979), provides data on the upsurge in drinking during the early decades of the nineteenth century.

2. Jed Dannenbaum, "The Origins of Temperance Activism and Militancy among American Women," *Journal of Social History* 15, no. 2 (1981): 235–52.

3. A sampling from the past several years includes Beth A. Salerno, *Sister Societies: Women's Antislavery Organizations in Antebellum America* (DeKalb: Northern Illinois University Press, 2005); Alisse Portnoy, *Their Right to Speak Women's Activism in the Indian and Slave Debates* (Cambridge: Harvard University Press, 2005); Susan Zaeske, *Signatures of Citizenship: Petitioning, Antislavery, and Women's Political Identity* (Chapel Hill: University of North Carolina Press, 2003); Michael D. Pierson, *Free Hearts and Homes: Gender and American Antislavery Politics* (Chapel Hill: University of North Carolina Press, 2003); and Deborah B. Van Broekhoven, *The Devotion of These Women: Rhode Island in the Antislavery Network* (Amherst: University of Massachusetts Press, 2002).

4. On prohibition as an abject failure, see Richard Hofstader's classic *The Age of Reform* (New York: Vintage Books, 1955); Andrew Sinclair, *Era of Excess: A Social History of Prohibition* (New York: Harper and Row, 1962); and, more recently, Edward Behr, *Prohibition: Thirteen Years that Changed America* (New York: Arcade Publishers, 1996). Behr's book was the accompaniment to a BBC television film of the same name. Many works of women's history argue for the centrality of abolition to the women's rights movement. A recent textbook by Kathryn Kish Sklar, *Women's Rights Emerges within the Anti-Slavery Movement, 1830–1870: A Brief History with Documents* (Boston: Bedford, 2000), makes this point succinctly.

5. Carol Mattingly, *Well-Tempered Women: Nineteenth-Century Temperance Rhetoric* (Carbondale: Southern Illinois University Press, 1998), 22–23; Elizabeth Cady Stanton, Susan B. Anthony, and Matilda Joslyn Gage, eds., *History of*

Woman Suffrage (hereafter *HWS*) vol. 1 (New York: Fowler and Wells, 1881), 512–13; Ida Husted Harper, *The Life and Work of Susan B. Anthony*, vol. 1 (Indianapolis: Hollenbeck, 1898), 95.

6. There are some exceptions to this generalization. See, for instance, Mattingly, *Well-Tempered Women*, and Janet Zollinger Giele, *Two Paths to Women's Equality: Temperance, Suffrage, and the Origins of Modern Feminism* (New York: Twayne Publishers, 1995). In her *Woman Suffrage and the Origins of Liberal Feminism in the United States, 1820–1920* (Cambridge: Harvard University Press, 1996), Suzanne M. Marilley acknowledged the importance of the WCTU and Frances Willard's "sophisticated ideological trickery" (221) in the drive for woman suffrage but attributed its influence to Willard's canny deployment of a "feminism of fear," rather than the "feminism of personal development" that would ultimately win the day and result in the passage of the Nineteenth Amendment.

7. For more on the continuing salience of antebellum temperance ideology, especially as it related to gender, see David Kyvig, *Repealing National Prohibition*, 2nd ed. (Kent: Kent State University Press, 2000); Ruth Bordin, *Woman and Temperance: The Quest for Power and Liberty, 1873–1900* (New Brunswick: Rutgers University Press, 1990); Kenneth D. Rose, *American Women and the Repeal of Prohibition* (New York: New York University Press, 1996); Catherine Gilbert Murdock, *Domesticating Drink: Women, Men, and Alcohol in America, 1870–1940* (Baltimore: Johns Hopkins University Press, 1998); and Elaine Frantz Parsons, *Manhood Lost: Fallen Drunkard and Redeeming Women in the Nineteenth-Century United States* (Baltimore: Johns Hopkins University Press, 2003).

8. This appears to be a propitious time to embark on an analysis of the impact of class formation on gender ideology and the temperance movement. As Gary J. Kornblith noted recently, *"class is back* in the study of late eighteenth- and early nineteenth-century American history" after roughly two decades of eclipse by the cultural turn in history and related disciplines. See his "Introduction to the Symposium on Class in the Early Republic," *Journal of the Early Republic* 25, no. 4 (2005): 523–26 (quote on 523). In addition, I have found the following particularly provocative and useful: Mary P. Ryan, *Cradle of the Middle Class: The Family in Oneida County, New York, 1790–1865* (New York: Cambridge University Press, 1981); Karen Halttunen, *Confidence Men and Painted Women: A Study in Middle-Class Culture in America, 1830–1870* (New Haven: Yale University Press, 1982); Carroll Smith-Rosenberg, *Disorderly Conduct: Visions of Gender in Victorian America* (New York: Oxford University Press, 1985); Stuart M. Blumin, *The Emergence of the Middle Class: Social Experience in the American City, 1760–1900* (New York: Cambridge University Press, 1989); Richard L. Bushman, *The Refinement of America: Persons, Houses, Cities* (New York: Knopf, 1992); Catherine E. Kelly, *In the New England Fashion: Reshaping Women's Lives in the Nineteenth Century* (Ithaca: Cornell University Press, 1999); and Brian Roberts, *American Alchemy: The California Gold Rush and Middle-Class Culture* (Chapel Hill: University of North Carolina Press, 2000).

9. John Marsh, *A Half Century Tribute to the Cause of Temperance* (New York: American Temperance Union, 1851), 27. For more on the extent of temperance publication, see Mark Y. Hanley, *Beyond a Christian Commonwealth: The Protestant Quarrel with the American Republic, 1830–1860* (Chapel Hill: University of North Carolina Press, 1994). On print culture in the early nineteenth-century United States, see Ronald Zboray, *A Fictive People: Antebellum Economic Development and the American Reading Public* (New York: Oxford University Press, 1993); and Isabelle Lehuu, *Carnival on the Page: Popular Print Media in Antebellum America* (Chapel Hill: University of North Carolina Press, 2000).

10. On separate spheres, see Nancy Cott, *The Bonds of Womanhood: "Woman's Sphere" in New England, 1780–1835* (New Haven: Yale University Press, 1977). Though women's historians have dissected this concept, questioning its validity as an accurate description of the antebellum society and gender arrangements, it remains an important point of reference. If antebellum Americans did not actually organize their lives according to the doctrine of separate spheres, they did talk about it endlessly, often using it to justify actions and social arrangements. Thus for a discussion of middle-class ideology, separate spheres remains an essential construct. For more on separate spheres, including recent criticism of its unreflective use, see the articles in Cathy N. Davidson and Jessamyn Hatcher, eds., *No More Separate Spheres!* (Durham: Duke University Press, 2002).

11. Scott C. Martin, "'A Star that Gathers Lustre from the Gloom of Night': Wives, Marriage and Gender in Early Nineteenth-Century American Temperance Reform," *Journal of Family History* 29, no. 3 (2004): 274–92; and Scott C. Martin, "Violence, Gender and Intemperance in Early National Connecticut," *Journal of Social History* 24, no. 2 (2000): 309–25.

12. See, for example, Nancy Hewitt, *Women's Activism and Social Change: Rochester, New York, 1822–1872* (Ithaca: Cornell University Press, 1984); Lori D. Ginzberg, *Women and the Work of Benevolence: Morality, Politics and Class in the Nineteenth-Century United States* (New Haven: Yale University Press, 1990); Elizabeth R. Varon, *We Mean to Be Counted: White Women and Politics in Antebellum Virginia* (Chapel Hill: University of North Carolina Press, 1998); and Bruce Dorsey, *Reforming Men and Women: Gender in the Antebellum City* (Ithaca: Cornell University Press, 2002).

13. Brian Harrison, *Drink and the Victorians: The Temperance Question in England, 1815–1872* (Pittsburgh: University of Pittsburgh Press, 1971); Janet Saltzman Chafetz and Anthony Gary Dworkin, *Female Revolt: Women's Movements in World and Historical Perspective* (Totowa: Rowman and Allanheld, 1986); Lillian Lewis Shiman, *Women and Leadership in Nineteenth-Century England* (New York: St. Martin's Press, 1992); Craig Heron, *Booze: A Distilled History* (Toronto: Between the Lines, 2003).

14. John Quist, *Restless Visionaries: The Social Roots of Antebellum Reform in Alabama and Michigan* (Baton Rouge: Louisiana State University Press, 1998), 7, 15, 465, 463.

1—Female Intemperance

1. A. B. Johnson, *An Address to the Utica Temperance Society . . . July 29, 1829* (Utica: William Williams, 1829), 12–13; Charles Sprague, *An Address . . . May 31, 1827* (Boston: R. Butts, 1827), 13; Stephen P. Hill, *Sermon on the Subject of Temperance . . . published at its request* (Baltimore: Sands and Neilson, 1836), 13.

2. Tyrrell, "Women and Temperance," 139, and *Sobering Up*, 181; Harry Gene Levine, "Temperance and Women in 19th-Century United States," in *Alcohol and Drug Problems in Women: Research Advances in Alcohol and Drug Problems*, Vol. 5, ed. Orianna Josseau Kalant (New York: Plenum Press, 1980), 34; Mark Lender, "A Special Stigma: Women and Alcoholism in the Late 19th and Early 20th Centuries," in *Alcohol Interventions*, ed. David L. Strug, S. Priyandarsini, and Merton M. Hyman, 41–57 (Binghamton: Haworth Press, 1986); Nicholas O. Warner, *Spirits of America: Intoxication in Nineteenth-Century American Literature* (Norman: University of Oklahoma Press, 1997), 183.

3. Jessica Warner, "The Sanctuary of Sobriety: The Emergence of Temperance as a Feminine Virtue in Tudor and Stuart England," *Addiction* 92, no. 1 (1997): 97–111; A. Lynn Martin, "Deviant Drinking or Deviant Women?" www.arts. adelaide.edu.au/CentreFoodDrink/Articles/DeviantDrinking.html (accessed 22 May, 2003); Barbara Leigh, "'A Thing so Fallen, and so Vile': Images of Drinking and Sexuality

in Women," *Contemporary Drug Problems* 22, no. 3 (1995): 415–34: Gregory Austin, *Alcohol in Western Society from Antiquity to 1800* (Santa Barbara: ABC Clio, 1985); and Marian Sandmaier, *The Invisible Alcoholics: Women and Alcohol Abuse in America* (New York: McGraw Hill, 1980).

4. W. J. Rorabaugh, *The Alcoholic Republic*, 12; *The Constitution of the Massachusetts Society for the Suppression of Intemperance . . . and Members of Said Society* (Boston: Sewell Phelps, 1818), 10; *Facts to Think About, and What's the Remedy?* (Philadelphia: C. Sherman, 1850), 42; Robert M. Hartley, *Intemperance in Cities and Large Towns: Showing Its Physical, Social, and Moral Effects; also The Means for Its Prevention and Removal* (New York: John F. Trow, 1851), 207.

5. *A Warning Voice Against Intemperance* 1, no. 1 (Philadelphia: John Clarke, 1828), 4; *The Genius of Temperance, Philanthropist and People's Advocate* 7, no. 28 (1830): 1; *Genius of Temperance* 7, no. 33 (1833): 3; *New York Organ and Temperance Safeguard* 7, no. 13 (25 Sep 1847): 102; *New York Organ* 7, no. 14 (1847): 108.

6. Levine, "Temperance and Women," 34; Alexander Gunn, *A Sermon on the Prevailing Vice of Intemperate Drinking . . . New Year, 1813* (New York: Whiting and Watson, 1813), 16; Joseph Harrington, *Address, Delivered at Roxbury . . . June 30, 1820* (Boston: Joseph T. Buckingham, 1820), 6; Thomas J. O'Flaherty, *A Medical Essay on Drinking, by Thomas J. O'Flaherty, M.D.* (Hartford: Hudson and Skinner, 1828), 28–29; "A Drunken Woman," *The Dew Drop* 2, no. 17 (1844): 1; "Drunken Women," *Journal of the American Temperance Union* 22, no. 8 (1858), 157.

7. T. S. Arthur, *The Ruined Family and Other Tales* (Philadelphia: Godey & M'Michael, 1843); Lydia H. Sigourney, "Louisa Wilson," in *Water-drops* (New York: Robert Carter, 1848); Osgood Bradbury, *The Distiller's Daughter: Or, The Power of Woman* (n.p., [1844?]); Walt Whitman, *Franklin Evans, or the Inebriate. A Tale of the Times* (New York: J. Winchester, 1842).

8. David S. Reynolds, "Black Cats and Delirium Tremens: Temperance and the American Renaissance," in *The Serpent in the Cup: Temperance in American Literature*, ed. Reynolds and Debra J. Rosenthal (Amherst: University of Massachusetts Press, 1997), 22–23, 24–25; Isaac F. Shepard, "Confessions of a Female Inebriate (1842)," in *Drunkard's Progress: Narratives of Addiction, Despair, and Recovery*, ed. John W. Crowley (Baltimore: Johns Hopkins University Press, 1999), 78–79; Bradbury, *Distiller's Daughter*, 47; Sigourney, "Louisa Wilson," in *Water-drops*, 118; *The History of the Bottle* (New York: Oliver and Brother, 1848), 28.

9. *Who Slew All These? An Authentic Narrative*, in *The Temperance Volume* (New York: American Tract Society, 1834), 2–3; "The Double Victim," *Columbia Washingtonian* (Hudson, New York) 1, no. 49 (1843): 1; "Horrible," *The Pearl* 1, no. 11 (1846): 86; *The Old Brewery, and the New Mission House at the Five Points. By the Ladies of the Mission* (New York: Stringer and Townsend, 1854), 199.

10. Thomas H. Appleton, Jr., "'Moral Suasion Has Had Its Day,': From Temperance to Prohibition in Antebellum Kentucky," in *A Mythic Land Apart: Reassessing Southerners and Their History*, ed. John David Smith and Thomas H. Appleton, Jr., (Westport: Greenwood Press, 1997) 19–20; Jane H. Pease and William H. Pease, *Ladies, Women and Wenches: Choice and Constraint in Antebellum Charleston and Boston* (Chapel Hill: University of North Carolina Press, 1990), 145; *Report of a Committee Appointed by the Pennsylvania Society . . . February 14, 1828* (Philadelphia: Atkinson and Alexander, 1828), 7; *Plain Facts . . . Massachusetts Temperance Society* (Boston: Ford and Damrell, 1834), 21; *Ceremonies, Etc. New York State Inebriate Asylum, Binghamton, New York* (New York: Wynkoop, Hallenbeck and Thomas, 1859), 175.

11. Tyrrell, "Women and Temperance," 139, and *Sobering Up*, 181.

12. Levine, "Temperance and Women," 34.

13. Baron Stow, *An Address . . . Nov. 26, 1829* (Portsmouth: Miller and Brewster, 1830), 13; John T. Kirkland, *A Sermon . . . May 27, 1814* (Boston: John Eliot, 1814), 8; Luther Fraseur Dimmick, *Intemperance: A Sermon . . . April 1, 1824* (Newburyport: Charles Whipple, 1824), 12; *On Intemperance,* in *The Publications of the American Tract Society* (Boston: Flagg and Gould, 1824), 48.

14. Joshua Bates, *Two Sermons on Intemperance . . . April 8, 1813* (Boston: Samuel T. Armstrong, 1813), 11; *On Intemperance,* 64; Stephen Badger, *The Substance of Two Discourses . . . Minister of that Place* (Boston: Samuel T. Armstrong, 1811), 16–17.

15. Drunken wives appeared seldom as objects of scorn or criticism in temperance literature. Though wives received their share of criticism from temperance advocates, it was usually for not supporting their husbands' sobriety, rather than for their own drunkenness. Most frequently wives appeared as victims of male drunkenness. On wives in the temperance movement, see Scott C. Martin, "'A Star That Gathers Lustre from the Gloom of Night,'" 274–92.

16. *The Minutes of a Temperance Convention . . . the 28th and 29th of November, 1837* (Maysville: L. Collins, 1837), 8; *Annals of the Ladies' American Home Education Society and Temperance Union, Vol. IX* (Boston: J. Howe, 1847), 9; Albert Barnes, "Are You a Mother?" *Journal of the American Temperance Union* 1, no. 8 (1837): 116.

17. *Address of the Chillicothe Association . . . Use of Ardent Spirits* (Chillicothe: John Andrews, 1815), 11; Harrington, *Address,* 16.

18. Thomas Trotter, *An Essay, Medical, Philosophical . . . on the Human Body* (Philadelphia: Anthony Finley, 1813), 132; William B. Carpenter, *The Physiology of Temperance . . . on the Healthy Human System* (London: Henry G. Bohn, 1853), 36, 37, 38.

19. "A Dialogue between a Father and Son," 18; and "My Mother," 24, both in *The Evils of Intemperance, Exemplified in Poetry and Prose* (Boston: N. Boynton, 1829).

20. Lindsly, "Essay," 135.

21. R. D. Mussey, *An Address on Ardent Spirit . . . June 5, 1827* (n.p., n.d.), 8; Daniel Frost, Jr., *An Address . . . Canterbury, Conn.* (New Bedford: B. Lindsey & Son, 1829), 7; *The Constitution and Address of the Baltimore Temperance Society . . . of Maryland* (Baltimore: J. D. Troy, 1830), 33; George W. Bethune, *The Substance of an Address . . . at Rome* (Utica: William Williams, 1833), 12; Frederic A. Whitney, *Address on Temperance . . . Dec. 21, 1845* (Boston: Benjamin H. Greene, 1846), 18; Justin Edwards, *The Temperance Manual* (New York: American Tract Society, n.d.), 38.

22. Lunsford P. Vandell, "Doctor Vandell's Address," *Proceedings and Second Annual Report of the Kentucky Temperance Society . . . Lundsford P. Vandell, M.D.* (Frankfurt: A. G. Hodges, 1832), 13; Marcus E. Cross, *The Mirror of Intemperance, and History of the Temperance Reform* (Philadelphia: John T. Lange, 1849), 207; "Doings of a Grog Shop," *The Temperance Annual and Cold Water Magazine* (Philadelphia: Drew & Scammell, 1843), 23.

23. Shepard, "Confessions of a Female Inebriate," 74; Reynolds, "Black Cats and Delirium Tremens," 28; Maria Lamas, *The Glass; or, The Trials of Helen More* (Philadelphia: Martin E. Harmstead, 1849), 22.

24. Thomas Skinner, *Another Voice from the Grave . . . Dying Request* (Philadelphia: Religious Tract Society, 1819), 6; Hartley, *Intemperance in Cities,* 139, 121, 122.

25. *Macbeth* II, iii; Benjamin Rush, "An Inquiry into the Effects of Ardent Spirits upon the Human Body and Mind" (1784), reprinted as "The Effects of Ardent Spirits upon the Human Body and Mind," in *The Temperance Volume; Embracing the Temperance Tracts of the American Tract Society* (New York: American Tract Society, 1834), 266; *Inquiries and Observations, upon the Diseases of the Mind* (Philadelphia: Kimber and Richardson, 1812), quoted in Ronald Walters, *Primers for Prudery: Sexual Advice to Victorian America* (Englewood Cliffs: Prentice Hall, 1974),

111. On alcohol's role as an aphrodisiac, see David T. Courtwright, *Forces of Habit: Drugs and the Making of the Modern World* (Cambridge: Harvard University Press, 2001), 100–102; Harrison, *Drink and the Victorians*, 39; and the sources cited in footnote 3. The connection in the popular mind between drinking and female promiscuity persisted in the public mind throughout the nineteenth century and into the twentieth. See Sandmaier, *The Invisible Alcoholics*; and Murdock, *Domesticating Drink*, esp. 71–79.

26. Badger, *Substance of Two Discourses*, 8–9.

27. Daniel O. Morton, *"Wine is a Mocker, Strong Drink is Raging": A Discourse . . . Vermont Temperance Society* (Montpelier: E. P. Morton, 1828), 11; Aikin, *Moral Reform*, 16; Nathaniel S. Prime, *The Pernicious Effects of Intemperance . . . Nov. 5, 1811* (Brooklyn: Adlen Spooner, 1812), 8; Thomas Herttell, *An Expose of the Causes . . . Obviated* (New York: E. Conrad, 1819), 28; *The Evils of Drunkenness* (New York: D. Fanshaw, 1820), 3; David M'Conaughy, A. M., *Drunkenness Excludes from Heaven . . . V.I, 10* (Gettysburg: Robert G. Harper, 1827), 8; "Intemperance," *New York Washington Reformer and Ladies' Literary Journal* 1, no. 16 (1843): 108.

28. Leigh, "A Thing So Fallen," 421; Rush, "Inquiry," 2; Orson S. Fowler, *Fowler on Matrimony . . . Companions for Life*, Stereotype edition, 20th Thousand (New York: O. S. and L. N. Fowler, 1842), 73; E. P. Rogers, *Poems Delivered at the Delavan Union, from 1845 to 1850* (Newark: A. Stephen Holbrook, 1850), 6.

29. Michael Ryan, *Prostitution in London . . . Abuses of the Reproductive Function* (London: H. Bailliere, 1839), 236, 237, 238; E. L. Cleveland, *A Discourse . . . Oct. 21st, 1850* (New Haven: J. H. Benham, 1850), 11; William Sanger, *The History of Prostitution: Its Extent, Causes and Effects throughout the World* (New York: Eugenics Publishing Co., 1939; orig. pub. 1858), 541; *Constitution and By-Laws of Washington Union . . . February 9, 1846* (Cincinnati: Caleb Clark, 1846), 11. On the connection between intemperance and prostitution in England, see also Harrison, *Drink and the Victorians*, 50, 175, and A. Lynn Martin, "Deviant Drinking."

30. Ryan, *Prostitution*, 218; Sanger, *History of Prostitution*, 518–19, 489.

31. Larry Whiteaker, *Seduction, Prostitution, and Moral Reform in New York, 1830–1860* (New York: Garland Publishing, 1997), 36, ff. 10; Ryan, *Prostitution*, 219; Skinner, *Another Voice from the Grave*, 6; Justin Edwards, *Joy in heaven over the Penitent . . . December 18, 1825* (Boston: T. R. Marvin, 1825), 17; *Constitution of the Society and Directors of the Penitent Female's Refuge. Adopted April 14, 1819* (Boston: True and Weston, 1819), 5; *Ninth Annual Report . . . Read at their Annual Meeting* (Boston: T. R. Marvin, 1828), 13; *Report of the Managers of the Magdalen Society for 1840* (Philadelphia: Joseph and William Kite, 1841), 5.

32. *The First Annual Report . . . October 26, 1818* (New York: J. Seymour, 1818), 16; "I Am Afraid There Is a God," in *Temperance Tales*, vol. 1 (Boston: Whipple & Damrell, 1838), 30; Bradbury, *The Distiller's Daughter* (n.p., n.d.), 40, 29.

33. Ryan, *Prostitution*, 238; *The Anniversary Report . . . Published by the Society* (Philadelphia: Henry H. Porter, 1831), 15.

34. *A Voice from Leverett Prison . . . March 16, 1836* (orig.: Boston: Printed for the Proprietor, 1836), 10th ed., 21; John Marsh, *A Discourse . . . in Several Churches of the City* (New York: American Temperance Union, 1848), 15. The verse is from Robert Pollok (1798–1827), *The Course of Time: A Poem in Ten Books* (London: T. Cadell, 1827).

35. Whitman, *Franklin Evans*, 144; Mrs. Maria Buckley, *Edith Moreton* (Philadelphia: Stavely and M'Calla, 1852), 41; *To the Honorable the Senate and House of Representatives of the Commonwealth of Pennsylvania* (1849), 5.

36. Levine, "Temperance and Women," 34.

37. Louis Hartz, *The Liberal Tradition in America: An Interpretation of American Political Thought since the Revolution* (New York: Harcourt Brace, 1955), 51–52. The

literature on middle-class formation is large. I have found the following useful: Blumin, *The Emergence of the Middle Class*; and Brian Roberts, *American Alchemy*.

38. Thomas L. Nichols, *Woman, in All Ages and Nations: . . . to the Present Time* (New York: Fowler and Wells, 1849), xi, 159; "Female Warriors," *New York Organ and Temperance Safeguard* 7, no. 20 (1847): 156.

39. Nichols, *Woman, in All Ages*, 224, viii. On binary thinking and gender, see Judith Butler, *Gender Trouble: Feminism and the Subversion of Identity* (New York: Routledge, 1990); Eve Kosofsky Sedgwick, *Epistemology of the Closet* (Berkeley: University of California Press, 1990), and *Between Men: English Literature and Homosocial Desire* (New York: Columbia University Press, 1992); Laura Lengel and John T. Warren, "Casting Gender," in their edited volume, *Casting Gender: Women and Performance in Intercultural Contexts* (New York: Peter Lang, 2005), 1–18; and Timothy B. Powell's "Introduction," 1–13 in his edited volume, *Beyond the Binary: Reconstructing Cultural Identity in a Multicultural Context* (New Brunswick: Rutgers University Press, 1999).

40. Leigh, "A Thing So Fallen," 427; E. Anthony Rotundo, *American Manhood: Transformations in Masculinity from the Revolution to the Modern Era* (New York: Basic Books, 1993), 3, 6, 22; Nancy Cott, "Passionlessness: An Interpretation of Victorian Sexual Ideology, 1790–1850," *Signs* 4, no. 2 (1978): 219–36.

41. Nichols, *Woman, in All Ages*, xi, 159; Charles Jewett, "Intemperance as a Vice of Individual Man," in *Speeches, Poems, and Miscellaneous Writings . . . and the Liquor Traffic* (Boston: John P. Jewett, 1849), 70; Philip B. Streit, *Address . . . Hampshire County Temperance Society* (Romney: William Harper, 1842), 15; "A Plantation in Ruins, or the History of John and Peter Hay," in *The Temperance Volume; Embracing the Temperance Tracts of the American Tract Society* (New York: American Tract Society, n.d.), 10.

42. *Opinions of the Press in Relation to the Liquor Traffic and the Morals of Boston* (Boston: Temperance Standard Press, 1846), 58; "A Drunken Woman," *The Dew Drop* 2, no. 17 (1844): 1.

43. Whitman, *Franklin Evans*, 72, 74.

44. Philadelphius, *The Moral Plague of Civil Society . . . this National Evil* (Philadelphia, 1821), 4; Bethune, *The Substance of an Address*, 12; *Report on the Agency of Intemperance in the Production of Pauperism* (Philadelphia: J. Van Cort, 1836), 7; *Journal of Health* 1, no. 7 (1829): 98; *The Evils of Drunkenness*, 4.

45. "Brooklyn Martha Washingtonian Society," *Journal of the American Temperance Union* 7, no. 1 (1843): 13; *The Third Anniversary Report . . . Published by the Society* (Philadelphia: John Clarke, 1832), 12; *Report on the Agency of Intemperance*, 6.

46. *Crime, Pauperism and Intemperance* (Providence: City Temperance Society, 1841), n.p.; *Plain Facts*, 24; Charles T. Woodman, *Narrative of Charles T. Woodman, a Reformed Inebriate. Written by Himself* (Boston: Theodore Abbot, 1843), 29; Henrietta Rose, *Nora Wilmot: A Tale of Temperance and Women's Rights* (Columbus: Osgood and Pierce, 1858), 100, 106–7.

47. *Evils of Drunkenness*, 3; Lindsly, "Essay," 129; Hartley, *Intemperance in Cities*, 139; "Female Inebriates," *The Pearl* 2, no. 37 (1848): 292.

48. *Thoughts on the Moral Physiology and Pathology of the Disease Liquor Drinking, with Advice Hints* (Boston: Redding & Co., 1862), 27.

49. Nicholas O. Warner, *Spirits*, 183; H. R. Storer, "Appendix," in *Methomania: A Treatise on Alcoholic Poisoning*, ed. Albert Day, (Boston: James Campbell, 1867), reprinted in *Nineteenth-Century Medical Attitudes toward Alcohol Addiction*, ed. Gerald Grob (New York: Arno Press, 1981) 62, 64–65.

50. *Opinions*, 54; Jewett, *Speeches*, 77.

51. Ellen Hickey Grayson, "Social Order and Psychological Disorder: Laughing Gas Demonstrations, 1800–1850," in *Freakery: Cultural Spectacles of the Extraordinary Body*, ed. Rosemarie G. Thompson (New York: New York University Press, 1996), 115. On opiate addiction, see David Courtwright, *Dark Paradise: A History of Opiate Addiction in America* (Cambridge: Harvard University Press, 2001); Nicholas O. Warner, *Spirits*, 73; Ann Braude, *Radical Spirits: Spiritualism and Women's Rights in Nineteenth-Century America* (Boston: Beacon Press, 1989).

2—Victims and Exemplars

1. John Watson, *An Alarming Portraiture . . . Advice Relative to the Subject* (Philadelphia: Kimbert and Conrad, 1813), 17–18; Frances B. Norris, *Reasons for Hating Strong Drink, and a Plea for Suffering Humanity, that the Plague May be Stayed* (Boston: W. & E. Howe, 1860), 8.

2. On cultural anxiety about failure, see Scott A. Sandage, *Born Losers: A History of Failure in America* (Cambridge: Harvard University Press, 2005).

3. Lorenzo Dow Johnson, *Martha Washingtonianism, or, A History of the Ladies' Temperance Benevolent Societies* (New York: Saxton & Miles, 1843), 7; *Addresses of Miss Anne E. Tomkins and Mr. William J. Hoge . . . 22nd of May, 1847* (Nashville: J. G. Sheperd, 1847), 5; Mary S. B. Shindler, "The Lost Youth," in *The Temperance Lyre, A Collection of Original Songs, Arranged and Adapted to the Most Popular Music of the Day, and Designed for Temperance Meetings* (New York: Dayton and Newman, 1842), 26–27; Anonymous, *"License" or "No License": A Calm Appeal to the Electors of Ulster County* (New York, 1846), 13.

4. Rose, *Nora Wilmot*, 58–59; Mrs. J. Thayer, *Picnic Tales, Number Three. The Drunkard's Daughter* (Boston: William S. Damrell, 1842), 84.

5. John Marsh, *Hannah Hawkins, The Reformed Drunkard's Daughter* (New York: The American Temperance Union, 1846), 30; "The Drunkard's Daughter," *The Lily* 1, no. 8 (1849): 59; "Affecting Incident," *The Lily* 1, no. 9 (1849): 67.

6. Mrs. E. N. Gladding, "Minnie—A Temperance Tale," in *Leaves from an Invalid's Journal, and Poems* (Providence: George H. Whitney, 1858), 110; Lucius M. Sargent, *The Cranberry Meadow* (Boston: John Ford, 1835), 3; Thomas Mitchell, ed., *The Maine Law Songster* (Lansingburgh: Thomas Mitchell and Richards and Harch, 1854), 82–86.

7. A Physician, "The Dying Drunkard," *The Dew Drop* 2, no. 21 (1845): 1; "A Drunkard's Home," *The Temperance Almanac for the Year of Our Lord 1843* (New York: L. D. Dewey, 1843), 47; "Correspondence of the Boston Traveller, A Horrible Sight—Rum's Doing and Death Doings," *The Lily* 2, no. 6 (1850): 45. The daguerreotype was an early and relatively affordable form of portrait photography that became popular, especially among the middle class. Considering the high rate of infant and child mortality, as well as Anglo-American culture's somewhat morbid fascination with death, it is not surprising that daguerreotypes of dead children found favor in the middle decades of the nineteenth century. See Karen Sanchez-Eppler, "Then When We Clutch Hardest: On the Death of a Child and the Replication of an Image," in Mary Chapman and Glenn Hendler, eds., *Sentimental Men: Masculinity and the Politics of Affect in American Culture* (Berkeley: University of California Press, 1999) 64–85.

8. Joshua B. Flint, *An Address . . . May 29, 1828* (Boston: Bowles and Dearborn, 1828), 7; "The Mother's Appeal," in *Chrystal Fount: or, Songs for the Sons and Daughters of Temperance* (New York: Philip J. Cozans, 1860), 25; "The Mother's Lament, for a Son who died of Intemperance," *The Temperance Offering*, T. S. Arthur, ed. (New York: Leavitt and Allen, [185?]), 105; *The Appeal of a Wife and Mother, Temperance Tract No. 1* (Providence: S. R. Weeden, [1840?]), 9, 16.

9. Mrs. R. S. Harvey, "A Single Glass of Wine," in *The Fountain and the Bottle; comprising Thrilling Examples of the Opposite Effects of Temperance and Intemperance,* ed. A Son of Temperance (Boston: Horace Wentworth, 1850), 164.

10. "The Drunkard's Will," *The Investigator and General Intelligencer* 1, no. 23 (1828): 4; Lydia Sigourney, "Hymn," *Journal of the American Temperance Union* 1, no. 1 (1837): 16; J. Blanchard, Jr., "Extract from an Address delivered before the Temperance Society of Wethersfield, VT, Sept. 16, 1831," Appendix C in *The Third Annual Report of the Richmond Society for the Promotion of Temperance. Presented January 16, 1832* (Richmond: J. MacFarlan, 1832), 22.

11. Sprague, *An Address,* 11; "Experience and Counsel of a Friend," *The Temperance Offering* 1, no. 6 (1845): 199–200; E. D., "Soliloquy of the Drunkard's Wife," *The Dew Drop* 2, no. 24 (1845): 1; "The Miseries of Intemperance," *The Lily* 1, no. 4 (1849): 28.

12. "A Village Scene," *The Temperance Offering* 1, no. 1 (1845): 11; *Confessions of a Reformed Inebriate* (New York: American Temperance Union, 1844), 128–29; "An Incident," *The Lily* 2, no. 2 (1850): 13–14.

13. Alexander Gunn, *A Sermon,* 9; Stephen Foster, *A Sermon on Intemperance . . . 21st of April, 1833* (Knoxville: F. S. Heiskell, 1833), 12; *Scenes of Intemperance, Exhibited in Familiar Conversations between a Mother and Her Children* (Philadelphia: American Sunday School Union, 1833), 9–10; "Characteristic," *The Dew Drop* 2, no. 2 (1844): 2.

14. *Proceedings of the Temperance Society of Columbia, South Carolina . . . and Prosperity of the Country* (Columbia: M'Morris and Wilson, 1829), 22, 17; *Crime, Pauperism and Intemperance,* n.p.; William B. M'Clure, *Temperance Address . . . Sons of Temperance* (Pittsburgh: Kennedy and Brother, 1852), 16.

15. David Pickering, *The Effects of Intemperance . . . at the Universalist Chapel* (Taunton: Samuel W. Mortimer, 1827), 16; Bethune, *The Substance of an Address,* 12; James Laird Vallandigham, A.B., *An Address . . . November 16, 1833* (Georgetown: J. S. M'Calla, 1833), 6.

16. *"License" or "No License,"* 6; Marsh, *A Half Century Tribute,* 15; M. M. C., *"To the Editress of the Olive Plant" The Olive Plant* 1, no. 19 (1842): 147; A Lady, "The Poor Man's House Repaired; or, The Wretched Made Happy," in *The Temperance Volume* (New York: American Tract Society, 1834), 3.

17. T. S. Arthur, "The Cold Water Fanatic," in *The Temperance Offering for 1853,* ed. T. S. Arthur (New York: Cornish, Lamport & Co., 1853), 65; William Jenks, A. M., *A Sermon . . . with the Annual Report* (Boston: Phelps and Farnham, 1821), 11; Henry P. Grattan, *The Bottle, a Poem . . . Engraved by Tudor Horton* (New York: Talbot Watts, 1848), n.p., Plate Seven.

18. *The Investigator and General Intelligencer* 2, no. 9 (1828): 3; *The Cold Water Girl* 1, no. 1 (1843): n.p.; S. R. L., "The Wedding Glass," in *The Cold Water Magazine* 1, no. 3 (n.d.): 95; *The Temperance Almanac for the year of our Lord 1839* (Boston: Whipple & Damrell, 1838), n.p.; *The History of The Bottle, as Originally Published in the New York Organ, from Engravings designed by Cruikshank* (New York: Oliver and Brothers, 1848), 28.

19. N. A. Keyes, *A Temperance Sermon . . . Pennsylvania* (Lancaster: John H. Pearsol, 1852), 14; Rev. James Nelson Hume, *Temperance versus Intemperance . . . February 25, 1840* (Boston: D. H. Lea, 1840), 24.

20. John Gough, "The Inebriate's Lament," *Journal of the American Temperance Union* 7, no. 12 (1843): 185; Mrs. R. H. Riley, "The Dying Wife's Pleas to her Husband," in *Temperance Offering for 1853,* ed. Arthur, 161–62.

21. Nathan S. S. Beman, *A Discourse delivered in Stephenstown . . . of Those*

Towns (Troy: F. Adancourt, 1829), 16–17; "Appeal to the Ladies," in *"License" or "No License,"* 13–14; "A Drunkard's Home," *The Temperance Almanac for the Year of Our Lord 1843*, 47–48; Carolo Emilio, *Intemperance: Its Effects . . . or, The Means of Its Cure* (Philadelphia, 1856), 21. For a fascinating discussion of how the antebellum era's popular culture made female victims objects of desire, see Patricia Cline Cohen, *The Murder of Helen Jewett* (New York: Knopf, 1998), esp. 266–90.

22. *The Hypocrisy and Cowardice of Pilate . . . and Good* (n.p., [1840s?]), 6–7. See the discussion of the undutiful wife, below.

23. *American Temperance Magazine and Sons of Temperance Offering* 1, no. 1 (1851): 65; Mrs. Whitman, "Woman's Love," in *Temperance Offering for 1853*, ed. Arthur, 23.

24. William Caruthers, *The Drunkard from Cradle to Grave . . . Feb. 26* (Savannah: W. T. Williams, 1840), 16.

25. Bloomer quote in *HWS*, vol. 1, 483; Susan B. Anthony, "Letter on Temperance, August 26, 1852," in *Elizabeth Cady Stanton/Susan B. Anthony: Correspondence, Writings, Speeches*, ed. Ellen Carol DuBois (New York: Schocken Books, 1981), 38, 40; *HWS*, vol. 1, 485. For a good discussion of the feminist wing of the temperance movement and their views on divorce, custody, and property rights, see Elizabeth Pleck, *Domestic Tyranny: The Making of Social Policy against Family Violence from Colonial Times to the Present* (New York: Oxford University Press, 1987), 54–63.

26. "Intemperance—An Extract," *The Lily* 1, no. 5 (1849): 34; "Influence of the Young," *The Lily* 1, no. 7 (1849): 52; Mary C. Vaughn, "The Drunkard's Wife and Home," *The Lily* 4, no. 2 (1852): 16. On *The Lily's* changing emphasis, see E. Claire Jerry, "*The Lily*, 1849–1856: From Temperance to Woman's Rights," in Martha A. Solomon, ed., *A Voice of Their Own: The Woman Suffrage Press, 1840–1910* (Tuscaloosa: University of Alabama Press, 1991), 30–47.

27. On this point, see Cohen, *Murder*, 277.

28. "William Carleton; or, The Reformed Drunkard," *Temperance Almanac for the Year of Our Lord 1843* (Albany: C. Van Benthuysen, 1843), n.p.

29. *American Temperance Magazine and Sons of Temperance Offering* (New York) 3, no. 1 (1852); *Temperance Recorder* (Albany) 2, no. 9 (1833): 70.

30. *The Second Annual Report of the Female Total Abstinence Society of Philadelphia* (Philadelphia: H. Probasco, 1838), 4; Emilio, *Intemperance*, 24–25, 36.

31. "Female Influence," *New York Washington Reformer and Ladies' Literary Journal*, 1, no. 16 (1843): 106; Eliza, "An Address to the Female Readers of the Female Advocate," *Genius of Temperance* 6, no. 41 (1832): 1; *Anniversary Celebration of Howard Union, No.3, Daughters of Temperance. Wednesday Evening, Oct. 25, 1848* ([Providence?], 1848); Elvira, "Female Duties," *Genius of Temperance* 6, no. 41 (1832): 1.

32. "Celebration of July Fourth," *New York Organ* 7, no. 45 (1848): 356; "Bristol County Temperance Convention," *The Dew Drop* 2, no. 1 (1844): 2; "A Severe Rebuke," *The Dew Drop* 2, no. 10 (1844): 1; "Alcohol for Pickles," *The Lily* 1, no. 0 (1849): 67.

33. "Ladies," *The Dew Drop* 2, no. 4 (1844): 1; Bradbury, *The Distiller's Daughter* (1844), 9.

34. John Neal, *Address . . . February 11, 1829* (Portland: Day and Fraser, 1829), 14; "Daughters of Temperance," *New York Organ* 7, no. 29 (1848): 228; "Temperance," *Staunton Spectator and General Advertiser* (4 Dec. 1845), 4; "Resolutions of U. S. Temperance Convention, May 24, 1833, Philadelphia," in *The Temperance Almanac for the Year of Our Lord 1843* (New York, L. D. Dewey, 1843), 27.

35. *American Temperance Magazine* (New York) 1, no. 1 (1851): cover; *Journal of the American Temperance Union* 7, no. 1 (1843): 9.

36. *American Temperance Magazine* 1, no. 1 (1851); "A Sunday School Signing the Pledge," *Journal of the American Temperance Union* 7, no. 1 (1843): 9; R. Carpen-

ter, "Woman's Influence," *New York Washingtonian and Ladies' Literary Pearl* 2, no. 2 (1847): 12; "Female Aid Required," in *Temperance Hymn Book and Minstrel: A Collection of Hymns, Songs and Odes, for Temperance Meetings and Festivals,* ed. John Marsh (New York: American Temperance Union, 1841), 46–47.

37. Abel Fletcher, *The History, Objects, and Principles . . . December 2, 1844* (Philadelphia: Gihon & Porter, 1845), 25, 26; "Daughters of America," *New York Organ* 7, no. 1 (1847): 4; Thomas H. Flandrau, *Address . . . May 9, 1842* (Utica: Woodland & Donaldson, 1842), 8.

38. T. S. Arthur, "The Cold Water Wedding," in *The Ruined Family and Other Tales* (Philadelphia: Godey & M'Michael, 1843), 94; Arthur, ed., *The Temperance Offering,* 102.

39. *Temperance Almanac for the Year of Our Lord 1843,* 23, 24; *The Mother Rewarded and the Son Reclaimed* (Portland: William Hyde & Son, 1851), 29, 30. On republican motherhood, see Linda Kerber, *Women of the Republic: Intellect and Ideology in Revolutionary America* (New York: Norton, 1986), esp. 265–88.

40. Marsh, *Hannah Hawkins,* 25. Karen Sanchez-Eppler has argued that a strong theme of incest runs through tales of children reforming their intemperate fathers. See her "Temperance in the Bed of a Child: Incest and Social Order in Nineteenth-Century America," *American Quarterly Temperance Magazine* 47, no. 1 (1995): 1–33. My reading of temperance literature does not support this interpretation.

41. *The Dew Drop* 2, no. 26 (1845): 3; Mrs. Wilber, "The Moral Power of Woman," *The Lily* 1, no. 7 (1849): 52.

42. Thayer, *Picnic Tales, Number Three,* 87, 90.

43. Caroline Lee Hentz, "The Drunkard's Daughter," in *Courtship and Marriage, or, The Joys and Sorrows of American Life* (Philadelphia: T. B. Peterson, 1856), 376.

44. "Good Wives," *New York Organ* 7, no. 22 (1847): 172; "Heaven on Earth," *New York Organ* 7, no. 48 (1848): 380; A. N., "My Wife's Influence," *Investigator and General Intelligencer* 1, no. 26 (1828): 4; Mary Hinckley, *The Camphene Lamp; or, Touch Not, Taste Not, Handle Not* (Lowell: James P. Walker, 1852), 14, 19.

45. John Ellis, *Marriage and Its Violations, Licentiousness and Vice* (New York: John Ellis, 1860), 19–20; "William Carleton; or, the Reformed Drunkard," *Temperance Almanac for the Year of Our Lord 1843,* n.p.; Philip P. Neely, "Idella Pemberton," *Daughter of Temperance* 1, no. 4 (1850): 1; "A Judicious Wife," *The Dew Drop* 2, no. 8 (1844): 1.

46. "The Husband Tamer," *New York Washingtonian and Ladies Literary Pearl* 2, no. 6 (1847): 41; "If My Husband Were to Do So: A Domestic Incident," in *The Temperance Offering,* ed. Arthur, 83, 86.

47. "Miss Anthony's Address to the State Temperance Convention," *The Lily* 4, no. 7 (1852): 57; Mary C. Vaughn, "The Drunkard's Wife and Home," *The Lily* 4, no. 2 (1852): 16.

48. Mrs. E. F. Ellett, "A Country Recollection, or, The Reformed Inebriate," in *The Adopted Daughter and Other Tales,* ed. Alice Carey (Philadelphia: J. B. Smith, 1859), 138; A Lady of Baltimore, *The Price of a Glass of Brandy* (Baltimore: Robert Neilson, 1841), 22, 24.

3—The Suffering Woman

1. Charles D. Meigs, *Females and their Diseases: A Series of Lectures to His Class* (Philadelphia: Lea and Blanchard, 1848), 38, 41.

2. Lydia H. Sigourney, "The Intemperate," 7–22, in *The Intemperate and the Reformed. Shewing the Awful Consequences of Intemperance, and the Blessed Effects of the Temperance Reformation* (Boston: Seth Bliss, 1833). "The Intemperate" first appeared in

the gift book *The Religious Souvenir for 1834* (Philadelphia: Dey, Miellee and Biddle 1833), and was later reprinted in *Sketches* (Amherst: J.S.&C. Adams, 1834) and in Sigourney's collection of temperance writings, *Water-drops*. The engraving (Figure 5) appeared as the frontispiece of *Remarks on the Utility and Necessity of Asylums or Retreats for the Victims of Intemperance* (Philadelphia: Brown, Bickering & Guilbert, 1840).

3. Ibid., 9, 10.

4. Meigs, *Females and their Diseases*, 44.

5. Rebecca J. Tannenbaum, "Earnestness, Temperance, Industry: The Definition and Uses of Professional Character among Nineteenth-Century Physicians," *Journal of the History of Medicine and Allied Sciences* 49 (1994): 252, 257; Ronald L. Numbers, "The Fall and Rise of the American Medical Profession," in *Sickness and Health in America*, ed. Judith Leavitt and Ronald Numbers (Madison: University of Wisconsin Press, 1985), 185–96; Karen Haltunnen, *Confidence Men and Painted Women: A Study in Middle-Class Culture in America* (New Haven: Yale University Press, 1982).

6. Daniel Drake, "Physiological Temperance Society," *Boston Medical and Surgical Journal* 26, no. 7 (1842): 114.

7. Lebbeus Armstrong, *The Temperance Reformation* (New York: Fowler and Wells, 1853); Massachusetts Temperance Society, *The Physiological Effects of Alcoholic Drinks . . . in the State of Massachusetts* (Boston: Massachusetts Temperance Society, 1848), 2, 43–47; *Fourteenth Annual Report . . . November 5, 1827* (Boston: N. S. Simpkins and Co., 1827), 4; *The Anniversary Report*, 4.

8. Robert Macnish, *The Anatomy of Drunkenness* (New York: D. Appleton &. Co., 1835), 16; Carpenter, *The Physiology of Temperance and Total Abstinence*, 53; Samuel A. Cartwright, "Hygenics of Temperance, or Water and Alcohol, contrasted on the People Proper," *Boston Surgical and Medical Journal* 49, no. 1 (1853): 9.

9. Charles Jewett, MD, *Speeches, Poems and Miscellaneous Writings . . . and the Liquor Traffic* (Boston: John P. Jewett, 1849), 16; William Sweetser, MD, *A Dissertation on Intemperance . . . Massachusetts Medical Society* (Boston: Hilliard and Gray, 1829), 72; Storer, "Appendix," in *Methomania*, Day, 64–65.

10. J. C. Lettsom, *History of Some of the Effects of Hard Drinking*, 6th ed. (London: W. Darton and Co., 1791), 1; *The Constitution and Address of the Baltimore Temperance Society . . . in the University of Maryland* (Baltimore: J. D. Troy, 1830), 31; Lindsly, "Essay," 171–72.

11. Shepard, "Confessions of a Female Inebriate," 71–72; Thayer, *Picnic Tales Number Three*, 15.

12. Thomas L. Nichols, *Woman, in All Ages and Nations*, 159, 160.

13. John C. Wiltbank, *The Introductory Lecture to the Course of Midwifery in the Medical Department of Pennsylvania College, for the Session of 1853–54* (Philadelphia: Edward Grattan, 1854), 7; John C. Wiltbank, *The Peculiarities of the Female . . . November 6, 1845* (Philadelphia: Barrett & Jones, 1845), 9.

14. Sweetser, *Dissertation*, 56; Lindsly, "Essay," 135.

15. Sweetser, *Dissertation*, 69–70; *Constitution and Address*, 31; *Proceedings of the Physiological Temperance Society of the Medical Institute of Louisville* (Louisville: N. H. White, 1842), 6.

16. Sweetser, *Dissertation*, 41; Macnish, *Anatomy*, 117; Lindsly, "Essay," 128.

17. Lettsom, *History*, 7, 8–9; James Jackson, "On a Peculiar Disease resulting from the use of Ardent Spirits," *New England Journal of Medicine and Surgery* 11, no. 4 (1822): 352; Sweetser, *Dissertation*, 46.

18. Lettsom, *History*, 5–6.

19. Nichols, *Woman in All Ages*, 160; Macnish, *Anatomy*, 14.

20. Thomas Trotter, *An Essay*, 189; Macnish, *Anatomy*, 167. William Sweetser

(*Dissertation,* 93) attributes the story to Benjamin Rush; it also appears in Lindsly, "Essay," 181–82.

21. Mussey, *An Address on Ardent Spirit,* 11; "Spontaneous Combustion," *The Medical Repository* VII:2 (1822), 245; Macnish, *Anatomy,* 139–52; Drake, *A Discourse . . . to a Popular Audience,* 43, 79.

22. Trotter, *Essay,* 86, 87. Robert Macnish also noted that some "writers allege that unmarried women, especially if somewhat advanced in years, are more given to liquor than those who are married," though he declined to decide the issue. See Macnish, *Anatomy,* 16.

23. Jessica Warner, "Old and In the Way: Widows, Witches, and Spontaneous Combustion in the Age of Reason," *Contemporary Drug Problems* 23 (Summer 1996): 197–220, quote from 216. See also Carol Karlsen, *The Devil in the Shape of a Woman* (New York: Vintage Books, 1989), 255–57.

24. "An Incident," *The Lily* 1, no. 1 (1849): 2.

25. Drake, *Discourse,* 51; Flint, *An Address,* 6; Marcus E. Cross, *The Mirror of Intemperance, and History of the Temperance Reform* (Philadelphia: John T. Lange, 1849), 180.

26. Sigourney, "The Intemperate," 8–9.

27. Ibid., 15.

28. Ibid., 14–15.

29. Ibid., 22.

30. L. H. Sigourney, *Letters of Life* (New York: D. Appleton and Company, 1866), 354; Ann Douglas, *The Feminization of American Culture* (New York: Avon Books, 1977), 53. Sigourney hoped to "quicken" her female readers to impress "upon the tender minds committed to their charge the subjugation of the appetites, and the wisdom and beauty of self-control" (*Letters of Life,* 354).

31. Sigourney, "Letters to Females," in *Water-drops,* 262–63.

32. *The Afflicted Family . . . hunger and cruel neglect* (New York: Printed for the Publisher, 1842), 5, 13, 22.

33. Unless otherwise cited the biographical data on Meigs was taken from entries in *The National Cyclopaedia of American Biography* (New York: White and Co., 1929), 390; *The Dictionary of American Biography* (New York: Scribner, 1964), 503–4; and *American National Biography Online* (New York: Oxford University Press, 2000), www.anb.org. maurice.bgsu.edu:80/articles/12/12-00605.html; (accessed 22 May 2007).

34. Robert Baker, "The Kappa Lambda Society of Hippocrates: The Secret Origins of the American Medical Association," *Fugitive Leaves . . . Physicians of Philadelphia,* 3rd ser., 11, no. 2 (1996): 4; *Report of the Committee . . . May Deem Proper* (Philadelphia: John Clarke, 1829); *The Anniversary Report.*

35. *National Cyclopedia,* 390.

36. Meigs, *Females and their Diseases,* 37, 36, 49. Meigs's other writings also manifest this fascination with ovaries, as well as his attribution to them of enormous influence over female health and character. In *Obstetrics: The Science and the Art* (Philadelphia: Lea and Blanchard, 1849), Meigs proclaimed that the ovary's "great influence is exhibited in pronouncing the single word, sex, for the ovary is the sex of the woman, or the female. But if the ovary be her sex, then the whole peculiar physical, moral, and intellectual character of the female are derived from it, as their source . . . they are conformed to its wants, its powers, its offices—and often modified by its conditions" (112).

37. Ibid., 44, 46, 36, 43, 46, 49.

38. Meigs's reference to specific details in his remarks on the print—Mrs. Harwood losing the farm that had been her dowry, for instance—suggests that the doctor was familiar with Sigourney's story. As noted in note 2, "The Intemperate" also appeared as the

frontispiece illustration for *Remarks on the Utility and Necessity of Asylums or Retreats for the Victims of Intemperance,* suggesting its popularity and relevance in Philadelphia temperance circles. Explicating the print, the *Remarks* observed that the "wife, whom he has solemnly and sincerely vowed to love and cherish, would still be fair and beautiful, if neglect and abuse had not broken her loving heart, and poverty and despair become her portion. She bears her sick boy in her arms, while the babe clings to her neck, and the only remaining one of the little circle that might be so happy around a cheerful fireside, is brought to premature sorrow, and instead of the bright smile and joyous leap of childhood, he is doomed to tears and suffering and grief. The storm rages! The man who once was so tender of his wife that he 'would not suffer the winds of heaven to visit her face too roughly' is now changed to a monster!" (3).

39. Meigs, *Females and their Diseases,* 46.

40. Ibid, 49.

41. Ibid, 46.

42. On women's legal and social status, see Marylynn Salmon, *Women and the Law of Property in Early America* (Chapel Hill: University of North Carolina Press, 1986); Michael Grossberg, *Governing the Hearth: Law and Family in Nineteenth-Century America* (Chapel Hill: University of North Carolina Press, 1985); Pleck, *Domestic Tyranny.* On medical attitudes toward women, see G. J. Barker-Benfield, *The Horrors of the Half-Known Life: Male Attitudes toward Women and Sexuality in Nineteenth-Century America* (New York: Harper and Row, 1976), and Carroll Smith-Rosenberg and Charles Rosenberg, "The Female Animal: Medical and Biological Views of Woman and Her Role in Nineteenth-Century America," *Journal of American History* 60, no. 2 (1973): 332–56.

43. For a description of "The Bad Husband," see Gale Research Company, *Currier and Ives: A Catalogue Raisonné* (Detroit: Gale Research Co., 1984), 38. Apparently, Currier and Ives reissued this print later in the 1870s as "The Fruits of Intemperance."

4—Female Moral Suasion

1. "Influence of Woman," *The Temperance Almanac for the Year of Our Lord 1839,* n.p.

2. The literature on domesticity is large. I have found especially useful Cott's *The Bonds of Womanhood* and Alexander's "'We are Engaged as a Band of Sisters.'"

3. Benjamin Wadsworth, *Female Charity an Acceptable Offering . . . November 7, 1816* (Andover: Flagg and Gould, 1817), 25; Edwards, *Joy in Heaven over the Penitent,* 10. Both Wadsworth and Edwards became actively involved in the temperance movement.

4. *Temperance Recorder,* (Albany) 2, no. 9 (1833): 70; *Temperance Almanac for 1845* (Troy: B. H. Boynton, 1845), no pagination; M'Clure, *Temperance Address,* 18; Susan B. Anthony, Daughters of Temperance Oration, March 1, 1849, Canajoharie, New York, quoted in Ida Husted Harper, *The Life and Work of Susan B. Anthony,* vol. 1 (Indianapolis: The Hollenbeck Press, 1898), 55.

5. Aikin, *Moral Reform,* 15; *Annals of the American Female Home Education Society and Temperance Union,* vol. 4 (Boston: The Society, 1842), 2; *Temperance Offering* 1, no. 5 (1845): 169.

6. "Female Influence," *American Quarterly* 2, no. 1 (1834): 29; Nathaniel W. Chittenden, *The Influence of Woman . . . October 3rd, 1837* (New York: Scottherd and Adams, 1837), 17; "Female Influence," *The Fountain* 1, no. 3 (1838): 10; "The Good Wife," *New York Washingtonian and Ladies' Literary Pearl* 2, no. 6 (1847): 44; *The Hypocrisy and Cowardice of Pilate* (n.p., n.d.), 15.

7. "Female Influence," *New York Washington Reformer and Ladies' Literary Journal* 1, no. 16 (1843): 106; "Noble," *The Dew Drop* 2, no. 13 (1844): 3; Letter from Sarah M. Adams, *New York Washingtonian and Ladies' Literary Pearl* 2, no. 7 (1847): 52.

8. "Young Ladies," *The Pearl* 1, no. 30 (1846): 238; Alonzo Potter, "Address on the Drinking Usages of Society," 25–26, in *Addresses* (Boston: Massachusetts Temperance Society, 1861); M'Clure, *Temperance Address,* 18–19.

9. Potter, *Addresses,* 25; "Gin Drinking in England," in *The Temperance Family Almanac for the Year of Our Lord 1835 . . . TEMPERANCE* (Boston: Russell, Odiorne & Metcalf, 1835), 34.

10. Leonard Bacon, *A Discourse . . . in the City of New Haven* (New Haven: B. L. Hamlen, 1838), 40; Albert Barnes, *The Cause of Intemperance in Cities and Large Towns* (Philadelphia: George, Latimer & Co., 1834), 35; "Magnificent Drinking Saloons," *New York Organ* 7, no. 34 (1848): 268.

11. "Female Influence," *The Pearl* 1, no. 13 (1846): 100.

12. William R. DeWitt, *Profanity and Intemperance, Prevailing Evils. A Discourse* (Harrisburg: Fenn & Wallace, 1840), 4; "She Wished It Well," *Temperance Offering* 1, no. 6 (1845): 207; "Why Is It?" *The Pearl* 1, no. 2 (1846): 12; "Influence of Women," *The Temperance Almanac for the Year of our Lord 1839,* n.p.

13. Beman, *A Discourse,* 26; "Am I My Brother's Keeper?" *The Olive Plant* 1, no. 2 (1841): 12; "Woman's Labor in the Cause," *The Olive Plant* 2, nos. 3 & 4 (1842): 21; "Letter from L. J. B.," *The Olive Plant* 1, no. 2 (1841): 12.

14. Potter, *Addresses,* 25–26; Neal, *Address,* 16, 15; "To the Ladies of the United States," *Temperance Almanac, 1838* (Albany: Packard and Benthuysen, 1838), 31.

15. Potter, *Addresses,* 26.

16. Lamas, *The Glass,* 7, 8, 27.

17. C. L. C., "Charles Hastings; or, The Effects of Female Influence," *The Pearl* 1, no. 18 (1846): 137.

18. Grenville Mellen, *The First Glass* (Southwark, Philadelphia: Wm. F. Geddes, 1834), 2, 3, 4.

19. "The Bridal Feast," 63–64, in *Chrystal Fount; or, Songs for the Sons and Daughters of Temperance* (New York: Philip J. Cozans, 1860); "Wine on the Wedding Night," in Miss C. B. Porter, *The Silver Cup of Sparkling Drops, from Many Fountains for the Friends of Temperance* (Buffalo: Derby and Co., 1852), 181–82.

20. Thomas P. Hunt, *The Wedding Days of Former Times* (Philadelphia: Griffith & Simon, 1845), 11, 15–16, 27.

21. "Brandied Peaches," in *The Temperance Offering for 1853,* ed. Arthur, 153.

22. T. S. Arthur, "A Story for Wives," in *The Temperance Offering,* ed. Arthur, 17, 24, 30.

23. Letter from M. M. C., *The Olive Plant* 1, no. 19 (1842): 147; "The Gleasons; or, Trials and Triumphs," *The Pearl* 1, no. 2 (1846): 14.

24. "Women's Labor in the Cause," *The Olive Plant* 2, nos. 3 & 4 (1842); 21; Letter from "F. M. H.," *The Lily* 1, no. 3 (1849): 23; "New Year's Day," *The Lily* 3, no. 1 (1851): 23; Mrs. Wilber, "The Moral Power of Woman," *The Lily* 1, no. 7 (1849): 52.

25. Marsh, *A Half Century Tribute,* 18; Hunt, *Wedding Days,* 73. On the temperance movement's changing tactics in the 1840s and 1850s, see Tyrrell, *Sobering Up,* especially 225–89; and Dannenbaum, *Drink and Disorder.*

26. "Influence of Woman," *The Temperance Almanac for the Year of our Lord 1839,* n.p.; "The Drunkard's Wife," in *Chrystal Fount,* 30.

27. Lydia Sigourney, "The Widow and her Son," in *Water-drops,* 45–46, 48–49, 51.

28. Elisha Mitchell, *Arguments for Temperance . . . at their Request* (Raleigh: J. Gales and Son, 1831), 10; "Bristol County T. A. Society in Fall River," *The Dew Drop*

2, no. 10 (1844): 2; "The Merciless Rumseller," *The Pearl* 1, no. 19 (1846): 150.

29. Drake, *A Discourse*, 32–33; *Journal of Health* 1, no. 7 (1829): 98, 99; "Causes of Drunkenness," *Journal of the American Temperance Union* 1, no. 10 (1837): 145; *The History of The Bottle*, 6.

30. "Fifth Report," *Permanent Temperance Documents of the American Temperance Society* (New York: Arno Press, 1972), 41; Philadelphius, *The Moral Plague*, 4; Bethune, *The Substance of an Address*, 12; *The Evils of Drunkenness*, 4.

31. Julia L. Dumont, "The First Temperance Pledge," in *Life Sketches from Common Paths: A Series of American Tales* (New York: D. Appleton & Co., 1856), 39, 38; *The Mother Rewarded and the Son Reclaimed*, 29.

32. John W. Frick, *Theatre, Culture and Temperance Reform in Nineteenth-Century America* (Cambridge: Cambridge University Press, 2003), 67, 71, 125. *The Drunkard, or the Fallen Saved* is reprinted in Richard Moody, ed., *Dramas from the American Theatre, 1762–1909* (Boston: Houghton Mifflin, 1969). On the play's relation to middle-class formation, see also Jeffrey D. Mason's discussion of *The Drunkard* in his *Melodrama and the Myth of America* (Bloomington: University of Indiana Press, 1993), 61–88.

33. *Confessions of a Reformed Inebriate*, 115; *Three Experiments in Drinking, or, Three Eras in the Life of An Inebriate* (Boston: Otis, Broaders, & Co., 1837), 25.

34. Buckley, *Edith Moreton*, 6, 7, 13, 14, 39.

35. Ibid., 43, 46.

36. Ibid., 24, 25.

37. Ibid., 26–27.

38. Ibid., 33–34.

39. *Edith Moreton*'s publication date, 1852, may be significant in this regard, as it followed closely the passage of state prohibition a year earlier in Maine. On the shift in reform tactics, see Ginzberg, *Women and the Work of Benevolence*, especially 98–132.

5—Toward Legislation

1. Hartley, *Intemperance in Cities and Large Towns*, 139–40. On alcohol consumption and the middle class, see Rorabaugh, *The Alcoholic Republic*, 8, 232–33; Thomas R. Pegram, *Battling Demon Rum: The Struggle for a Dry America, 1800–1933* (Chicago: Ivan R. Dee, 1998), 31–32; Paul Johnson, *A Shopkeeper's Millennium: Society and Revivals in Rochester, New York, 1815–1837* (New York: Hill and Wang 1978); and Blumin, *The Emergence of the Middle Class*, esp. 194–204.

2. James Trecothick Austin, *An Address . . . May 27, 1830* (Boston: John H. Eastburn, 1830), 18; Bacon, *A Discourse on the Traffic in Spirituous Liquors*, 4–5; Rorabaugh, *Alcoholic Republic*, 169. On responses to Irish and German immigrants, see Pegram, *Battling Demon Rum*, 33–34; Tyrell, *Sobering Up*, 264–68; and Dannenbaum, *Drink and Disorder*, esp. 106–53.

3. Gunn, *A Sermon*, 24; Dimmick, *Intemperance*, 12; Streit, *Address*, 4. See also Pegram, *Battling Demon Rum*, 32–33.

4. Roberts, *American Alchemy*, 263.

5. Cross, *The Mirror of Intemperance*, 36, 37; William J. Armstrong, *The Evils of Intemperance . . . Presbyterian Church* (Richmond: J. MacFarlan, 1829), 4; "A Chapter in the History of Our Country," *Temperance Almanac for 1837* (Albany: Packard and Van Bethuysen, 1837), 16; Hill, *Sermon*, 11. On the continued resonance of depicting alcoholic invasions of the middle-class home in temperance literature and discourse, see Parsons, *Manhood Lost*, 126–56.

6. Bellamy Storer, *An Address . . . February, 1833* (Cincinnati: F. S. Benton,

1833), 8, 9; *The Appeal of a Wife and Mother* (Providence: S. R. Weeden, 1840?), 2.

7. Benjamin Wadsworth, *Intemperance a National Evil . . . June 29, 1815* (Salem: Thomas C. Cushing, 1815), 11.

8. James Trecothick Austin, *Address*, 18; Edward Hitchcock, *An Essay on Alcoholic and Narcotic Substances, as Articles of Common use. Addressed Particularly to Students* (Boston: J. S. & C. Adams & Co., 1830), 39, and *An Essay on Temperance, Addressed Particularly to Students, and the Young Men of America* (Amherst: J. S. & C. Adams, 1830), 29.

9. "The Drunkard," *Temperance Almanac of the Massachusetts Temperance Union, for the Year of Our Lord 1845* (Boston: Mass. Temperance Union, 1844), 30; Vallandigham, *An Address*, 5; Flint, *An Address*, 6; *Opinions of the Press*, 16.

10. Tyrrell, *Sobering Up*, 6, 7.

11. Flint, *Address*, 24; Hartley, *Intemperance*, 105; Marsh, *A Half Century Tribute*, 6–7.

12. Alvan Stewart, *An Essay on the Evils of Intemperance . . . of Oneida* (Utica: Gardiner Tracy, 1833), 7; George Russell, "The Rum Seller's Song," *Temperance Almanac of the Massachusetts Temperance Union, for the Year of Our Lord 1845* (Boston: Mass. Temperance Union, 1844), 29.

13. Joseph Harvey, *An Appeal to Christians . . . May 5th, 1831* (Middletown: William D. Starr, 1831), 21; Solomon Adams, *An Address . . . Cumberland Co. Temperance Society* (Portland: Shirley, Hyde and Co., 1830), 12–13; James Rodgers, *A Discourse . . . January 1st, 1834* (n.p., n.d.), 1.

14. Frick, *Theatre, Culture, and Temperance Reform in Nineteenth-century America*, 75.

15. Scott C. Martin, ed., *Cultural Change and the Market Revolution in America, 1789–1860* (Lanham, Maryland: Rowman and Littlefield, 2005); Charles Sellers, *The Market Revolution: Jacksonian America, 1815–1846* (New York: Oxford University Press, 1991), esp. 237–68; Tyrrell, *Sobering Up*, 109, 237; and Dannenbaum, *Drink and Disorder*, 91.

16. *A Hasty Defense . . . Temperance Societies, & c.* (York: W. C. Smyth, 1833), 2, 7, 12; "Resolutions of Grocers," Appendix to Leonard Bacon, *A Discourse on the Traffic in Spirituous Liquors* (New Haven: B. L. Hamlen, 1838), 51; A Friend of Temperance and Equal Rights, *An Address to the Leaders of the Abstinence Enterprise* (Philadelphia, 1831), 4.

17. John Gregory, *The Bramble* (Methuen: S. J. Varney, 1837); Leonard Withington, *A Review of the Late Temperance Movements in Massachusetts* (Boston: James Munroe, 1840), 5, 12, 22, 27; E. B. Cooke, *Infidelity and Benevolent Societies* (Waterbury: E. B. Cooke and Co., 1848), 5.

18. Anonymous, *Reasons for Not Joining the Temperance Society by a Clergyman* (Richmond: n.p., 1836), 34; Harrison Gray Otis, *Letter from an Aged . . . on Coercive Measures in Aid of Temperance* (Boston: Eastburn's Press, 1848), 11; D. C. Lansing, *A Remedy for Intemperance* (Utica: Hastings and Tracy, 1832), 6; *Proceedings of the State Temperance Convention . . . January 13 and 14, 1841* (Harrisburg: John Weishampel, 1841), 14.

19. *Second Annual Report of . . . Philadelphia* (Philadelphia: H. Probasco, 1838), 4; George S. Burleigh, *Memoirs of Alcohol . . . and of His Daughter Gin* (Hartford: Robinson & Pratt, 1834), 10, 22; *Temperance Recorder* 2, no. 7 (1833): 49; *Address to the People of the Commonwealth Relative to the License Question* (n.p., 1846), 5; Hume, *Temperance versus Intemperance*, 14; Rev. H. Harabaugh, *A Word in Season . . . the Evils of Intemperance* (Chambersburg: German Reformed Church, 1846), 18; Jesse Torrey, Jr., *The Intellectual Torch . . . Including Essays on the Use of Distilled Spirits* (Ballston Spa: J. Comstock, 1817), 23; Hume, *Temperance versus Intemperance*, 16.

20. Harvey, *An Appeal to Christians*, 19, 22; Adams, *Address*, 14.

21. Albert Barnes, *The Immorality of the Traffic in Ardent Spirits . . . April 13, 1834* (Philadelphia: George, Latimer & Co., 1834), 4; Rev. L. J. Halsey, *Legal Prohibition . . . April and July, 1855* (Louisville: J. F. Brennan, 1855), 24; "Doings of a Grog Shop," *The Temperance Annual and Cold Water Magazine for 1843* (Philadelphia: Drew &

Scammell, 1843), 22; Bacon, *Discourse,* 43; "The Spider and the Fly," *Temperance Almanac for the Year of Our Lord 1840* (n.p., n.d.); Frederick A. Fickhardt, "The Sons of Temperance, A Brief History of Temperance in the United States, and Narrative of the Origin, Character and Progress of the Order of Sons of Temperance of America," in *The Temperance Offering,* Arthur, [185?], 257.

22. Lansing, *Remedy for Intemperance,* 7; Herttell, *An Expose,* 5–7; Halsey, *Legal Prohibition,* 7; Marsh, *Half Century Tribute,* 20.

23. J. H. Agnew, *Address . . . April 20, 1829* (Philadelphia: W. F. Geddes, 1829), 4, 5, 6; Samuel Chipman, *The Temperance Lecturer* (Albany, 1846), 64; *Temperance, Its Rise and Progress . . . by a "Son."* (Sandusky: Amos Moore, 1848), 9, 23.

24. Philadelphius, *Moral Plague,* 2; "How It Destroys the Sensibilities," *Temperance Recorder* 2, no. 9 (1833): 68–69; Lucius M. Sargent, *"Licensed Houses." An Examination of the License Law of the Commonwealth of Massachusetts* (Boston: J. Ford, 1833), 39; "Traffic," *Temperance Almanac of the Massachusetts Temperance Union, for the Year of Our Lord 1841* (Boston: Whipple and Damrell, 1840), n.p.; Justin Edwards, *The Temperance Manual* (New York: American Tract Society, [1847?]), 85–86.

25. "Fourth Report," *Permanent Temperance Documents,* 46; Gladding, "Minnie —A Temperance Tale," in *Leaves from an Invalid's Journal,* 109, 110; *Tenth Annual Report of the Maryland State Temperance Society* (Baltimore: Samuel Sands, 1841), 10; Harabaugh, *A Word in Season,* 17, 27–28.

26. On the religious influences that led Arthur to, quite literally, demonize drink, see Francis Lauricella, Jr., "The Devil in Drink: Swedenborgianism in T. S. Arthur's *Ten Nights in a Bar-room* (1854)," in *Perspectives in American History,* vol. 12 (1979), ed. Donald Fleming (Cambridge: Charles Warren Center, 1979), 351–86, and Graham Warder, "Temperance Nostalgia, Market Anxiety, and the Reintegration of Community in T. S. Arthur's *Ten Nights in a Bar-room,*" in *Cultural Change and Market Revolution,* ed. Scott Martin, 217–45.

27. T. S. Arthur, *Ten Nights in a Bar-Room, and What I Saw There,* ed. Jon Miller (Acton: Copley Publishing Group, 2002), 13, 99.

28. Arthur, *Ten Nights,* 10, 29.

29. Ibid., 9, 85, 13, 94.

30. Tim Ruppel, "Gender Training: Male Ambitions, Domestic Duties, and Failure in the Magazine Fiction of T. S. Arthur," in *Prospects: An Annual Review of American Cultural Studies,* vol. 24 (Cambridge: Cambridge University Press, 1999), 311–37.

31. Arthur, *Ten Nights,* 15, 44. Arthur did allow that in "exceptional cases" women acquiesced in their husbands' trafficking in liquor, sometimes even opening taverns themselves. But these were "women of bad principles and worse hearts" (45), whose exception proved the rule of feminine virtue.

32. Ibid., 11, 92, 6, 66, 181, 159, 161.

33. Ibid., 20, 42, 43.

34. Ibid., 117, 120, 125.

35. Ibid., 133.

36. Ibid., 184.

37. Harabaugh, *A Word in Season,* 11. On the temperance movement's transition from moral suasion to legal coercion, see Blocker, *American Temperance Movements,* 46–47, 51–60; Pegram, *Battling Demon Rum,* 24–42; and Tyrrell, *Sobering Up.*

6—Protecting the Home

1. *License or No License, That is the Question. To the Voters of Ohio* (n.p., n.d. [1840s]); Henry Lobdell, *The Religious, Moral and Political Evils of the Liquor Traffic . . . Cause of Temperance* (New York: William Osborn, 1848), 9.

2. William R. Alger, *The Facts of Intemperance, and their Claims on the Public Action of the People* (Boston: Crosby, Nichols and Company, 1852), 18; Albert Barnes, *The Throne of Iniquity . . . Intoxicating Beverages* (New York: American Temperance Union, 1852), 18, 19.

3. Charles W. Flanders, *A Temperance Address delivered before the Concord Temperance Society* (Concord: Jones & Cogswell, 1858), 18; Orlando Lund, *Maine Law Documents for the People* (Elmira: L. Baldwin, Jr., 1853), 21; Henry S. Clubb, *The Maine Liquor Law . . . Including a life of Hon. Neal Dow* (New York: Fowler and Wells, 1856), 105.

4. Lobdell, *Evils of the Liquor Traffic,* 24; Samuel M. Smucker, *Considerations . . . the Sale of Ardent Spirits in Pennsylvania* (Philadelphia: 1852), 4–5.

5. Tyrrell, "Women and Temperance," 142; Clubb, *Maine Liquor Law,* 263.

6. Tyrrell, "Women and Temperance," 144; Dannenbaum, "The Origins of Temperance Activism," 243; Dexter C. Bloomer, *Life and Writings of Amelia Bloomer* (Boston, 1895), 160; "Caroline M. Sweet," *The Lily* 1, no. 8 (1849): 62.

7. Clifford S. Griffin, *Their Brothers' Keepers: Moral Stewardship in the United States, 1800–1860* (New Brunswick: Rutgers University Press, 1960), 147; Neal Dow, *The Reminiscences of Neal Dow: Recollections of Eighty Years* (Portland: Evening Express Publishing Co., 1898), 273–75. For discussions of the Maine Law and its antecedents, see Tyrrell, *Sobering Up,* 252–60; Blocker, Jr., *American Temperance Movements,* 51–60. A copy of the Maine Law can be found in Rev. John Marsh, *The Napoleon of Temperance . . . Author of the Maine Liquor Law* (New York: American Temperance Union, 1852); Lund, *Maine Law Documents,* is also useful.

8. "Right has Triumphed," *The Lily* 1, no. 6 (1849): 45; "Light Breaking," *The Lily* 1, no. 5 (1849): 37. See also "Another Victim," *The Lily* 1, no. 4 (1849): 30; "You Are Going Too Far!," *The Lily* 1, no. 5 (1849): 37–38; "New Law in Wisconsin," *The Lily* 1, no. 5 (1849): 38; "A Good Law," *The Lily* 2, no. 3 (1850): 20.

9. Henry A. Wing, *Maine's War upon the Liquor Traffic* (Portland: Portland Evening Express, 1909), 14, 15; P. T. Winskill, *The Temperance Movement and its Workers* (London: Blackie and Son, 1892), 269; *Proceedings, Speeches and Addresses of the Fourth National Temperance Convention . . . with the Maine Law* (New York: American Temperance Union, 1851), 26.

10. Anonymous, *The Unjust Judge; or, The Evils of Intemperance on Judges, Lawyers, and Politicians* (Mansfield, Ohio: Wesleyan Methodist Connection, 1854), 183, 185. On temperance and prohibition as difficult political issues, see Michael F. Holt's *The Political Crisis of the 1850s* (New York: W. W. Norton and Co., 1978), 155, and *The Rise and Fall of the American Whig Party: Jacksonian Politics and the Onset of the Civil War* (New York: Oxford University Press, 1999), esp. 950–60.

11. "Temperance and Politics," *The Lily* 2, no. 3 (1850): 20; William B. Brown, *The Massachusetts Liquor Law Just and Timely* (Andover: John D. Flagg, 1852), 12. For a splendid discussion of the political dimension of temperance during the Second Party system, see Dannenbaum, *Drink and Disorder.*

12. Tyrrell, "Women and Temperance," 143; *Proceedings of the Rhode-Island Total Abstinence Society . . . January 25, 1854* (Providence: Albert Crawford Green, 1854), 16.

13. "Temperance and Anti-Temperance at the Polls," *The Lily* 4, no. 4 (1852): 29; Stanton quoted in *The Lily* 4, no. 7 (1852): 58; Dannenbaum, "The Origins of Temperance Activism," 241.

14. Dannenbaum, "Origins," 239, 236.

15. *The Whole World's . . . September 1st and 2nd 1853* (New York: Fowler and Wells, 1853), 8.

16. *HWS,* vol. 1, 476; Tyrrell, "Women and Temperance," 146.

17. *Whole World's Temperance Convention,* 2, 8; *HWS,* vol. 1, 500.

18. John Watson, *Observations on the Customary Use of Distilled Spirituous*

Liquors (Philadelphia: Kimber and Conrad, 1810), 24; *Intemperance . . . Fairfield County* (Hartford: Peter B. Gleason, 1813), 23, 24; *Circular addressed to the Members of the Massachusetts Society for the Suppression of Intemperance* (Boston: Samuel T. Armstrong, 1814), 10, 12, 13. On the MSSI, see Robert L. Hampel, *Temperance and Prohibition in Massachusetts, 1813–1852* (Ann Arbor: UMI Research Press, 1982).

19. Thomas Herttell, *An Expose*, 9–10, 13; John Ware, MD, *An Address . . . May, 1825* (Boston: Christian Register, 1826), 8.

20. *Three Experiments in Drinking*, 32; *The Temperance Text Book: A Collection of Facts and Interesting Anecdotes, illustrating the Evils of Intoxicating Drinks*, 3rd ed. (Philadelphia: E. L. Carey and A. Hart, 1837) 80; DeWitt, *Profanity and Intemperance*, 10; J. Henry Clark, *The Present Position and Claims of the Temperance Enterprise* (New York: Baker and Scribner, 1847), 15.

21. Halttunen, *Confidence Men and Painted Women*, 61, 64; "Fashion," *The Pearl* 1, no. 19 (1846): 147.

22. Flandrau, *Address*, 8; G. J. Grosvenor, *An Address on the Importance of Female Influence to the Temperance Reformation* (Geneva: Ira Merrell, 1842), 17.

23. Anna Cora Mowatt, *Fashion*, in Richard Moody, ed., *Dramas from the American Theatre, 1762–1909* (Cleveland: World Publishing, 1966); Mrs. S. A. Southworth, *The Inebriate's Hut; or, The First Fruits of the Maine Law* (Boston: Phillips, Sampson & Co., 1854), 45; John K. Cornyn, *Dick Wilson, the Rumseller's Victim; or, Humanity Pleading for the Maine Law* (Buffalo: Derby, Orton and Mulligan, 1853), 87, 95, 105–6; Southworth, *Inebriate's Hut*, 32; Metta V. Fuller, *Fashionable Dissipation* (Philadelphia: See, Peters & Co., 1854), 12–13, 41. On the evolution of fashion, see also Jeanette C. Lauer and Robert H. Lauer, "The Battle of the Sexes: Fashion in 19th Century America," *Journal of Popular Culture* 13, no. 4 (1980): 581–89; and Linzy A. Brekke, "The 'Scourge of Fashion': Political Economy and the Politics of Consumption in the Early Republic," *Early American Studies* 3, no. 1 (2005): 111–39.

24. Jonathan French Stearns, *Female Influence and the True Christian Mode of Its Exercise* (Newburyport: J. G. Tilton, 1837), 9; Grosvenor, *Address*, 21; "Female Influence," *The Temperance Monitor* (June 1836), 5; *Temperance Text Book*, 100.

25. "Ladies in Grog Shops," *The Pearl* 1, no. 9 (1846): 69; "Plain Dealing," *The Pearl* 1, no. 24 (1846): 188; "Magnificent Drinking Saloons," *New York Organ* 7, no. 34 (1848): 268; Johnson, *Martha Washingtonianism*, 26, 27.

26. Potter, *Addresses*, 10.

27. Glenn Hendler, *Public Sentiments: Structures of Feeling in Nineteenth-Century American Literature* (Chapel Hill: University of North Carolina Press, 2001), 35, 32; see also Hendler's "Bloated Bodies and Sober Sentiments: Masculinity in 1840s Temperance Narratives," in *Sentimental Men: Masculinity and the Politics of Affect in American Culture*, ed. Mary Chapman and Glenn Hendler (Berkeley: University of California Press, 1999), 125–48. On the Washingtonian movement, see Blocker, Jr., *American Temperance Movements*, 30–61; Tyrrell, *Sobering Up*, 159–190, and Dannenbaum, *Drink and Disorder*, esp. 32–68; and John B. Gough, *Autobiography and Personal Recollections . . . as a Public Speaker* (Springfield: Bill, Nichols and Co., 1870), as well as his other published works.

28. "Moral Suasion of Women," *The Olive Plant* 2, no. 14 (1843): 107. The author of this article cautioned women "not to do what others have done before her, denounce and threaten" when they make their "appeal to the conscience and heart . . . denunciation will not accomplish the object." On Martha Washington societies, see Johnson, *Martha Washingtonianism*; and Alexander, "'We are Engaged as a Band of Sisters.'"

29. Clubb, *Maine Liquor Law*, 15; L. J. Halsey, *Legal Prohibition the Only Remedy for Drunkenness* (Louisville: J. F. Brennan, 1855), 12, 13; Opinions of the Press, 60.

30. "The 'Organ' vs. the 'Pearl': Legal Force vs. Moral Suasion," *The Pearl* 1, no. 40 (1847): 338; "The Organ and the Pearl," *The Pearl* 1, no. 44 (1847): 348; "An Awkward Apology," *The Pearl* 1, no. 44 (1847): 356.

31. *The Dew Drop* 2, no. 8 (1844): 3; "Light Breaking," *The Lily* 1, no. 5 (1849): 37; Marsh, *A Half Century Tribute*, 20; *Temperance Tracts for the People, Nos. 1–12* (New York: New York State Temperance Society, 1854), 2; Smucker, *Considerations*, 14.

32. Charles W. Flanders, *A Temperance Address . . . April 8, 1858* (Concord: Jones & Cogswell, 1858), 19; Joel Wakeman, *The Mysterious Parchment; or, The Satanic License. Dedicated to Maine Law Progress* (Boston: John P. Jewett and Company, 1853), 23; Southworth, *The Inebriate's Hut*, 37; Pharcellus Church, *Mapleton; or, More Work for the Maine Law* (Boston: Jenks, Hickling and Swan, 1852), 52.

33. Church, *Mapleton*, 161; Metta V. Fuller, *The Senator's Son; or, The Maine Law; A Last Refuge* (Cleveland: Tooker and Gatchel, 1853), 116, 212; *Unjust Judge*, 138.

34. Church, *Mapleton*, 52; *Unjust Judge*, 188, 245, 177. By the mid-1840s, dissatisfaction with moral suasion spread through the temperance movement and beyond throughout the Benevolent Empire, as the myriad of antebellum reform movements came to be called. See Lori Ginzberg, "'Moral Suasion is Moral Balderdash': Women, Politics, and Social Activism in the 1850s," *Journal of American History* 73, no. 3 (1986): 601–22.

35. Nancy A. Hewitt, *Women's Activism and Social Change*, 162–65; "Woman's Work in the Temperance Cause," *The Lily* 1, no. 4 (1849): 21; "Caroline M. Sweet," *The Lily* 1, no. 8 (1849), 61. See also "You are Going Too Far!" *The Lily* 1, no. 5 (1849): 37–38; and "Protection for Married Women," *The Lily* 1, no. 5 (1849): 40. On Mary Vaughn's change of heart, see Ginzberg, *Women and the Work of Benevolence*, 114–15. For a discussion of the growing woman's rights militancy of *The Lily*, consult Jerry, "*The Lily*, 1849–1856: From Temperance to Woman's Rights."

36. *The Layman's Argument against the Interdiction of Intoxicating Liquors by Church or State* (Richmond: C. H. Wynn's Steam-Powered Printing Press, 1853), 4; "Two Worlds' Temperance Conventions," *New York Evangelist* 24, no. 20 (19 May 1853), 78; "Temperance and Woman's Rights," *New York Times*, February 8, 1853, 8; "The Amazons," *New York Times*, February 9, 1853, 4; "From the Era," *The Huntress* 16, no. 15 (1853): 2; "California Correspondence," *Spirit of the Times* 24, no. 51 (1855): 608.

37. "What Woman is Doing," *New York Washingtonian and Ladies' Literary Pearl* 2, no. 10 (1847): 76; "Sympathy of Woman," *New York Organ* 7, no. 11 (1847): 84; "John Marsh and the Order," *New York Organ* 7, no. 11 (1847): 86; "Downright Plagiarism," *New York Organ* 7, no. 9 (1847): 76.

38. E. Francis, ed., *The Beauties of . . . Sisters of Temperance* (Philadelphia: W. A. Leary and Co., 1851), 64, 65; "Original Daughter of Temperance," *The Pearl* 1, no. 33 (1847): 261; "To the Editress of the Pearl," *The Pearl* 1, no. 37 (1847): 293; "Geneva Union and Grand Union, Daughters of Temperance," *The Pearl* 1, no. 39 (1847): 308.

39. "Daughters of Temperance," *New York Organ* 7, no. 42 (1848): 332; "National Union of Daughters of Temperance," *New York Organ* 7, no. 44 (1848): 348; "Daughters of Temperance," *New York Organ* 8, no. 3 (1848): 20; *New York Organ* 8, no. 12 (1848): 95, 96; *Journal of Proceedings of the National Union of Daughters of Temperance of North America*, Third Annual Meeting, Boston June 12–14, 1850 (Philadelphia: William F. Geddes, 1850), 3, back cover.

40. Henry Hickock, *The Duty of Christian Women to Convert the Social Heart to the Principles of Temperance* (Rochester: Lee, Mann and Co., 1853), 12; Samuel V. Leech, *The Influence of Woman on the Temperance Reformation* (Baltimore: James Young, 1865), 6.

41. Hickock, *Duty of Christian Women*, 23; *Female Influence for the Maine Law* (New York: American Temperance Union, 1855), 2, 3, 4; Leech, *Influence of Woman*, 6.

42. Tyrrell, *Sobering Up*, 125–31; for temperance nostalgia, see Warder, "Temperance Nostalgia," 217–45.

43. *HWS*, vol. 1, 505–6.

Conclusion—The Legacy of Middle-Class Temperance Ideology

1. Elizabeth Cady Stanton to Susan B. Anthony, 20 June 1853, in DuBois, ed., *Elizabeth Cady Stanton/Susan B. Anthony,* 57.

2. S. F. Carey, *Ritual for the Admission of Females into the Order of the Sons of Temperance* (Trenton: H. B. Howell, 1860), 2. On the Carson League, see J. C. Furnas, *The Life and Times of the Late Demon Rum* (New York: Capricorn Books, 1965), 262; and Pegram, *Battling Demon Rum,* 41. For the Good Templars, consult Jane E. Stebbins, *Fifty Years History of the Temperance Cause* (Hartford: J. P. Fitch, 1876); I. N. Pierce, *The History of the Independent Order of Good Templars* (Philadelphia: Daughaday & Becker, 1869); David Fahey, *Temperance and Racism: John Bull, Johnny Reb, and the Good Templars* (Lexington: University Press of Kentucky, 1996); and Tyrrell, *Sobering Up.*

3. On women and the Sanitary Commission, see Nancy S. Garrison, *With Courage and Delicacy: Civil War on the Peninsula and the U.S. Sanitary Commission* (Cambridge: Da Capo, 2003); Judith Ann Giesberg, *Civil War Sisterhood: The U.S. Sanitary Commission and Women's Politics in Transition* (Boston: Northeastern University Press, 2000).

4. Wendy F. Hammand, "The Woman's National Loyal League: Feminist Abolitionists and the Civil War," *Civil War History* 35, no. 1 (1989): 39–58.

5. On the Woman's Crusade, see Mother [Mrs. Eliza Daniel] Stewart, *Memories of the Crusade: A Thrilling Account of the Women of Ohio in 1873, against the Liquor Crime* (Columbus: Wm. G. Hubbard & Co., 1888); Bordin, *Woman and Temperance,* 15; Jack Blocker Jr.'s *"Give to the Wind thy Fears": The Women's Temperance Crusade, 1873–1874* (Westport: Greenwood Press, 1985), and *American Temperance Movements,* 61–64, 75–79; and Michelle J. Stecker, "A Respectable Revolution: The Dynamics of Religion and Gender in the Ohio Woman's Temperance Crusade, 1873–1874" (Ph.D. dissertation, University of Toledo, 2000). On the WCTU, see Bordin, *Woman and Temperance;* Ian R. Tyrrell, *Woman's World, Woman's Empire: The Woman's Christian Temperance Union in International Perspective* (Chapel Hill: University of North Carolina Press, 1991).

6. On the antebellum experience of postbellum activists, see Stebbins, *Fifty Years;* Stewart, *Memories,* 17–21; Ruth Bordin, *Frances Willard: A Biography* (Chapel Hill: University of North Carolina Press, 1986).

7. Parsons, *Manhood Lost,* 168. On the WCTU's use of gendered rhetoric, see also Mattingly, *Well-Tempered Women.* For the linkage of home protection to suffrage, consult Frances E. Willard, *Home Protection Manual: Containing an Argument for the Temperance Ballot for Woman, and How to Obtain It, as a Means of Home Protection* (New York: The Independent, 1879).

8. Murdock, *Domesticating Drink,* 9. On this and similar points, see also Giele, *Two Paths to Women's Equality.*

9. For discussions of women, prohibition, and repeal, see David E. Kyvig, "Women against Prohibition," *American Quarterly* 28, no. 4 (1976): 465–82, and *Repealing National Prohibition* (Kent: Kent State University Press, 2000); Caryn E. Neumann, "The End of Gender Solidarity: The History of the Women's Organization for National Prohibition Reform in the United States, 1929–1933," *Journal of Women's History* 9, no. 2 (1997): 31–51; and Rose, *American Women and the Repeal of Prohibition*.

10. Glenn Hendler, "Bloated Bodies and Sober Sentiments," quote on 127.

11. For example, see Nancy D. Campbell, *Using Women: Gender, Drug Policy, and Social Justice* (New York: Routledge, 2000), 19–28.

Works Cited

Newspapers and Periodicals

The American Quarterly Temperance Magazine (Albany, NY)
American Temperance Magazine and Sons of Temperance Offering (New York)
Boston Medical and Surgical Journal
The Cold Water Girl (Philadelphia)
Columbia Washingtonian (Hudson, NY)
Daughter of Temperance (Naperville, IL)
The Dew Drop (Taunton, MA)
The Fountain (Philadelphia)
The Genius of Temperance, Philanthropist and People's Advocate (New York)
The Huntress (Washington, D.C.)
The Investigator and General Intelligencer (Providence, RI)
Journal of Health (Philadelphia)
Journal of the American Temperance Union (Philadelphia)
The Lily (Seneca Falls, NY)
The Medical Repository (New York)
The New York Evangelist
New York Organ and Temperance Safeguard
New York Times
New York Washington Reformer and Ladies' Literary Journal
New York Washingtonian and Ladies' Literary Pearl
The Olive Plant and Ladies' Temperance Advocate (New York)
The Pearl, A Ladies' Weekly Literary Gazette Devoted to the Advocacy of Various Ladies' Total Abstinence Associations (New York)
Spirit of the Times (New York)
Staunton Spectator and General Advertiser (Virginia)
The Temperance Monitor (Philadelphia)
The Temperance Offering (Salem, MA)
Temperance Recorder (Albany)

Articles and Books

Adams, Solomon. *An Address, delivered at North-Yarmouth, April 28, 1830, before the Cumberland Co. Temperance Society.* Portland: Shirley, Hyde and Co., 1830.

Address to the People of the Commonwealth Relative to the License Question. N.p., 1846.

Addresses of Miss Anne E. Tomkins and Mr. William J. Hoge before Sumner Division, No. 20, Sons of Temperance at Gallatin, Tennessee on the 22nd of May, 1847. Nashville: J. G. Sheperd, 1847.

The Afflicted Family, and Awful Effects of Intemperance: deleniated [sic] in a Brief Relation of the Melancholy Particulars that Attended the Unfortunate Family of James Ellison, (comprised of himself, wife, and five helpless children,) in their attempted remove in the winter of 1841, from the extreme part of the state of Pennsylvania . . . when through the beastly inebriation of their father, three of his children perished by reason of hunger and cruel neglect. New York: Printed for the Publisher, 1842.

Agnew, J. H. *Address on Intemperance in the Use of Ardent Spirits. Delivered Before the Temperance Society of Connellsville, Pennsylvania, April 20, 1829.* Philadelphia: W. F. Geddes, 1829.

Aikin, S. C. *Moral Reform. A Sermon delivered at Utica, on Sabbath Evening, February 16, 1834.* Utica: R. B. Shepherd, 1834.

Alexander, Ruth M. "'We are Engaged as a Band of Sisters': Class and Domesticity in the Washingtonian Temperance Movement, 1840–1850." *Journal of American History* 75, no. 3 (1988): 763–85.

Alger, William R. *The Facts of Intemperance, and their Claims on the Public Action of the People.* Boston: Crosby, Nichols and Company, 1852.

American National Biography Online. New York: Oxford University Press, 2000.

Annals of the American Female Home Education Society and Temperance Union, vol. 4. Boston: The Society, 1842.

Annals of the Ladies' American Home Education Society and Temperance Union, Vol. IX. Boston: J. Howe, 1847.

Anniversary Celebration of Howard Union, No. 3, Daughters of Temperance. Wednesday Evening, Oct. 25, 1848. [Providence?]: 1848.

The Anniversary Report of the Managers of the Pennsylvania Society for Discouraging the Use of Ardent Spirits. Read on the 27th May, 1831, and Ordered to be Published by the Society. Philadelphia: Henry H. Porter, 1831.

The Appeal of a Wife and Mother. Temperance Tract No. 1. Providence: S. R. Weeden, [1840?].

Appleton, Thomas H. "'Moral Suasion Has Had Its Day': From Temperance to Prohibition in Antebellum Kentucky." In *A Mythic Land Apart: Reassessing Southerners and Their History,* edited by John David Smith and Thomas H. Appleton, Jr. Westport: Greenwood Press, 1997.

Armstrong, Lebbeus. *The Temperance Reformation.* New York: Fowler and Wells, 1853.

Armstrong, William J. *The Evils of Intemperance, and the Duty of the Temperate: A Sermon, Preached at the First Presbyterian Church, Richmond, VA, on the Day of Fasting and Prayer on Account of Intemperance, appointed by the General Assembly of the Presbyterian Church.* Richmond: J. MacFarlan, 1829.

Arthur, T. S. *The Ruined Family and Other Tales.* Philadelphia: Godey & M'Michael, 1843.

———. *Ten Nights in a Bar-Room, and What I Saw There,* edited by Jon Miller. Acton: Copley Publishing Group, 2002.

———, ed. *The Temperance Offering.* New York: Leavitt and Allen, [185?].

———, ed. *The Temperance Offering for 1853.* New York: Cornish, Lamport & Co., 1853.

Austin, Gregory. *Alcohol in Western Society from Antiquity to 1800.* Santa Barbara: ABC Clio, 1985.

Austin, James Trecothick. *An Address Delivered before the Massachusetts Society for the Suppression of Intemperance, May 27, 1830.* Boston: John H. Eastburn, 1830.

Bacon, Leonard. *A Discourse on the Traffic in Spirituous Liquors, delivered in the Center Church, New Haven, February 6, 1838, with an Appendix, Exhibiting the Present State and Influence of the Traffic in the City of New Haven.* New Haven: B. L. Hamlen, 1838.

Badger, Stephen. *The Substance of Two Discourses on Intemperance; Delivered at Natick; by the Late Rev. Stephen Badger, Minister of that Place.* Boston: Samuel T. Armstrong, 1811.

Baker, Robert. "The Kappa Lambda Society of Hippocrates: The Secret Origins of the American Medical Association." In *Fugitive Leaves from the Historical Collections, Library of the College of Physicians of Philadelphia*, 3rd ser., 11, no. 2 (1996).

Baltimore Temperance Society. *The Constitution and Address of the Baltimore Temperance Society; to which is added An Address, delivered before the Society, by N. R. Smith, M.D., Professor of Surgery in the University of Maryland.* Baltimore: J. D. Troy, 1830.

Barker-Benfield, G. J. *The Horrors of the Half-known Life: Male Attitudes toward Women and Sexuality in Nineteenth-Century America.* New York: Harper and Row, 1976.

Barnes, Albert. *The Cause of Intemperance in Cities and Large Towns.* Philadelphia: George, Latimer & Co., 1834.

———. *The Immorality of the Traffic in Ardent Spirits: A Discourse, Delivered in the First Presbyterian Church in Philadelphia, April 13, 1834.* Philadelphia: George, Latimer & Co., 1834.

———. *The Throne of Iniquity, or Sustaining Evil by Law: A Discourse in Behalf of a Law Prohibiting the Traffic in Intoxicating Beverages.* New York: American Temperance Union, 1852.

Bates, Joshua. *Two Sermons on Intemperance, Delivered on the Day of the Annual Fast, April 8, 1813.* Boston: Samuel T. Armstrong, 1813.

BBC. *Prohibition: Thirteen Years that Changed America.* London: British Broadcasting Company, 1996.

Behr, Edward. *Prohibition: Thirteen Years that Changed America.* New York: Arcade Publishers, 1996.

Beman, Nathan S. S. *A Discourse delivered in Stephenstown, Dec. 25, 1828, and in Troy, Sabbath Evening, Jan. 11, 1829 before the Temperance Societies of Those Towns.* Troy, NY: F. Adancourt, 1829.

Bethune, George W. *The Substance of an Address in Favor of Temperance Societies. Delivered on the 26th of February, 1833, at Rome.* Utica: William Williams, 1833.

Blocker, Jack. Jr, *American Temperance Movements: Cycles of Reform.* Boston: Twayne Publishers, 1989.

———. *"Give to the Wind thy Fears": The Women's Temperance Crusade, 1873–1874.* Westport: Greenwood Press, 1985.

Bloomer, Dexter C. *Life and Writings of Amelia Bloomer.* Boston, 1895.

Blumin, Stuart M. *The Emergence of the Middle Class: Social Experience in the American City, 1760–1900.* New York: Cambridge University Press, 1989.

Bordin, Ruth. *Frances Willard: A Biography.* Chapel Hill: University of North Carolina Press, 1986.

———. *Woman and Temperance: The Quest for Power and Liberty, 1873–1900.* New Brunswick: Rutgers University Press, 1990.

Bradbury, Osgood. *The Distiller's Daughter: Or, The Power of Woman.* N.p., [1844?].

Braude, Ann. *Radical Spirits: Spiritualism and Women's Rights in Nineteenth-century America.* Boston: Beacon Press, 1989.

Brekke, Linzy A. "The 'Scourge of Fashion': Political Economy and the Politics of Consumption in the Early Republic." *Early American Studies* 3, no. 1 (2005): 111–39.

Brown, William B. *The Massachusetts Liquor Law Just and Timely.* Andover: John D. Flagg, 1852.

Buckley, Maria. *Edith Moreton, or, Temperance versus Intemperance.* Philadelphia: Stavely and M'Calla, 1852.

Burleigh, George C. *Memoirs of Alcohol. Written by Himself. Including Biographical Sketches of His Sons Brandy, Rum, and Whiskey; and of His Daughter Gin.* Hartford: Robinson & Pratt, 1834.

Bushman, Richard L. *The Refinement of America: Persons, Houses, Cities.* New York: Knopf, 1992.

Butler, Judith. *Gender Trouble: Feminism and the Subversion of Identity.* New York: Routledge, 1990.

Campbell, Nancy D. *Using Women: Gender, Drug Policy, and Social Justice.* New York: Routledge, 2000.

Carey, S. F. *Ritual for the Admission of Females into the Order of the Sons of Temperance.* Trenton: H. B. Howell, 1860.

Carpenter, William B. *The Physiology of Temperance and Total Abstinence, being an Examination of the Effects of the Excessive, Moderate, and Occasional Use of Alcoholic Liquors on the Healthy Human System.* London: Henry G. Bohn, 1853.

Caruthers, William. *The Drunkard from Cradle to Grave. A lecture, delivered before the Savannah Temperance Society, at the First Presbyterian Church, Jan. 15, and repeated Feb. 26.* Savannah: W. T. Williams, 1840.

Ceremonies, Etc. New York State Inebriate Asylum, Binghamton, New York. New York: Wynkoop, Hallenbeck and Thomas, 1859.

Chafetz, Janet Saltzman, and Anthony Gary Dworkin. *Female Revolt: Women's Movements in World and Historical Perspective.* Totowa: Rowman and Allanheld, 1986.

Chillicothe Association for Promoting Morality and Good Order. *Address of the Chillicothe Association for Promoting Morality and Good Order, to the Fellow Citizens, on Profane Swearing, the Violation of the Sabbath, and the Intemperate Use of Ardent Spirits.* Chillicothe: John Andrews, 1815.

Chipman, Samuel B. *The Temperance Lecturer.* Albany, 1846.

Chittenden, Nathaniel. *The Influence of Woman upon the Destinies of a People; Being an Oration delivered at the Annual Commencement of Columbia College, October 3rd, 1837.* New York: Scottherd and Adams, 1837.

Chrystal Fount: or, Songs for the Sons and Daughters of Temperance. New York: Philip J. Cozans, 1860.

Church, Pharcellus. *Mapleton; or, More Work for the Maine Law.* Boston: Jenks, Hickling and Swan, 1852.

Circular addressed to the Members of the Massachusetts Society for the Suppression of Intemperance. Boston: Samuel T. Armstrong, 1814.

Clark, J. Henry. *The Present Position and Claims of the Temperance Enterprise.* New York: Baker and Scribner, 1847.

Cleveland, E. L. *A Discourse on the Existing State of Morals in the City of New Haven, delivered before the New Haven Washington Temperance Union, in the Court Street Church, Sabbath Evening, Oct. 13, and Repeated in the Center Church, Sabbath Evening, Oct. 21st, 1850.* New Haven: J. H. Benham, 1850.

Clubb, Henry S. *The Maine Liquor Law: Its Origin, History, and Results, Including a life of Hon. Neal Dow.* New York: Fowler and Wells, 1856.

Cohen, Patricia Cline. *The Murder of Helen Jewett.* New York: Knopf, 1998.

Confessions of a Reformed Inebriate. New York: American Temperance Union, 1844.

Constitution and By-Laws of Washington Union, Number 1, Daughters of Temperance of the City of Cincinnati, Instituted February 9, 1846. Cincinnati: Caleb Clark, 1846.

Constitution of the Society and Directors of the Penitent Female's Refuge. Adopted April 14, 1819. Boston: True and Weston, 1819.

Cooke, E. B. *Infidelity and Benevolent Societies.* Waterbury: E. B. Cooke and Co., 1848.

Cornyn, John K. *Dick Wilson, the Rumseller's Victim; or, Humanity Pleading for the Maine Law.* Buffalo: Derby, Orton and Mulligan, 1853.

Cott, Nancy. *The Bonds of Womanhood: "Woman's Sphere" in New England, 1780–1835.* New Haven: Yale University Press, 1977.

———. "Passionlessness: An Interpretation of Victorian Sexual Ideology, 1790–1850." *Signs* 4, no. 2 (1978): 219–36.

Courtwright, David T. *Dark Paradise: A History of Opiate Addiction in America.* Cambridge: Harvard University Press, 2001.

———. *Forces of Habit: Drugs and the Making of the Modern World.* Cambridge: Harvard University Press, 2001.

Crime, Pauperism and Intemperance. Providence: City Temperance Society, 1841.

Cross, Marcus E. *The Mirror of Intemperance, and History of the Temperance Reform.* Philadelphia: John T. Lange, 1849.

Dannenbaum, Jed. *Drink and Disorder: Temperance Reform in Cincinnati from the Washingtonian Revival to the WCTU.* Urbana: University of Illinois Press, 1984.

———. "The Origins of Temperance Activism and Militancy among American Women." *Journal of Social History* 15, no. 2 (1981): 235–52.

Davidson, Cathy N., and Jessamyn Hatcher, eds. *No More Separate Spheres!* Durham: Duke University Press, 2002.

DeWitt, William R. *Profanity and Intemperance, Prevailing Evils. A Discourse.* Harrisburg: Fenn & Wallace, 1840.

"A Dialogue between a Father and Son." In *The Evils of Intemperance, Exemplified in Poetry and Prose. With Engravings. By a Friend to Temperance,* 18. Boston: N. Boynton, 1829.

The Dictionary of American Biography. New York: Scribner, 1964.

Dimmick, Luther Fraseur. *Intemperance: A Sermon, delivered at the North Church in Newburyport, on the Occasion of the Publick Fast, April 1, 1824.* Newburyport: Charles Whipple, 1824.

Dorsey, Bruce. *Reforming Men and Women: Gender in the Antebellum City.* Ithaca: Cornell University Press, 2002.

Douglas, Ann. *The Feminization of American Culture.* New York: Avon Books, 1977.

Dow, Neal. *The Reminiscences of Neal Dow: Recollections of Eighty Years.* Portland: Evening Express Publishing Co., 1898.

Drake, Daniel. *A Discourse on Intemperance; Delivered at Cincinnati, March 1, 1828, before the Agricultural Society of Hamilton County, and Subsequently Pronounced, by Request, to a Popular Audience.* Cincinnati: Looker and Reynolds, 1828.

DuBois, Ellen Carol, ed. *Elizabeth Cady Stanton/Susan B. Anthony: Correspondence, Writings, Speeches.* New York: Schocken Books, 1981.

Dumont, Julia L. *Life Sketches from Common Paths: A Series of American Tales.* New York: D. Appleton & Co., 1856.

Edwards, Justin. *Joy in heaven over the Penitent. A Sermon, delivered in Park Street Church, Before the Penitent Female's Refuge Society, on the Evening of Sabbath, December 18, 1825.* Boston: T. R. Marvin, 1825.

———. *The Temperance Manual.* New York: American Tract Society, [1847?].

Ellett, Mrs. E. F. "A Country Recollection, or, The Reformed Inebriate." In *The Adopted Daughter and Other Tales,* edited by Alice Carey. Philadelphia: J. B. Smith, 1859.

Ellis, John. *Marriage and Its Violations, Licentiousness and Vice.* New York: John Ellis, 1860.

Emilio, Carolo. *Intemperance: Its Effects, Physical, Intellectual, and Moral; Its History and Origin, and How the Habit is Formed. Together with a View of Redemption; or, The Means of Its Cure.* Philadelphia, 1856.

The Evils of Drunkenness. New York Religious Tract Society, No. 83. New York: D. Fanshaw, 1820.

Facts to Think About, and What's the Remedy? Philadelphia: C. Sherman, 1850.

Fahey, David. *Temperance and Racism: John Bull, Johnny Reb, and the Good Templars.* Lexington: University Press of Kentucky, 1996.

Female Influence for the Maine Law. New York: American Temperance Union, 1855.

The First Annual Report of the Managers of the Society for the Prevention of Pauperism in the City of New York. Read and Accepted October 26, 1818. New York: J. Seymour, 1818.

Flanders, Charles W. *A Temperance Address delivered before the Concord Temperance Society, in the First Baptist Church, Fast Day, April 8, 1858.* Concord: Jones & Cogswell, 1858.

Flandrau, Thomas H. *Address: Delivered at a Meeting of the Female Washingtonian and Other Temperance Societies of the City of Utica, May 9, 1842.* Utica: Woodland & Donaldson, 1842.

Fletcher, Abel. *The History, Objects, and Principles of the Order of the Sons of Temperance: An Address, delivered in Richmond, VA, December 2, 1844.* Philadelphia: Gihon & Porter, 1845.

Flint, Joshua B. *An Address Delivered before the Massachusetts Society for the Suppression of Intemperance, May 29, 1828.* Boston: Bowles and Dearborn, 1828.

Foster, Stephen. *A Sermon on Intemperance; Delivered in the First Presbyterian Church in Knoxville, Tenn., on the 21st of April, 1833.* Knoxville: F. S. Heiskell, 1833.

Fowler, Orson S. *Fowler on Matrimony: or, Phrenology and Physiology Applied to the Selection of Congenial Companions for Life.* Stereotype edition, 20th Thousand. New York: O. S. and L. N. Fowler, 1842.

Francis, E., ed. *The Beauties of Temperance; or, The Principles and Organization of the Sons, Daughters, Cadets, and Juvenile Sisters of Temperance.* Philadelphia: W. A. Leary and Co., 1851.

Frick, John W. *Theatre, Culture and Temperance Reform in Nineteenth-century America.* Cambridge: Cambridge University Press, 2003.

A Friend of Temperance and Equal Rights. *An Address to the Leaders of the Abstinence Enterprise.* Philadelphia, 1831.

Frost, Daniel, Jr. *An Address, delivered November 12, 1828, before the Temperance Society, of Canterbury, Conn.* New Bedford: B. Lindsey & Son, 1829.

Fuller, Metta V. *Fashionable Dissipation.* Philadelphia: See, Peters & Co., 1854.

———. *The Senator's Son; or, The Maine Law; A Last Refuge.* Cleveland: Tooker and Gatchel, 1853.

Furnas, J. C. *The Life and Times of the Late Demon Rum.* New York: Capricorn Books, 1965.

Gale Research Company. *Currier and Ives: A Catalogue Raisonné.* Detroit: Gale Research Co., 1984.

Garrison, Nancy S. *With Courage and Delicacy: Civil War on the Peninsula and the U.S. Sanitary Commission.* Cambridge: Da Capo, 2003.

Giele, Janet Zollinger. *Two Paths to Women's Equality: Temperance, Suffrage, and the Origins of Modern Feminism.* New York: Twayne Publishers, 1995.

Giesberg, Judith Ann. *Civil War Sisterhood: The U.S. Sanitary Commission and Women's Politics in Transition.* Boston: Northeastern University Press, 2000.

Ginzberg, Lori D. "'Moral Suasion is Moral Balderdash': Women, Politics, and Social Activism in the 1850s." *Journal of American History* 73, no. 3 (1986): 601–22.

———. *Women and the Work of Benevolence: Morality, Politics and Class in the Nineteenth-Century United States.* New Haven: Yale University Press, 1990.

Gladding, Mrs. E. N. "Minnie—A Temperance Tale." In *Leaves from an Invalid's Journal, and Poems.* Providence: George H. Whitney, 1858.

Gough, John B. *Autobiography and Personal Recollections of John B. Gough, With Twenty-six Years Experience as a Public Speaker.* Springfield: Bill, Nichols and Co., 1870.

Grattan, Henry P. *The Bottle, a Poem Suggested by the Celebrated Designs of Geo. Cruikshank, reduced and Engraved by Tudor Horton.* New York: Talbot Watts, 1848.

Grayson, Ellen Hickey. "Social Order and Psychological Disorder: Laughing Gas Demonstrations, 1800–1850." In *Freakery: Cultural Spectacles of the Extraordinary Body,* edited by Rosemarie G. Thompson. New York: New York University Press, 1996.

Gregory, John. *The Bramble.* Methuen: S. J. Varney, 1837.

Griffin, Clifford S. *Their Brothers' Keepers: Moral Stewardship in the United States, 1800–1860.* New Brunswick: Rutgers University Press, 1960.

Grob, Gerald. *Nineteenth-Century Medical Attitudes toward Alcohol Addiction.* New York: Arno Press, 1981.

Grossberg, Michael. *Governing the Hearth: Law and Family in Nineteenth-Century America.* Chapel Hill: University of North Carolina Press, 1985.

Grosvenor, G. J. *An Address on the Importance of Female Influence to the Temperance Reformation.* Geneva: Ira Merrell, 1842.

Gunn, Alexander. *A Sermon on the Prevailing Vice of Intemperate Drinking, Delivered in the Reformed Church, Bloomingdale, in the City of New York, on Friday, The First Day of the New Year, 1813.* New York: Whiting and Watson, 1813.

Halsey, Rev. L. J. *Legal Prohibition the Only Remedy for Drunkenness; being the Substance of Two Discourses, delivered in the Chestnut St. Church, Louisville, on the First Sabbaths of April and July, 1855.* Louisville: J. F. Brennan, 1855.

Halttunen, Karen. *Confidence Men and Painted Women: A Study in Middle-class Culture in America, 1830–1870.* New Haven: Yale University Press, 1982.

Hammand, Wendy F. "The Woman's National Loyal League: Feminist Abolitionists and the Civil War." *Civil War History* 35, no. 1 (1989): 39–58.

Hampel, Robert L. *Temperance and Prohibition in Massachusetts, 1813–1852.* Ann Arbor: UMI Research Press, 1982.

Hanley, Mark Y. *Beyond a Christian Commonwealth: The Protestant Quarrel with the American Republic, 1830–1860.* Chapel Hill: University of North Carolina Press, 1994.

Harabaugh, Rev. H. *A Word in Season, or, A Plea for Legislative Aid in Putting Down the Evils of Intemperance.* Chambersburg: German Reformed Church, 1846.

Harper, Ida Hustedt. *The Life and Work of Susan B. Anthony.* 2 vols. Indianapolis: Hollenbeck, 1898.

Harrington, Joseph. *Address, Delivered at Roxbury, before the Roxbury Auxiliary Society for the Suppression of Intemperance, June 30, 1820.* Boston: Joseph T. Buckingham, 1820.

Harrison, Brian. *Drink and the Victorians: The Temperance Question in England, 1815–1872.* Pittsburgh: University of Pittsburgh Press, 1971.

Hartley, Robert M. *Intemperance in Cities and Large Towns: Showing Its Physical, Social, and Moral Effects; also The Means for Its Prevention and Removal.* New York: John F. Trow, 1851.

Hartz, Louis. *The Liberal Tradition in America: An Interpretation of American Political Thought since the Revolution.* New York: Harcourt Brace, 1955.

Harvey, Joseph. *An Appeal to Christians, on the Immorality of Using or Vending Distilled Liquors, as an Article of Luxury or Diet. Delivered Before the Temperance Society in East-Hampton, Conn. May 5th, 1831.* Middletown: William D. Starr, 1831.

Harvey, Mrs. R. S. "A Single Glass of Wine." In *The Fountain and the Bottle; comprising Thrilling Examples of the Opposite Effects of Temperance and Intemperance,* edited by A Son of Temperance. Boston: Horace Wentworth, 1850.

A Hasty Defense of the Farmers and Distillers of York County, against the Aspersion of the Temperance Societies, & c. York: W. C. Smyth, 1833.

Hendler, Glenn. "Bloated Bodies and Sober Sentiments: Masculinity in 1840s Temperance Narratives." In *Sentimental Men: Masculinity and the Politics of Affect in American Culture,* edited by Mary Chapman and Glenn Hendler. Berkeley: University of California Press, 1999.

———. *Public Sentiments: Structures of Feeling in Nineteenth-Century American Literature.* Chapel Hill: University of North Carolina Press, 2001.

Hentz, Caroline Lee. *Courtship and Marriage, or, The Joys and Sorrows of American Life.* Philadelphia: T. B. Peterson, 1856.

Heron, Craig. *Booze: A Distilled History.* Toronto: Between the Lines, 2003.

Herttell, Thomas. *An Expose of the Causes of Intemperate Drinking, and the Means by which it may be Obviated.* New York: E. Conrad, 1819.

Hewitt, Nancy. *Women's Activism and Social Change: Rochester, New York, 1822–1872.* Ithaca: Cornell University Press, 1984.

Hickock, Henry. *The Duty of Christian Women to Convert the Social Heart to the Principles of Temperance.* Rochester: Lee, Mann and Co., 1853.

Hill, Stephen P. *Sermon on the Subject of Temperance. Delivered on the 27th Day of December, 1835, in accordance with the call made on the Rev. Clergy by the Executive Committee of the Maryland State Temperance Society, to unite in a simultaneous temperance effort on that day; and published at its request.* Baltimore: Sands and Neilson, 1836.

Hinckley, Mary. *The Camphene Lamp; or, Touch Not, Taste Not, Handle Not.* Lowell: James P. Walker, 1852.

The History of the Bottle. New York: Oliver and Brother, 1848.

Hitchcock, Edward. *An Essay on Alcoholic and Narcotic Substances, as Articles of Common use. Addressed Particularly to Students.* Boston: J. S. & C. Adams & Co., 1830.

———. *An Essay on Temperance, Addressed Particularly to Students, and the Young Men of America.* Amherst: J. S. & C. Adams, 1830.

Hofstader, Richard. *The Age of Reform.* New York: Vintage Books, 1955.

Holt, Michael. *The Political Crisis of the 1850s.* New York: W. W. Norton and Co., 1978.

———. *The Rise and Fall of the American Whig Party: Jacksonian Politics and the Onset of the Civil War.* New York: Oxford University Press, 1999.

Hume, James Nelson. *Temperance versus Intemperance: An Address, or Concise Treatment on the Nature and Effects of Alcohol. Delivered in the Brick Church, Montpelier, Vt., before the Temperance Society of that Place, on the Day of Simultaneous Meetings throughout the World, February 25, 1840.* Boston: D. H. Lea, 1840.

Hunt, Thomas P. *The Wedding Days of Former Times.* Philadelphia: Griffith & Simon, 1845.

Husted Harper, Ida. *The Life and Work of Susan B. Anthony.* Vol. 1. Indianapolis: Hollenbeck, 1898.

The Hypocrisy and Cowardice of Pilate Less Objectionable than the Hypocrisy and Cowardice of Many Men of Our Day who are Called Both Brave and Good. N.p.: [1840s?].

"I Am Afraid There Is a God." In *Temperance Tales.* Vol. 1. Boston: Whipple & Damrell, 1838.

Inquiries and Observations, upon the Diseases of the Mind. Philadelphia: Kimber and Richardson, 1812. Quoted in Ronald Walters, *Primers for Prudery: Sexual Advice to Victorian America,* 111. Englewood Cliffs: Prentice Hall, 1974.

Intemperance. An Address to the Churches and Congregations of the Western District of Fairfield County. Hartford: Peter B. Gleason, 1813.

Jackson, James. "On a Peculiar Disease resulting from the use of Ardent Spirits." *New England Journal of Medicine and Surgery* 11, no. 4 (1822).

Jenks, William. *A Sermon, delivered before the Massachusetts Society for the Suppression of Intemperance, at their Annual Meeting, June 1, 1821, with the Annual Report.* Boston: Phelps and Farnham, 1821.

Jerry, E. Claire. "*The Lily*, 1849–1856: From Temperance to Woman's Rights." In *A Voice of Their Own: The Woman Suffrage Press, 1840–1910*, edited by Martha A. Solomon, 30–47. Tuscaloosa: University of Alabama Press, 1991.

Jewett, Charles. *Speeches, Poems, and Miscellaneous Writings, on Subjects connected with Temperance and the Liquor Traffic.* Boston: John P. Jewett, 1849.

Johnson, A. B. *An Address to the Utica Temperance Society, Delivered at the Second Presbyterian Church, July 29, 1829.* Utica: William Williams, 1829.

Johnson, Lorenzo Dow. *Martha Washingtonianism, or, A History of the Ladies' Temperance Benevolent Societies.* New York: Saxton & Miles, 1843.

Johnson, Paul. *A Shopkeeper's Millennium: Society and Revivals in Rochester, New York, 1815–1837.* New York: Hill and Wang, 1978.

Journal of Proceedings of the National Union of Daughters of Temperance of North America. Third Annual Meeting, Boston, June 12–14, 1850. Philadelphia: William F. Geddes, 1850.

Karlsen, Carol. *The Devil in the Shape of a Woman.* New York: Vintage Books, 1989.

Kelly, Catherine E. *In the New England Fashion: Reshaping Women's Lives in the Nineteenth Century.* Ithaca: Cornell University Press, 1999.

Kerber, Linda. *Women of the Republic: Intellect and Ideology in Revolutionary America.* New York: Norton, 1986.

Keyes, N. A. *A Temperance Sermon, delivered February 8th, 1852, before the Lancaster Temple of Honor No. 48, of the State of Pennsylvania.* Lancaster: John H. Pearsol, 1852.

Kirkland, John T. *A Sermon, Delivered before the Massachusetts Society for Suppression of Intemperance, at their Annual Meeting in Boston, May 27, 1814.* Boston: John Eliot, 1814.

Kornblith, Gary. "Introduction to the Symposium on Class in the Early Republic." *Journal of the Early Republic* 25, no. 4 (2005): 523–26.

Kyvig, David E. *Repealing National Prohibition.* 2nd ed. Kent: Kent State University Press, 2000.

———. "Women against Prohibition." *American Quarterly* 28, no. 4 (1976): 465–82.

A Lady of Baltimore. *The Price of a Glass of Brandy.* Baltimore: Robert Neilson, 1841.

Lamas, Maria. *The Glass; or, The Trials of Helen More, A Thrilling Temperance Tale.* Philadelphia: Martin E. Harmstead, 1849.

Lansing, D. C. *A Remedy for Intemperance.* Utica: Hastings and Tracy, 1832.

Lauer, Jeanette C., and Robert H. Lauer. "The Battle of the Sexes: Fashion in 19th Century America." *Journal of Popular Culture* 13, no. 4 (1980): 581–89.

Lauricella, Francis, Jr. "The Devil in Drink: Swedenborgianism in T. S. Arthur's *Ten Nights in a Bar-room* (1854)." In *Perspectives in American History*, vol. 12, edited by Donald Fleming, 351–86. Cambridge: Charles Warren Center, 1979.

The Layman's Argument against the Interdiction of Intoxicating Liquors by Church or State. Richmond: C. H. Wynn's Steam-Powered Printing Press, 1853.

Leech, Samuel V. *The Influence of Woman on the Temperance Reformation.* Baltimore: James Young, 1865.

Lehuu, Isabelle. *Carnival on the Page: Popular Print Media in Antebellum America.* Chapel Hill: University of North Carolina Press, 2000.

Leigh, Barbara. "A Thing So Fallen, and So Vile: Images of Drinking and Sexuality in Women." *Contemporary Drug Problems* 22, no. 3 (1995): 415–34.

Lender, Mark. "A Special Stigma: Women and Alcoholism in the Late 19th and Early 20th Centuries." In *Alcohol Interventions*, edited by David L. Strug, S. Priyandarsini, and Merton M. Hyman, 41–57. Binghamton, NY: Haworth Press, 1986.

Lengel, Laura, and John T. Warren. "Introduction: Casting Gender." In *Casting Gender: Women and Performance in Intercultural Contexts*, edited by Laura Lengel and John T. Warren, 1–18. New York: Peter Lang, 2005.

Lettsom, J. C. *History of Some of the Effects of Hard Drinking.* 6th ed. London: W. Darton and Co., 1791.

Levine, Harry Gene. "Temperance and Women in 19th-Century United States." In *Alcohol and Drug Problems in Women.* Research Advances in Alcohol and Drug Problems, 5, edited by Orianna Josseau Kalant. New York: Plenum Press, 1980.

"License" or "No License": A Calm Appeal to the Electors of Ulster County. New York, 1846.

License or No License, That is the Question. To the Voters of Ohio. N.p., n.d. [1840s].

Lindsly, Harvey. "An Essay on the Origin and Introduction into Medical Practice, & c., of Ardent Spirits." In *Temperance Prize Essays*, by R. D. Mussey and H. Lindsly, 171–72. Washington: Duff Green, 1835.

Lobdell, Henry. *The Religious, Moral and Political Evils of the Liquor Traffic, and their Remedy. "Prevention is Better than Cure." An Appeal for Present Action in the Cause of Temperance.* New York: William Osborn, 1848.

Lund, Orlando. *Maine Law Documents for the People.* Elmira: L. Baldwin, Jr., 1853.

Macnish, Robert. *The Anatomy of Drunkenness.* New York: D. Appleton &. Co., 1835.

Marilley, Suzanne M. *Woman Suffrage and the Origins of Liberal Feminism in the United States, 1820–1920.* Cambridge: Harvard University Press, 1996.

Marsh, John. *A Discourse on the Extent and Evils of the Sunday Liquor Traffic in Cities. Delivered before the New York Tenth Ward Temperance Society, and in Several Churches of the City.* New York: American Temperance Union, 1848.

———. *A Half Century Tribute to the Cause of Temperance. Originally Delivered before the Ulster County Society, January 8, 1851. With an Appendix, Containing all the Principal Temperance Incidents & Publications of the Last Half Century.* New York: American Temperance Union, 1851.

———. *Hannah Hawkins, The Reformed Drunkard's Daughter.* New York: American Temperance Union, 1846.

———. *The Napoleon of Temperance, Sketches of the Life and Character of the Hon. Neal Dow, Mayor of Portland, and Author of the Maine Liquor Law.* New York: American Temperance Union, 1852.

———, ed. *Temperance Hymn Book and Minstrel: A Collection of Hymns, Songs and Odes, for Temperance Meetings and Festivals.* New York: American Temperance Union, 1841.

Martin, A. Lynn. "Deviant Drinking or Deviant Women?" www.arts.adelaide.edu.au /CentreFoodDrink/Articles/DeviantDrinking.html (accessed 22 May 2003).

Martin, Scott C. "'A Star that Gathers Lustre from the Gloom of Night': Wives, Marriage and Gender in Early Nineteenth-century American Temperance Reform." *Journal of Family History* 29, no. 3 (2004): 274–92.

———. "Violence, Gender and Intemperance in Early National Connecticut." *Journal of Social History* 24, no. 2 (2000): 309–25.

———, ed. *Cultural Change and the Market Revolution in America, 1789–1860.* Lanham, MD: Rowman & Littlefield, 2005.

Mason, Jeffrey D. *Melodrama and the Myth of America.* Bloomington: University of Indiana Press, 1993.

Massachusetts Society for the Suppression of Intemperance. *The Constitution of the Massachusetts Society for the Suppression of Intemperance, as Revised and Altered, together with their Annual Report, for the Year 1818, and A List of Officers and Members of Said Society.* Boston: Sewell Phelps, 1818.

———. *Fourteenth Annual Report of the Massachusetts Society for the Suppression of Intemperance, with Resolutions Passed at a Public Meeting Held November 5, 1827.* Boston: N. S. Simpkins and Co., 1827.

Massachusetts Temperance Society. *The Physiological Effects of Alcoholic Drinks, from the British and Foreign Medical Review of Dr. Forbes; with Documents and Record of the Massachusetts Temperance Society, illustrating the Origin of the Temperance Reformation, and Its Progress in the State of Massachusetts.* Boston: Massachusetts Temperance Society, 1848.

―――. *Plain Facts, Addressed to the Inhabitants of Boston, on the City Expenses for the Support of Pauperism, Vice, and Crime. Published by the Council of the Massachusetts Temperance Society.* Boston: Ford and Damrell, 1834.

Mattingly, Carol. *Well-Tempered Women: Nineteenth-century Temperance Rhetoric.* Carbondale: Southern Illinois University Press, 1998.

M'Clure, William B. *Temperance Address delivered by William B. M'Clure, by Request. January 1, 1852, before Pittsburgh Division No. 42, Sons of Temperance.* Pittsburgh: Kennedy and Brother, 1852.

M'Conaughy, David, A. M. *Drunkenness Excludes from Heaven: A Discourse on 1st Corinthians, V.I, 10.* Gettysburg: Robert G. Harper, 1827.

Meigs, Charles D. *Females and their Diseases: A Series of Lectures to His Class.* Philadelphia: Lea and Blanchard, 1848.

―――. *Obstetrics: The Science and the Art.* Philadelphia: Lea and Blanchard, 1849.

Mellen, Grenville. *The First Glass.* Southwark, Philadelphia: Wm. F. Geddes, 1834.

The Minutes of a Temperance Convention, of Northern Kentucky, Held in Maysville, on the 28th and 29th of November, 1837. Maysville: L. Collins, 1837.

Mitchell, Elisha. *Arguments for Temperance: A Sermon Addressed to the Students of the University of North Carolina, March 13th, 1831, and Published at their Request.* Raleigh: J. Gales and Son, 1831.

Mitchell, Thomas, ed. *The Maine Law Songster.* Lansingburgh: Thomas Mitchell and Richards and Harch, 1854.

Moody, Richard, ed. *Dramas from the American Theatre, 1762–1909.* Boston: Houghton Mifflin, 1969.

Morton, Daniel O. *"Wine is a Mocker, Strong Drink is Raging": A Discourse, delivered at Montpelier, October 16, 1828, on the Formation of the Vermont Temperance Society.* Montpelier: E. P. Morton, 1828.

The Mother Rewarded and the Son Reclaimed. Portland: William Hyde & Son, 1851.

Mowatt, Anna Cora. *Fashion.* In *Dramas from the American Theatre, 1762–1909,* edited by Richard Moody. Cleveland: World Publishing, 1966.

Murdock, Catherine Gilbert. *Domesticating Drink: Women, Men, and Alcohol, 1870–1940.* Baltimore: Johns Hopkins University Press, 1998.

Mussey, R. D. *An Address on Ardent Spirit, read before the New-Hampshire Medical Society, at their Annual meeting, June 5, 1827.* Hanover: Thomas Mann, 1828.

"My Mother." In *The Evils of Intemperance, Exemplified in Poetry and Prose. With Engravings. By a Friend to Temperance,* 24. Boston: N. Boynton, 1829.

The National Cyclopaedia of American Biography. New York: White and Co., 1929.

Neal, John. *Address Delivered before the Portland Association for the Promotion of Temperance, February 11, 1829.* Portland: Day and Fraser, 1829.

Neumann, Caryn E. "The End of Gender Solidarity: The History of the Women's Organization for National Prohibition Reform in the United States, 1929–1933." *Journal of Women's History* 9, no. 2 (1997): 31–51.

Nichols, Thomas L. *Woman, in All Ages and Nations; A Complete and Authentic History of the Manners and Customs, Character and Condition of the Female Sex, in Civilized and Savage Countries, From the Earliest Ages to the Present Time.* New York: Fowler and Wells, 1849.

Ninth Annual Report of the Directors of the Penitent Females' Refuge, Read at their Annual Meeting. Boston: T. R. Marvin, 1828.

Norris, Frances B. *Reasons for Hating Strong Drink, and a Plea for Suffering Humanity, that the Plague May be Stayed.* Boston: W. & E. Howe, 1860.

Numbers, Ronald L. "The Fall and Rise of the American Medical Profession." In *Sickness and Health in America,* edited by Judith Leavitt and Ronald Numbers, 185–96. Madison: University of Wisconsin Press, 1985.

O'Flaherty, Thomas J. *A Medical Essay on Drinking, by Thomas J. O'Flaherty, M.D.* Hartford: Hudson and Skinner, 1828.

The Old Brewery, and the New Mission House at the Five Points. By the Ladies of the Mission. New York: Stringer and Townsend, 1854.

On Intemperance. In *The Publications of the American Tract Society.* Boston: Flagg and Gould, 1824.

Opinions of the Press in Relation to the Liquor Traffic and the Morals of Boston. Boston: Temperance Standard Press, 1846.

Otis, Harrison Gray. *Letter from an Aged and a Retired Citizen of Boston to a Member of the House of Representatives of Massachusetts, on Coercive Measures in Aid of Temperance.* Boston: Eastburn's Press, 1848.

Parsons, Elaine Frantz. *Manhood Lost: Fallen Drunkard and Redeeming Women in the Nineteenth-Century United States.* Baltimore: Johns Hopkins University Press, 2003.

Pease, Jane H., and William H. Pease. *Ladies, Women and Wenches: Choice and Constraint in Antebellum Charleston and Boston.* Chapel Hill: University of North Carolina Press, 1990.

Pegram, Thomas R. *Battling Demon Rum: The Struggle for a Dry America, 1800–1933.* Chicago: Ivan R. Dee, 1998.

The Pennsylvania Society. *The Anniversary Report of the Managers of the Pennsylvania Society for Discouraging the Use of Ardent Spirits. Read on the 7th May, 1831, and Ordered to be Published by the Society.* Philadelphia: Henry H. Porter, 1831.

———. *Report of a Committee Appointed by the Pennsylvania Society, for Discouraging the use of Ardent Spirits, to Examine and Report What Amendments Ought to be Made in the Laws of the Said State, for the Suppression of Vice and Immorality, Particularly those against Gaming. Read and Adopted February 14, 1828.* Philadelphia: Atkinson and Alexander, 1828.

———. *The Third Anniversary Report of the Managers of the Pennsylvania Society for Discouraging the Use of Ardent Spirits. Read on the 22nd May, 1832 and Ordered to be Published by the Society.* Philadelphia: John Clarke, 1832.

Permanent Temperance Documents of the American Temperance Society. New York: Arno Press, 1972.

Philadelphius. *The Moral Plague of Civil Society: or, The Pernicious Effects of the Love of Money on the Morals of Mankind: Exemplified in the Encouragement Given to the Use of Ardent Spirits in the United States, with the Proper Remedy for the Cure of this National Evil.* Philadelphia, 1821.

Pickering, David C. *The Effects of Intemperance: A Discourse, delivered on Sabbath Evening, January 14, 1827; at the Universalist Chapel.* Taunton: Samuel W. Mortimer, 1827.

Pierce, I. N. *The History of the Independent Order of Good Templars.* Philadelphia: Daughaday & Becker, 1869.

Pierson, Michael D. *Free Hearts and Homes: Gender and American Antislavery Politics.* Chapel Hill: University of North Carolina Press, 2003.

"A Plantation in Ruins, or the History of John and Peter Hay." In *The Temperance Volume; Embracing the Temperance Tracts of the American Tract Society.* New York: American Tract Society, n.d.

Pleck, Elizabeth. *Domestic Tyranny: The Making of Social Policy against Family Violence from Colonial Times to the Present.* New York: Oxford University Press, 1987.

Pollok, Robert. *The Course of Time: A Poem in Ten Books.* London: T. Cadell, 1827.

Porter, Miss C. B. "The Silver Cup of Sparkling Drops." In *Many Fountains for the Friends of Temperance.* Buffalo: Derby and Co., 1852.

Portnoy, Alisse. *Their Right to Speak: Women's Activism in the Indian and Slave Debates.* Cambridge: Harvard University Press, 2005.

Potter, Alonzo. *Addresses.* Boston: Massachusetts Temperance Society, 1861.

Powell, Timothy B. *Beyond the Binary: Reconstructing Cultural Identity in a Multicultural Context.* New Brunswick: Rutgers University Press, 1999.

Prime, Nathaniel S. *The Pernicious Effects of Intemperance in the Use of Ardent Spirits, and the Remedy of that Evil. A Sermon, delivered at the Opening of the Presbytery of Long-Island, at Aquebogue, Nov. 5, 1811.* Brooklyn: Adlen Spooner, 1812.

Proceedings of the Physiological Temperance Society of the Medical Institute of Louisville. Louisville: N. H. White, 1842.

Proceedings of the Rhode-Island Total Abstinence Society, at their Annual Meeting in Providence, January 25, 1854. Providence: Albert Crawford Green, 1854.

Proceedings of the State Temperance Convention: Held at Harrisburg, Penn. January 13 and 14, 1841. Harrisburg: John Weishampel, 1841.

Proceedings of the Temperance Society of Columbia, South Carolina, together with their Constitution, and Report of their Committee on the Influence of Intemperance Upon the Health, Morals, and Prosperity of the Country. Columbia: M'Morris and Wilson, 1829.

Proceedings, Speeches and Addresses of the Fourth National Temperance Convention, Held at Saratoga Springs, N.Y., August 20, 1851; with the Maine Law. New York: American Temperance Union, 1851.

Quist, John. *Restless Visionaries: The Social Roots of Antebellum Reform in Alabama and Michigan.* Baton Rouge: Louisiana State University Press, 1998.

Reasons for Not Joining the Temperance Society by a Clergyman. Richmond: n.p., 1836.

Remarks on the Utility and Necessity of Asylums or Retreats for the Victims of Intemperance. Philadelphia: Brown, Bickering & Guilbert, 1840.

Report of the Committee, Appointed by the Philadelphia Medical Society, January 24, 1829, to take into Consideration the Propriety of that Society Expressing their Opinion with Regard to the Use of Ardent Spirits, and to Frame such Resolutions as they May Deem Proper. Philadelphia: John Clarke, 1829.

Report of the Managers of the Magdalen Society for 1840. Philadelphia: Joseph and William Kite, 1841.

Report on the Agency of Intemperance in the Production of Pauperism. Philadelphia: J. Van Cort, 1836.

Reynolds, David S. "Black Cats and Delirium Tremens: Temperance and the American Renaissance." *The Serpent in the Cup: Temperance in American Literature,* edited by David S. Reynolds and Debra J. Rosenthal, 22–25. Amherst: University of Massachusetts Press, 1997.

Roberts, Brian. *American Alchemy: The California Gold Rush and Middle-class Culture.* Chapel Hill: University of North Carolina Press, 2000.

Rodgers, James. *A Discourse before the Noblestown Temperance Society, January 1st, 1834.* N.p., n.d.

Rogers, E. P. *Poems Delivered at the Delavan Union, from 1845 to 1850.* Newark: A. Stephen Holbrook, 1850.

Rorabaugh, William J. *The Alcoholic Republic: An American Tradition.* New York: Oxford University Press, 1979.

Rose, Henrietta. *Nora Wilmot: A Tale of Temperance and Women's Rights.* Columbus: Osgood and Pierce, 1858.

Rose, Kenneth D. *American Women and the Repeal of Prohibition.* New York: New York University Press, 1996.

Rotundo, E. Anthony. *American Manhood: Transformations in Masculinity from the Revolution to the Modern Era*. New York: Basic Books, 1993.

Ruppel, Tim. "Gender Training: Male Ambitions, Domestic Duties, and Failure in the Magazine Fiction of T. S. Arthur." In *Prospects: An Annual Review of American Cultural Studies*. Vol. 24. Cambridge: Cambridge University Press, 1999.

Rush, Benjamin. "An Inquiry into the Effects of Ardent Spirits upon the Human Body and Mind." 1784. Reprinted as "The Effects of Ardent Spirits upon the Human Body and Mind," in *The Temperance Volume; Embracing the Temperance Tracts of the American Tract Society*. New York: American Tract Society, 1834.

Ryan, Mary P. *Cradle of the Middle Class: The Family in Oneida County, New York, 1790–1865*. New York: Cambridge University Press, 1981.

Ryan, Michael. *Prostitution in London, with a Comparative View of that of Paris and New York, as Illustrative of the Capitals and Large Towns of all Countries; and Proving Moral Depravation to be the Most Fertile Source of Crime, and of Personal and Social Misery; with an Account of the Nature and Treatment of the Various Diseases, Caused by Abuses of the Reproductive Function*. London: H. Bailliere, 1839.

Salerno, Beth A. *Sister Societies: Women's Antislavery Organizations in Antebellum America*. DeKalb: Northern Illinois University Press, 2005.

Salmon, Marylynn. *Women and the Law of Property in Early America*. Chapel Hill: University of North Carolina Press, 1986.

Sanchez-Eppler, Karen. "Temperance in the Bed of a Child: Incest and Social Order in Nineteenth-Century America." *American Quarterly* 47, no. 1 (1995): 1–33.

———. "Then When We Clutch Hardest: On the Death of a Child and the Replication of an Image." In *Sentimental Men: Masculinity and the Politics of Affect in American Culture*, edited by Mary Chapman and Glenn Hendler, 64–85. Berkeley: University of California Press, 1999.

Sandage, Scott A. *Born Losers: A History of Failure in America*. Cambridge: Harvard University Press, 2005.

Sandmaier, Marian. *The Invisible Alcoholics: Women and Alcohol Abuse in America*. New York: McGraw Hill, 1980.

Sanger, William. *The History of Prostitution: Its Extent, Causes and Effects throughout the World*. New York: Eugenics Publishing Co., 1939.

Sargent, Lucius M. *The Cranberry Meadow*. Boston: John Ford, 1835.

———. "Licensed Houses." *An Examination of the License Law of the Commonwealth of Massachusetts*. Boston: J. Ford, 1833.

Scenes of Intemperance, Exhibited in Familiar Conversations between a Mother and Her Children. Philadelphia: American Sunday School Union, 1833.

The Second Annual Report of the Female Total Abstinence Society of Philadelphia. Philadelphia: H. Probasco, 1838.

Sedgwick, Eve Kosofsky. *Between Men: English Literature and Homosocial Desire*. New York: Columbia University Press, 1992.

———. *Epistemology of the Closet*. Berkeley: University of California Press, 1990.

Sellers, Charles. *The Market Revolution: Jacksonian America, 1815–1846*. New York: Oxford University Press, 1991.

Shepard, Isaac F. "Confessions of a Female Inebriate." In *Drunkard's Progress: Narratives of Addiction, Despair, and Recovery*, edited by John W. Crowley, 71–74. Baltimore: Johns Hopkins University Press, 1999.

Shiman, Lillian Lewis. *Women and Leadership in Nineteenth-century England*. New York: St. Martin's Press, 1992.

Shindler, Mary S. B. *The Temperance Lyre, A Collection of Original Songs, Arranged and Adapted to the Most Popular Music of the Day, and Designed for Temperance Meetings*. New York: Dayton and Newman, 1842.

Sigourney, Lydia H. "The Intemperate." In *The Intemperate and the Reformed. Shewing the Awful Consequences of Intemperance, and the Blessed Effects of the Temperance Reformation, 7–22*. Boston: Seth Bliss, 1833.

———. *Letters of Life*. New York: D. Appleton and Company, 1866.

———. *Water-drops*. New York: Robert Carter, 1848.

Sinclair, Andrew. *Era of Excess: A Social History of Prohibition*. New York: Harper and Row, 1962.

Skinner, Thomas. *Another Voice from the Grave: or the Power of Conscience exemplified in the Dying Confession and Exercises of an Unfortunate Female, Published According to her Dying Request*. Philadelphia: Religious Tract Society, 1819.

Sklar, Kathryn Kish. *Women's Rights Emerges within the Anti-Slavery Movement, 1830–1870: A Brief History with Documents*. Boston: Bedford, 2000.

Smith-Rosenberg, Carroll. *Disorderly Conduct: Visions of Gender in Victorian America*. New York: Oxford University Press, 1985.

Smith-Rosenberg, Carroll, and Charles Rosenberg. "The Female Animal: Medical and Biological Views of Woman and her Role in Nineteenth-century America." *Journal of American History* 60, no. 2 (1973): 332–56.

Smucker, Samuel M. *Considerations in Favor of the Constitutionality and Beneficial Operation of a Law Prohibiting the Sale of Ardent Spirits in Pennsylvania*. Philadelphia, 1852.

Southworth, Mrs. S. A. *The Inebriate's Hut; or, The First Fruits of the Maine Law*. Boston: Phillips, Sampson & Co., 1854.

Sprague, Charles. *An Address Delivered Before the Massachusetts Society for the Suppression of Intemperance, May 31, 1827*. Boston: R. Butts, 1827.

Stanton, Elizabeth Cady, Susan B. Anthony, and Matilda Joslyn Gage, eds. *History of Woman Suffrage*. 2 vols. New York: Fowler and Wells, 1881.

Stearns, Jonathan French. *Female Influence and the True Christian Mode of Its Exercise*. Newburyport: J. G. Tilton, 1837.

Stebbins, Jane E. *Fifty Years History of the Temperance Cause*. Hartford: J. P. Fitch, 1876.

Stecker, Michelle J. "A Respectable Revolution: The Dynamics of Religion and Gender in the Ohio Woman's Temperance Crusade, 1873–1874." Ph.D. dissertation, University of Toledo, 2000.

Stewart, Alvan. *An Essay on the Evils of Intemperance, pronounced in the First Presbyterian Church, in Utica, on the 26th February, 1833, at the Request of the Two Temperance Societies in the County of Oneida*. Utica: Gardiner Tracy, 1833.

Stewart, Eliza D. *Memories of the Crusade: A Thrilling Account of the Women of Ohio in 1873, against the Liquor Crime*. Columbus: Wm. G. Hubbard & Co., 1888.

Storer, Bellamy. *An Address delivered before the Cincinnati Temperance Society on the Twenty Sixth Day of February, 1833*. Cincinnati: F. S. Benton, 1833.

Storer, H. R. "Appendix." In Albert Day, *Methomania: A Treatise on Alcoholic Poisoning* (1867). Reprinted in *Nineteenth-century Medical Attitudes toward Alcohol Addiction: Six Studies, 1814–1867*, edited by Gerald Grob. New York: Arno Press, 1981.

Stow, Baron. *An Address, Delivered before the Temperance Society of South-Berwick, Maine, Nov. 26, 1829*. Portsmouth: Miller and Brewster, 1830.

Streit, Philip B. *Address by Philip B. Streit, Esq., delivered on the 4th of July, 1842, in the Presbyterian Church at Romney, at the Request of the Hampshire County Temperance Society*. Romney: William Harper, 1842.

Sweetser, William. *A Dissertation on Intemperance, to which was awarded the Premium offered by the Massachusetts Medical Society*. Boston: Hilliard, Gray, and Company, 1829.

Tannenbaum, Rebecca. "Earnestness, Temperance, Industry: The Definition and Uses of Professional Character among Nineteenth-century Physicians." *Journal of the History of Medicine and Allied Sciences* 49 (1994): 252, 257.

Temperance Almanac for 1837. Albany: Packard and Van Bethuysen, 1837.

Temperance Almanac, 1838. Albany: Packard and Benthuysen, 1838.

Temperance Almanac for 1845. Troy: B. H. Boynton, 1845.

Temperance Almanac for the Year of Our Lord 1839: The Sixty-third Year of American Independence. Boston: Whipple & Damrell, 1838.

Temperance Almanac for the Year of Our Lord 1840. N.p., n.d.

Temperance Almanac for the Year of Our Lord 1843. Albany: C. Van Benthuysen, 1843.

Temperance Almanac for the Year of Our Lord 1843. New York: L. D. Dewey, 1843.

Temperance Almanac of the Massachusetts Temperance Union, for the Year of Our Lord 1841. Boston: Whipple and Damrell, 1840. n.p.

Temperance Almanac of the Massachusetts Temperance Union, for the Year of Our Lord 1845. Boston: Mass. Temperance Union, 1844.

The Temperance Annual and Cold Water Magazine. Philadelphia: Drew & Scammell, 1843.

Temperance Family Almanac for the Year of Our Lord 1835: Containing Besides the Usual Astronomical Calculations, Many Valuable Suggestions and Important Statements on THE SUBJECT OF TEMPERANCE. Boston: Russell, Odiorne & Metcalf, 1835.

Temperance, Its Rise and Progress: Together with the Origins, Secrets, Objections and Legitimate Influence, of the Order of the Sons of Temperance, by a "Son." Sandusky: Amos Moore, 1848.

The Temperance Text Book: A Collection of Facts and Interesting Anecdotes, Illustrating the Evils of Intoxicating Drinks. 3rd ed. Philadelphia: E. L. Carey and A. Hart, 1837.

Temperance Tracts for the People, Nos. 1–12. New York: New York State Temperance Society, 1854.

The Temperance Volume. New York: American Tract Society, 1834.

Tenth Annual Report of the Maryland State Temperance Society. Baltimore: Samuel Sands, 1841.

Thayer, Mrs. J. *Picnic Tales Number Three. The Drunkard's Daughter*. Boston: William S. Damrell, 1842.

The Third Annual Report of the Richmond Society for the Promotion of Temperance. Presented January 16, 1832. Richmond: J. MacFarlan, 1832.

Thoughts on the Moral Physiology and Pathology of the Disease Liquor Drinking, with Advice Hints. Boston: Redding & Co., 1862.

Three Experiments in Drinking, or, Three Eras in the Life of An Inebriate. Boston: Otis, Broaders, & Co., 1837.

To the Honorable the Senate and House of Representatives of the Commonwealth of Pennsylvania, in General Assembly met. 1849.

Torrey, Jesse, Jr. *The Intellectual Torch; Developing an Original, Economical and Expeditious Plan for the Universal Dissemination of Knowledge and Virtue; by Means of Free Public Libraries. Including Essays on the Use of Distilled Spirits*. Ballston Spa: J. Comstock, 1817.

Trotter, Thomas. *An Essay, Medical, Philosophical, and Chemical, on Drunkenness, and Its Effects on the Human Body*. Philadelphia: Anthony Finley, 1813.

Tyrrell, Ian R. *Sobering Up: From Temperance to Prohibition in Antebellum America, 1800–1860*. Westport: Greenwood Press, 1979.

———. *Woman's World, Woman's Empire: The Woman's Christian Temperance Union in International Perspective*. Chapel Hill: University of North Carolina Press, 1991.

———. "Women and Temperance in Antebellum America, 1830–1860." *Civil War History* 28, no. 2 (1982): 128–52.

The Unjust Judge; or, The Evils of Intemperance on Judges, Lawyers, and Politicians. Mansfield, Ohio: Wesleyan Methodist Connection, 1854.

Vallandigham, James Laird. *An Address, delivered before the Berlin Temperance Society; Worcester County, Maryland, July 4th, 1833; and Re-Delivered before the Temper-*

ance Society of Concord and Middleford, Deleware, November 16, 1833. George-town: J. S. M'Calla, 1833.

Van Broekhoven, Deborah B. *The Devotion of These Women: Rhode Island in the Anti-slavery Network.* Amherst: University of Massachusetts Press, 2002.

Vandell, Lunsford P. "Doctor Vandell's Address." *Proceedings and Second Annual Report of the Kentucky Temperance Society: With an Address delivered before the Society, by Lunsford P. Vandell, M.D.* Frankfurt: A. G. Hodges, 1832.

Varon, Elizabeth R. *We Mean to Be Counted: White Women and Politics in Antebellum Virginia.* Chapel Hill: University of North Carolina Press, 1998.

A Voice from Leverett Prison, or the Life, Trial, and Confession of Simeon L. Crockett, Who was Executed for Arson, March 16, 1836. Orig.: Boston: Printed for the Proprietor, 1836. 10th edition.

Wadsworth, Benjamin. *Female Charity an Acceptable Offering. A Sermon delivered in the Brick Meeting House in Danvers, at the Request of the Charitable Female Cent Society in Danvers and Middleton, for Promoting Christian Knowledge, November 7, 1816.* Andover: Flagg and Gould, 1817.

———. *Intemperance a National Evil. A Discourse Delivered in the Brick Meeting House in Danvers, Before the Society in that Town for Suppressing Intemperance and Other Vices, and for Promoting Temperance and General Morality. June 29, 1815.* Salem: Thomas C. Cushing, 1815.

Wakeman, Joel. *The Mysterious Parchment; or, The Satanic License. Dedicated to Maine Law Progress.* Boston: John P. Jewett and Company, 1853.

Walters, Ronald. *Primers for Prudery: Sexual Advice to Victorian America.* Englewood Cliffs: Prentice Hall, 1974.

Warder, Graham. "Temperance Nostalgia, Market Anxiety, and the Reintegration of Community in T. S. Arthur's *Ten Nights in a Bar-room.*" In Martin, *Cultural Change and Market Revolution,* 217–45.

Ware, John, M.D. *An Address delivered before the Massachusetts Society for the Suppression of Intemperance at their Annual Meeting, May, 1825.* Boston: Christian Register, 1826.

Warner, Jessica. "Old and In the Way: Widows, Witches, and Spontaneous Combustion in the Age of Reason." *Contemporary Drug Problems* 23 (Summer 1996): 197–220.

———. "The Sanctuary of Sobriety: The Emergence of Temperance as a Feminine Virtue in Tudor and Stuart England." *Addiction* 92, no. 1 (1997): 97–111.

Warner, Nicholas O. *Spirits of America: Intoxication in Nineteenth-Century American Literature.* Norman: University of Oklahoma Press, 1997.

A Warning Voice Against Intemperance 1, no. 1. Philadelphia: John Clarke, 1828.

Watson, John. *An Alarming Portraiture of the Pernicious Effects of the Customary Use of Distilled Spirituous Liquors, with some Remarks and Advice Relative to the Subject.* Philadelphia: Kimbert and Conrad, 1813.

———. *Observations on the Customary Use of Distilled Spirituous Liquors.* Philadelphia: Kimber and Conrad, 1810.

Whiteaker, Larry. *Seduction, Prostitution, and Moral Reform in New York, 1830–1860.* New York: Garland Publishing, 1997.

Whitman, Walt. *Franklin Evans, or the Inebriate. A Tale of the Times.* New York: J. Winchester, 1842.

Whitney, Frederic A. *Address on Temperance, delivered in the Town Hall, Brighton, Sunday Evening, Dec. 21, 1845.* Boston: Benjamin H. Greene, 1846.

The Whole World's Temperance Convention, Held at Metropolitan Hall in the City of New York on Thursday and Friday, September 1st and 2nd, 1853. New York: Fowler and Wells, 1853.

"Who Slew All These? An Authentic Narrative." In *The Temperance Volume.* New York: American Tract Society, 1834.

Willard, Frances E. *Home Protection Manual: Containing an Argument for the Temperance Ballot for Woman, and How to Obtain It, as a Means of Home Protection.* New York: The Independent, 1879.

Wiltbank, John C. *The Introductory Lecture to the Course of Midwifery in the Medical Department of Pennsylvania College, for the Session of 1853–54.* Philadelphia: Edward Grattan, 1854.

———. *The Peculiarities of the Female: A Lecture Introductory to the Course in Obstetrics in the Medical Department of Pennsylvania College, for the Session of 1845–46. Delivered November 6, 1845.* Philadelphia: Barrett & Jones, 1845.

Wing, Henry A. *Maine's War upon the Liquor Traffic.* Portland: Portland Evening Express, 1909.

Winskill, P. T. *The Temperance Movement and its Workers.* London: Blackie and Son, 1892.

Withington, Leonard. *A Review of the Late Temperance Movements in Massachusetts.* Boston: James Munroe, 1840.

Woodman, Charles T. *Narrative of Charles T. Woodman, a Reformed Inebriate. Written by Himself.* Boston: Theodore Abbot, 1843.

Zaeske, Susan. *Signatures of Citizenship: Petitioning, Antislavery, and Women's Political Identity.* Chapel Hill: University of North Carolina Press, 2003.

Zboray, Ronald. *A Fictive People: Antebellum Economic Development and the American Reading Public.* New York: Oxford University Press, 1993.

Index